WEBSTER'S
NEW WORLD™

POCKET
VOCABULARY

Mark Alan Stewart

IDG Books

Webster's New World™ Pocket Vocabulary

Published by
Hungry Minds, Inc.
909 Third Avenue
New York NY 10022
www.hungryminds.com
www.hungryminds.com/wnw/wnw_index.html

ISBN 0-02863486-1

Manufactured in the United States of America
9 8 7 6 5 4 3 2

Dictionary Editorial Offices:
New World Dictionaries
850 Euclid Avenue
Cleveland OH 44114

Contents

Introduction

Vocabulary demonstrates a person's ability to communicate effectively—at any education level. By opening this book, you've made an important first step toward mastering difficult words—whether you're in middle school, college or graduate school. *Webster's New World Pocket Vocabulary* has been designed to help you understand, pronounce and learn words contextually using a variety of systems.

Level 1 ("Quick Vocabulary") and **Level 2** ("Advanced Quick Vocabulary") contain words sorted by difficulty, and for each listing include pronunciation, part of speech, definition, and a sample sentence. Note that the parts of speech are general rules since many words can be used in several different ways.

Level 3 ("Synonyms by Triplets") focuses on related words. This level contains 100 word groups; in each group a common, everyday word is followed by three synonyms for that word. (The first word in each group is the closest synonym.) Learning words by triplets will afford you additional perspective on the words as you learn them. Each listing at Level 3 provides pronunciation, part of speech, a definition, and a sample sentence.

Level 4 ("Synonyms and Antonyms"), like Level 3, features related words. However, Level 4 provides not only synonyms but also antonyms—in a thesaurus format. Each listing at Level 4 also provides pronunciation, part of speech, and a brief definition.

Level 5 ("Vocabulary Focus") features more difficult words and more detailed contextual material. Each listing provides related meanings of the word, multiple uses for the word, information about related words, and at least one sample sentence or quotation using the word. (*Note:* The sample sentences also contain other difficult words for you to explore using a dictionary.) Level 5 is the place to delve in depth into words and their meanings.

Level 6 ("Vocabulary of Academia") features 31 advanced academic and professional topics—with words and definitions related to each. The words are grouped into subject areas, to help you remember them and to use them properly. Here are the subject areas you'll find at Level 6:

- Anthropology
- Architecture
- Astronomy
- Biochemistry
- Botany
- Business, Economics, and Finance
- Civil Law

- Engineering and Construction
- Criminology (Crimes and Criminal Procedure)
- Ecology (Meteorology, Soil Science and the Environment)
- Gastronomy (the Art and Science of Good Eating)
- Geography
- Geology (Rock Formations, Minerals, and Metals)
- Government
- Linguistics
- Literature
- Mathematics
- Medicine and the Health Professions
- Metaphysics and the Afterlife
- Military Science
- Music and Musicology
- Philosophy, Critical Thinking and Logic
- Physics
- Political Science
- Psychology
- Religion (Institutions and Customs)
- Sociology
- Theater Arts and Public Speaking
- Visual Arts—General/Sculpture
- Visual Arts—Painting
- Zoology

Level 7 ("Confusing Word Groups") features the most advanced vocabulary study system. Each word group at this level contains words often confused with one another. By studying words in these groups you can clearly see their difference in meaning, spelling, and usage, thereby sharpening your vocabulary. (*Note:* Many of the listings at Level 7 also appear at other levels in this book.)

About the Phonetic Spellings (Pronunciation Guides) in This Book

Each phonetic spelling in this book "spells out" the word just the way it sounds when spoken—without the diacritical marks you find in dictionaries. The syllable receiving primary emphasis is spelled with capital letters. Phonetic spellings for some spoken sounds, especially vowel sounds, can be a bit confusing—at least until you become accustomed to them. The next two pages contain a guide to help you properly interpret the phonetic spellings used in this book.

Editor's Note: The following pronunciation key and the phonetic spellings in this book serve merely as quick, easy guides, not as precise indicators, to pronouncing vocabulary words. For more specific and precise pronunciations, see *Webster's New World College Dictionary, 4th Edition*, or any other Webster's New World dictionary.

phonetic spelling	sample word	word spelled phonetically
a	cat	KAT
ah	otter	AH ter

ay	state	STAYT
	airplane	AYR playn
aw	**awe**some	AW sum
ee	**nea**t	NEET
e *or* eh	**ne**cklace	NEK lis
	espouse	eh SPOWZ
i *or* ih	**i**ndicate	IN dih kayt
ing	outstand**ing**	owt STAN ding
y	k**i**te	KYT
oh	**o**pen	OH pin
	beh**o**ld	bee HOHLD
oo	bea**u**tiful	BYOO tih ful
or	**or**dinary	OR duh nayr ee
ow	c**ou**ch	KOWCH
u *or* uh	st**u**ck	STUK
	appreciate	uh PREE shee ayt
	b**u**lly	BUL ee
zh	excur**s**ion	eks KER zhun

Level 1

Quick Vocabulary

Level 1 contains words that are moderate in difficulty level. Each listing includes the pronunciation, part of speech, definition, and a sample sentence. Note that the parts of speech are general rules since many words can be used in several different ways.

abolish (uh BAHL ish) *v.* to do away with, as an institution: Slavery was *abolished* in Massachusetts shortly after the American Revolution.

abrasive (uh BRAY siv) *adj.* scraping or rubbing, annoyingly harsh or jarring: The high-pitched whine of the machinery was *abrasive* to my nerves.

absurd (ub SERD) *adj.* clearly untrue, nonsensical: The parents dismissed the child's story of meeting men from outer space as *absurd*.

accede (uh SEED) *v.* to consent: He *acceded* to their request.

acclaim (uh KLAYM) *v.* to applaud, approve loudly: The crowd in the square *acclaimed* their hero as the new president.

accustom (uh KUS tum) *v.* to get or be used to: The supervisor was not *accustomed* to having her instructions ignored.

adamant (AD uh munt) *adj.* inflexible, hard: She was *adamant* in her determination to succeed.

adhere (ad HEER) *v.* to hold, stick to, cling: Many persons *adhere* to their beliefs despite all arguments.

adjourn (uh JERN) *v.* to suspend proceedings, usually for the day: Since it is now five o'clock, I move that we *adjourn* until tomorrow morning.

adjunct (AJ unkt) *adj.* something joined to a thing but not necessarily part of it: An index is an *adjunct* to a book.

adroit (uh DROYT) *adj.* skillful in the use of the hands or mental faculties: The *adroit* juggler was impressive.

adulterate (uh DUL ter ayt) *v.* to corrupt or to make impure by addition of foreign substances: Many foods are *adulterated* by the addition of preservatives.

adverse (ad VERS) *adj.* opposing, contrary: *Adverse* winds slowed the progress of the ship.

affectation (af ek TAY shun) *n.* artificial behavior or attitudes: Her upper-class manner of speaking was nothing but an *affectation.*

affinity (uh FIH nih tee) *n.* relationship, kinship: There is a close *affinity* among many European languages, such as Spanish and Italian.

affix (uh FIKS) *v.* to attach, fasten: A price tag was *affixed* to each item.

affluence (AF loo uns) *n.* wealth: Ken's *affluence* made him the object of envy among his poorer relatives.

agenda (uh JEN duh) *n.* list of things to be done: The president's *agenda* included a press conference.

allege (uh LEJ) *v.* to declare without proof: The *alleged* attacker has yet to stand trial.

alleviate (uh LEE vee ayt) *v.* to lessen, make easier: The morphine helped to *alleviate* the pain.

aloof (uh LOOF) *adj.* distant, reserved or cold in manner: Her elegant appearance and formal politeness made her seem *aloof,* though in reality she was only shy.

altercation (ahl ter KAY shun) *n.* angry dispute: The *altercation* stopped just short of physical violence.

altruist (AL troo ist) *n.* person who acts unselfishly in the interests of others: She proved herself an *altruist* by volunteering to help the flood victims.

analogous (uh NAL uh gus) *adj.* having a similarity or partial likeness: Writers often see springtime as *analogous* to youth and winter to old age.

annals (AN uls) *n.* chronological records: The *annals* of the scientific societies reflect the advances of our era.

annihilate (uh NY uh layt) *v.* to destroy completely: If we do not act to preserve the few remaining herds, within ten years hunters will *annihilate* the species.

annotate (AN oh tayt) *v.* to provide explanatory notes: Editors *annotate* authors' manuscripts to help the authors refine their works.

antipathy (an TIP uh thee) *n.* dislike: His *antipathy* toward cats almost amounted to a phobia.

annotate (AN oh tayt) *v.* to provide explanatory notes: Editors *annotate* authors' manuscripts to help the authors refine their works.

antipathy (an TIP uh thee) *n.* dislike: His *antipathy* toward cats almost amounted to a phobia.

apathy (AP uh thee) *n.* lack of interest or emotion: Widespread *apathy* among the electorate resulted in a low voter turnout for the election.

apparition (ap uh RIH shun) *n.* phantom, anything that appears suddenly or unexpectedly: Dressed for Halloween, the youngster looked like an *apparition*.

appease (uh PEEZ) *v.* to give in to satisfy or make peace, to pacify: Only a heartfelt apology will *appease* his rage at having been slighted.

append (uh PEND) *v.* to attach as a supplement: Exhibits should be *appended* to the report.

apprehend (ap ree HEND) *v.* to arrest; to understand: The police moved to *apprehend* the suspect. I could not *apprehend* what she was trying to say.

apprise (uh PRYZ) *v.* to give notice to; inform: He was captured because none could *apprise* him of the enemy's advance.

apropos (ap ruh POH) *adj.* pertinent, relevant, to the point: His kind remarks were *apropos* for the funeral service.

arbitrary (AR buh trayr ee) *adj.* despotic, arrived at through will or caprice: An *arbitrary* ruling of the civil commission is being challenged in the courts.

archaic (ar KAY ik) *adj.* no longer in use: Some words like "thou," once a common form of address, are now *archaic*.

archives (AR kyvs) *n.* historic records: A separate building houses the United States *archives* in Washington.

articulate (ar TIH kyoo layt) *adj.* expressing oneself readily, clearly or effectively: The *articulate* child told of the day's events in school.

ascertain (as er TAYN) *v.* to find out with certainty: Because of a lack of evidence the police have been unable to *ascertain* who committed the crime.

ascribe (uh SCRYB) *v.* to attribute, assign as a cause: His death was *ascribed* to poison.

asinine (AS ih nyn) *adj.* stupid, silly: The argument was too *asinine* to deserve a serious answer.

assemblage (uh SEM blij) *n.* a group or collection of things or persons: Out of the *assemblage* of spare parts in the garage, we found the pieces to repair the bicycle.

assent (uh SENT) *v.* to concur, comply, consent: All parties involved *assented* to the statement.

assess (uh SES) *v.* to set a value on: The house has been *assessed* for taxes at far below its market value.

assure (uh SHOOR) *v.* to make something certain, guarantee; to promise with confidence: The fact that they left their tickets *assures* that they will return.

astute (uh STOOT) *adj.* difficult to deceive: An *astute* judge of character, he knew his opponent was bluffing.

atypical (ay TIH pih kul) *adj.* not normal or usual: The usually calm man's burst of temper was *atypical.*

averse (uh VERS) *adj.* having a dislike or reluctance: The local residents disliked tourists and were *averse* to having their pictures taken.

avert (uh VERT) *v.* to turn aside or ward off: By acting quickly we *averted* disaster.

avow (uh VOW) *v.* to declare openly: She *avowed* her belief in the political system.

banter (BAN ter) *n.* good-natured, witty joking or teasing; *(v.)* to speak in a witty, teasing manner: Her comments were mere *banter*, not intended to wound.

bar (BAR) *v.* to oppose, prevent, or forbid; to keep out: A felony conviction will *bar* you from voting.

barter (BAR ter) *v.* to trade by direct exchange of one commodity for another: At the Indian market I *bartered* my sleeping bag for a hand-woven poncho.

belie (bih LY) *v.* to lie about, to show to be false: Her laughing face *belied* her pretense of annoyance.

benign (bih NYN) *adj.* Doing little or no harm; not malignant; kindly: The new government regulation was *benign*, imposing only minor constraints on businesses.

bespeak (bih SPEEK) *v.* to indicate, to speak for, especially in advance: The success of the first novel *bespeaks* a promising career for the young author.

bestow (bih STOH) *v.* to grant or confer: The republic *bestowed* great honors upon its heroes.

blatant (BLAY tunt) *adj.* too noisy or obtrusive, impossible to ignore: The children's *blatant* disregard for conventional manners appalled their older relatives.

bolster (BOHL ster) *v.* to prop up, support: The announcement that refreshments were being served *bolstered* the flagging spirits of the company.

brazen (BRAY zun) *adj.* brassy, shameless: The delinquents showed a *brazen* contempt for the law.

brevity (BREV uh tee) *n.* conciseness, terseness: *Brevity* is the essence of journalistic writing.

brunt (BRUNT) *n.* the principal force or shock, greater part: The *brunt* of the attack was borne by the infantry.

cache (KASH) *n.* hiding place for loot or supplies: The *cache* left by the explorer was found many years later.

candid (KAN did) *adj.* honest, open: She was always *candid* about her feelings; if she liked you, you knew it.

carnage (KAR nij) *n.* destruction of life: The *carnage* of modern warfare is frightful to consider.

caustic (KAW stik) *adj.* biting, burning, stinging: Her *caustic* remarks alientated her teammates.

cerebral (ser REE brul) *adj.* pertaining to the brain: The stroke was the result of a *cerebral* hemorrhage.

chaos (KAY ahs) *n.* complete confusion or disorder: By the time the children had finished playing with all the toys, the room was in a state of *chaos.*

charlatan (SHAR luh tin) *n.* one who pretends to know more than one actually knows: *Charlatans* who pretend they can cure cancer have caused many deaths.

chastise (CHAS tyz) *v.* to punish or scold severely: The disobedient boy was *chastised* by being spanked.

circumvent (SER kum vent) *v.* to go around, frustrate: A technicality allowed him to *circumvent* the law.

clamor (KLAM er) *n.* loud, continuous noise; uproar: The *clamor* of the protesting mob was unbearable.

cliché (klih SHAY) *n.* trite, overworked expression: "White as snow" is a *cliché.*

coerce (koh AYRS) *v.* to compel, force: He did not sign the confession freely but was *coerced.*

cognizant (KAHG nuh zunt) *adj.* having knowledge: She was *cognizant* of the facts when she made her decision.

coherent (koh HEER unt) *adj.* logically connected or organized: They were too distraught to give a *coherent* account of the crash.

cohesion (koh HEE zhun) *n.* sticking together: The *cohesion* of molecules creates surface tension.

commend (kuh MEND) *v.* to praise: The supervisor *commended* them for their excellent work.

compel (kum PEL) *v.* to force: He was *compelled* by law to make pay for the damage to his neighbor's property.

competent (KAHM puh tunt) *adj.* fit, capable, qualified: I am not *competent* to judge the authenticity of this document; you should take it to an expert.

complacent (kum PLAY sunt) *adj.* self-satisfied: A *complacent* student seldom attains the level of success achieved by those who demand more of themselves.

comply (kum PLY) *v.* to go along with, obey: The crowd *complied* with the order to disperse.

comprehensible (kahm pree HEN suh bul) *adj.* able to be understood: The episode was only *comprehensible* to those who knew the story thus far.

comprise (kum PRYZ) *v.* to include, be made up of, consist of: The test will be *comprised* of the subject matter of the previous lessons.

compulsory (kum PUL ser ee) *adj.* required, forced: Attendance is *compulsory* unless one has a medical excuse.

concise (kun SYS) *adj.* brief, to the point: A summary must be *concise* yet cover the topic.

concoction (kun KAHK shun) *n.* combination of various ingredients: The drink was a *concoction* of syrup, soda and three flavors of ice cream.

concurrent (kahn KER unt) *adj.* running together, happening at the same time: *Concurrent* action by the police and welfare authorities reduced juvenile crime.

condone (kun DOHN) *v.* to pardon, overlook an offense: The law will not *condone* any act of violence by an adult against a minor.

conducive (kun DOO siv) *adj.* leading to, helping: Mattie found the waterbed *conducive* to a restful sleep.

confiscate (KAHN fuh skayt) *v.* to seize, take by authority: The government has no right to *confiscate* private property without just compensation.

connive (kuh NYV) *v.* to pretend ignorance of or assist in wrongdoing: The builder and the agent *connived* in selling overpriced homes.

consensus (kun SEN sus) *n.* general agreement: The *consensus* of the jury was that the defendant was guilty.

consolidate (kun SAH luh dayt) *v.* to combine into a single whole: Let us *consolidate* our forces before we fight the gang from the next neighborhood.

consonance (KAHN suh nuns) *n.* harmony, pleasant agreement: Their *consonance* of opinion in all matters made for a peaceful household.

constitute (KAHN stih toot) *v.* to set up, make up, compose: In industrialized countries farmers *constitute* only a small percentage of the population.

constrain (kun STRAYN) *v.* to force or compel; confine: She was *constrained* to make a full confession.

construe (kun STROO) *v.* to interpret, analyze: His critique was *construed* as opposition to the proposal.

contagious (kun TAY jus) *adj.* transmittable by direct or indirect contact: Hepatitis is a *contagious* disease.

contentious (kun TEN chus) *adj.* quarrelsome: One *contentious* student can ruin a debate.

contingent (kun TIN junt) *adj.* depending upon something's happening: Our plans were *contingent* on escrow closing by the end of the month.

contort (kun TORT) *v.* to twist out of shape: Rage *contorted* her features into a frightening mask.

contrive (kun TRYV) *v.* to devise, plan: They *contrived* a way to fix the unit using old parts.

convene (kun VEEN) *v.* to gather together, as an assembly: The alumni will *convene* at the campus.

converge (kun VERJ) *v.* to move nearer together, head for one point: The flock *converged* on the seeded field.

coordinate (koh OR duh nayt) *v.* to bring different elements into order or harmony: Office schedules should be *coordinated* to promote efficiency.

correlate (KOR uh layt) *v.* to bring into or show relation between two things: Studies have *correlated* smoking and heart disease.

countermand (KOWN ter mand) *v.* to revoke an order or command: The wise executive will not hesitate to *countermand* an unwise order.

crass (KRAS) *adj.* stupid, unrefined: The *crass* behavior of some tourists serves to discredit their nation.

credence (KREE duns) *n.* faith, belief: One should pay little *credence* to the word of a known swindler.

criterion (kry TEER ee un) *n.* standard of judging: Flavor was one *criterion* for judging the pie-baking contest.

cryptic (KRIP tik) *adj.* having a hidden meaning, mysterious: The computer hacker easily deciphered the *cryptic* message.

culmination (kul mih NAY shun) *n.* highest attainment: Graduation with highest honors was the *culmination* of her academic efforts.

curative (KYOOR uh tiv) *adj.* concerning or causing the cure of disease: The grandmother had faith in the *curative* powers of certain herbs.

cursory (KER ser ee) *adj.* superficial, hurried: *Cursory* examination of the scene revealed nothing amiss, but later we discovered that some jewelry was missing.

curtail (ker TAYL) *v.* to reduce, shorten (especially in length): The school principal decided to *curtail* the school day due to an impending snowstorm.

debilitate (dih BIL uh tayt) *v.* to enfeeble, weaken: Excesses can *debilitate* even the strongest constitution.

decelerate (dee SEL uh rayt) *v.* to slow down or to reduce the rate of progress: When you see a stop sign in the distance, it is wise to *decelerate.*

decimate (DES uh mayt) *v.* to destroy a large part (literally, one tenth) of a population: The Black Death *decimated* the town.

decrepit (dih KREP ut) *adj.* broken down by old age: With its crumbling brick and peeling paint, the building had a *decrepit* appearance.

decry (dih KRY) *v.* to clamor against: Most critics *decry* the lackluster performance of the lead actor in the play.

deem (DEEM) *v.* to judge, think: The newspaper publisher did not *deem* the event worthy of coverage.

deference (DEF runs) *n.* act of respect, respect for another's wishes: Out of *deference* to her age, we rose when she entered the room.

defiant (dih FY unt) *adj.* Openly or boldly resisting: Beth was *defiant* of the new anti-smoking regulations, openly lighting up in a public area.

deficient (dih FIH shunt) *adj.* not up to standard, inadequate: The child is *deficient* in reading ability but excels in arithmetic.

defray (dih FRAY) *v.* to pay down (costs): The company *defrayed* the costs of its annual convention by eliminating its employees' Christmas bonuses.

defunct (dih FUNKT) *adj.* dead, no longer functioning: The discotheque, now *defunct*, was the most popular night spot in town during the late 1970's.

degenerate (dih JEN er ayt) *v.* to decline from a higher or normal form: The discussion eventually *degenerated* into a shouting match.

degrade (dih GRAYD) *v.* to lower in status, value or esteem: The celebrity refused interviews, feeling that they *degraded* her by exposing her personal life.

delegation (del uh GAY shun) *n.* group of persons officially authorized to act for others: Our *delegation* to the United Nations is headed by the ambassador.

delineate (duh LIN ee ayt) *v.* to mark off the boundary of: They asked him to *delineate* the areas where smoking was permitted.

delinquent (dih LING qwunt) *adj.* delaying or failing to do what roles or law require: Since she was *delinquent* in paying her taxes, she had to pay a fine.

demean (dih MEEN) *v.* to degrade, debase: He would not *demean* himself by resorting to personal attacks against his political opponent.

demonstrable (dih MAHN struh bul) *adj.* able to be shown: Consumer taste tests are needed to achieve *demonstrable* superiority over competing soft drinks.

demote (dih MOHT) *v.* to lower in rank: The senior account executive was *demoted* to a junior rank for failing to meet his sales quota.

deplete (dih PLEET) *v.* to empty, use up: At the present rates of consumption, the known reserves will be *depleted* before the end of the century.

deplore (dih PLOR) *v.* to lament, disapprove strongly: Pacifists *deplore* violence even on behalf of a just cause.

depreciate (dih PREE shee ayt) *v.* to lessen in value: Property will *depreciate* rapidly if kept in poor repair.

deprive (dih PRYV) *v.* to take away, often by force: No person may be *deprived* of his liberty without due process of law.

derelict (DAYR uh likt) *adj.* abandoning duty, remiss: The policeman was *derelict* in his duties; instead of apprehending the speeding motorist he continued to eat his lunch.

derogatory (der AH guh tor ee) *adj.* disparaging, disdainful: Her *derogatory* remarks offended all of us.

despicable (dih SPIK uh bul) *adj.* contemptible: The villain in melodramas is always a *despicable* character.

destitute (DES tih toot) *adj.* in extreme want: Three years of crop failures left the farmers *destitute.*

deterrent (dih TER unt) *n.* a thing that discourages: The absolute certainty of apprehension is a powerful *deterrent* to some types of crime.

detonate (DET uh nayt) *v.* to explode: An electrical charge can be used to *detonate* certain explosives.

detract (dee TRAKT) *v.* to take away a part, lessen: The course engraving *detracted* from the jewelry's value.

deviate (DEE vee ayt) *v.* to stray, turn aside from: If we *deviate* from the main road we'll be late for the show.

devious (DEE vee us) *adj.* roundabout, indirect, underhanded: When no one would tell her anything, she resorted to *devious* means to uncover the truth.

devise (dih VYZ) *v.* to contrive, invent: I will *devise* a plan of escape.

dexterity (dek STAYR uh tee) *n.* quickness, skill and ease in some act: The art of juggling is one that calls for great *dexterity*.

digress (dy GRES) *v.* to wander from the subject: The speaker decided to *digress* from the main topic in order to recapture the audience's attention.

dilate (DY layt) *v.* to expand: Some drugs will cause the pupil of the eye to *dilate*.

dilemma (duh LEM uh) *n.* choice of two unpleasant alternatives, a problem: Eve solved her *dilemma* about which dress to wear by not attending the party at all.

diplomatic (dip loh MAT ik) *adj.* employing tact and conciliation in dealing with people, especially in stressful situations: It would be *diplomatic* not to constantly refer to that woman's previous husbands.

discern (dih SERN) *v.* to perceive, identify: The fog was so thick we could barely *discern* each side of the road.

disciple (dih SY pul) *n.* follower of a teacher: The renowned economist won over many *disciples* with her startling theories.

disclose (dih SKLOHZ) *v.* to reveal: The reporter refused to *disclose* the source of her information.

discordant (dis KOR dunt) *adj.* harsh, not harmonious: The *discordant* cries of the gulls made me long for the familiar sounds of the city.

discretion (dis KRESH un) *n.* power of decision, individual judgment: The penalty to be imposed in many cases is left to the *discretion* of the judge.

disdain (dis DAYN) *v.* to reject as unworthy: Many new graduates unwisely *disdain* a lowly job that might in time lead to the position they desire.

disengage (dis in GAYJ) *v.* to loosen or break a connection: Depressing the clutch *disengages* the driving force from the wheels.

disinterested (dis IN truh stud) *adj.* not involved in, unprejudiced: A *disinterested* witness is one who has no personal stake in the outcome of the case.

dispatch (dis PACH) *v.* to send on an errand: The bank *dispatched* a courier to deliver the documents by hand.

dispel (dis PEL) *v.* to drive away, make disappear: The good-humored joke *dispelled* the tension in the room.

disquieting (dis KWY uh teen) *adj.* disturbing, tending to make uneasy: There have been *disquieting* reports of a buildup of forces along the border.

disseminate (dih SEM uh nayt) *v.* to spread, broadcast: The Internet allows one to *disseminate* information worldwide almost instantaneously.

dissension (dih SEN shun) *n.* lack of harmony or agreement: There was *dissension* among the delegates about which candidate to support.

dissipate (DIS uh payt) *v.* to scatter aimlessly: His inheritance *dissipated* quickly during a series of impulsive shopping sprees.

distraught (dih STRAHT) *adj.* crazed, distracted: The young mother was *distraught* over her son's death.

diverge (duh VERJ) *v.* to extend in different directions from a common point: The map indicated a main road *diverging* into two smaller roads at the city limit.

divert (duh VERT) *v.* to amuse or entertain; to distract attention: A visit from her sister *diverted* the hospital patient from her pain.

divest (dy VEST) *v.* to deprive, strip: A court martial serves to *divest* military officer of his or her rank.

divisive (duh VY siv) *adj.* tending to divide, causing disagreement: Whether to allow the factory to pollute the river was a *divisive* issue among the townspeople.

divulge (duh VULJ) *v.* to reveal, make public: Newspaper reporters have long fought the courts for the right not to *divulge* their sources of information.

docile (DAH sul) *adj.* easily led: The child was *docile* until he discovered his mother was gone.

domicile (DAHM uh syl) *n.* residence: Some people have one *domicile* in winter, another in summer.

dwindle (DWIN dul) *v.* to become steadily less; to shrink: As we consume more oil, our supply *dwindles.*

eclectic (ee KLEK tik) *adj.* drawing from diverse sources or systems: His *eclectic* record collection included everything from Bach cantatas to rap music.

ecstasy (EK stuh see) *n.* extreme happiness: The lovers were in *ecstasy,* oblivious to their surroundings.

egocentric (ee goh SEN trik) *adj.* self-centered: The *egocentric* boss always ignored his employees' advice.

elate (ee LAYT) *v.* to make joyful, elevate in spirit: A grade of 100 will *elate* any student.

elicit (ee LIS it) *v.* to draw out, evoke: Her direct questions only *elicited* further evasions.

eligible (EL uh juh bul) *adj.* fit to be chosen, qualified: Veterans are *eligible* for many government benefits, including low-cost loans.

elusive (ee LOO siv) *adj.* hard to find or grasp: Because the problem is so complex, a solution seems *elusive.*

emanate (EM uh nayt) *v.* to derive from, issue forth: Louisiana law *emanates* largely from French law.

embody (em BAH dee) *v.* to render concrete, give form to: The writer tried to *embody* his ideas in his novel's characters.

emigrate (EM uh grayt) *v.* to leave a country permanently to settle in another: Many people applied for visas, wishing to *emigrate* and escape persecution at home.

enact (en AKT) *v.* to put into law, do or act out: A bill was *enacted* lowering the voting age to eighteen.

encroach (en KROHCH) *v.* to infringe or invade: Property values fall when industries *encroach* upon residential areas.

endeavor (en DEV er) *n.* to attempt by effort, try hard; *(n.)* an attempt or effort: I *endeavored* to contact them several times but they never returned my calls.

endorse (en DORS) *v.* to declare support or approval for: Community leaders were quick to *endorse* a project that would bring new jobs to the neighborhood.

engulf (en GULF) *v.* to swallow up: The rising waters *engulfed* the village.

ensue (en SOO) *v.* to follow immediately or as a result: One person raised an objection and a long argument *ensued.*

entail (en TAYL) *v.* to involve or make necessary: Getting the report out on time will *entail* working all weekend.

entitle (en TY tul) *v.* to give a right or claim to: This pass *entitles* the bearer to two free admissions.

enumerate (ee NOO mer ayt) *v.* to count, specify in a list: In her essay she *enumerated* her reasons for wanting to attend the school.

enunciate (ee NUN see ayt) *v.* to pronounce clearly: He could not *enunciate* certain sounds while chewing gum.

environs (en VY runs) *n.* surroundings, suburbs: We searched the campus and its *environs.*

epitome (ih PIT uh mee) *n.* an abstract, part that typically represents the whole: He prepared an *epitome* of his work to show to the editor.

epoch (EP uk) *n.* distinctive period of time: Hemingway's writings marked an *epoch* in American literature.

eradicate (ih RAD uh kayt) *v.* to pluck up by the roots, wipe out: They tried to *eradicate* the hordes of rabbits by introducing a deadly epidemic.

erode (ih ROHD) *v.* to eat into, wear away: The glaciers *eroded* the land, leaving deep valleys.

esoteric (es oh TAYR ik) *adj.* limited to a few, secret: Her *esoteric* poem was understood by only a few readers.

estranged (is TRAYNJD) *adj.* alienated, separated: His *estranged* wife left him for another man one year ago.

euphoria (yoo FOR ee uh) *n.* extreme sense of well-being: Their *euphoria* at their ascent of the mountain was heightened by their narrow escape from death.

evince (ih VINS) *v.* to make evident, display: His curt reply *evinced* his short temper.

exacting (ayg ZAK ting) *adj.* severe in making demands: She was an *exacting* tutor, never content with less than perfection from her pupils.

expel (ek SPEL) *v.* to push or force out: When a balloon bursts, the air is *expelled* in a rush.

exploit (EK sployt) *v.* to use, especially unfairly or selfishly: Some employers *exploit* illegal immigrants, who are afraid to complain about substandard wages.

exposé (ek spoh ZAY) *n.* exposure of a scandal: Due to the reporter's *exposé* of corruption at the state capitol, two senators were indicted for influence-peddling.

exquisite (ek SKWIZ ut) *adj.* perfect, especially in a lovely, finely tuned or delicate way: The handmade lace was *exquisite* in every detail.

extinct (ek STINKT) *adj.* no longer existing; no longer active, having died down or burnt out: Prehistoric animals are now all *extinct.*

extricate (EK struh kayt) *v.* to free from an entanglement: Carefully removing each prickly branch, she *extricated* herself from the briars.

facsimile (fak SIM uh lee) *n.* An exact reproduction or copy: The dip was a reasonable *facsimile* of that served at the prestigious restaurant.

fallible (FAL ih bul) *adj.* capable of erring or being deceived in judgment: It is a shock for children to discover that their parents are *fallible.*

falter (FAHL ter) *v.* to hesitate, stammer, flinch: The cliff diver died because he *faltered* when diving off the cliff.

fanatic (fuh NAT ik) *n.* person with an unreasoning enthusiasm: The *fanatics* were eager to die for the glory of their religion.

fatigue (fuh TEEG) *n.* mental or physical weariness: After a full day's work, their *fatigue* was understandable.

fickle (FIK ul) *adj.* likely to change: None is so *fickle* as a neglected lover.

finesse (fuh NES) *n.* artifice, subtlety of contrivance to gain a point: She directed the actor with such *finesse* that the actor believed the direction to be his own idea.

finite (FY nyt) *adj.* having a limit, bounded: There was only a *finite* number of applicants to be considered.

flaunt (FLAWNT) *v.* to display freely, defiantly, or ostentatiously; *Flaunting* expensive jewelry in public may be an invitation to robbery.

flourish (FLOOR ish) *v.* to achieve success; to prosper or thrive: A baby will not *flourish* with much attention.

forfeit (FOR fit) *v.* to lose because of a fault: The team made a decisive error, causing it to *forfeit* its lead.

formidable (FOR muh duh bul) *adj.* causing fear or awe: He had a *formidable* enemy.

fortuitous (for TOO uh tus) *adj.* occurring by chance; bringing or happening by luck: It was *fortuitous* that I chose the winning lottery numbers.

forum (FOR um) *n.* place for public business or discussion: A television interview would be the best *forum* for calling our views to the public's attention.

forward (FOR werd) *v.* to promote, send, especially to a new address: The secretary promised to *forward* the request to the person in charge.

frail (FRAYL) *adj.* physically weak: Very old people are often *frail*.

fraud (FRAWD) *n. adj.* deceit or trickery: The real estate agent was charged with *fraud* for pocketing the check intended for the appraisal firm.

frenetic (fruh NET ik) *adj.* frenzied: *Frenetic* activity is evident in the dormitory just before exam time.

frivolous (FRIV uh lus) *adj.* not serious: The atmosphere of the gathering was entirely *frivolous* as everyone got dressed up in costumes and played children's games.

furnish (FER nish) *v.* to provide with what is needed: The army recruit will be *furnished* with uniforms and other equipment.

futile (FYOO tul) *adj.* trifling, useless, pointless: The racer fell so far behind the leader that continuing was *futile*.

generic (juh NER ik) *adj.* pertaining to a race or kind: The *generic* characteristics of each animal allow us to identify its species.

gist (JIST) *n.* essential part, core: That all men are not equal was the *gist* of his speech.

gorge (GORJ) *v.* to eat greedily: The neighborhood children *gorged* themselves on Halloween candy.

gracious (GRAY shus) *adj.* socially graceful, courteous, kind: A *gracious* host puts his guests at ease and is concerned only that they enjoy themselves.

grandeur (GRAN jer) *n.* splendor, magnificence, stateliness: The *grandeur* of the lofty mountains was admired by all.

grapple (GRAP ul) *v.* to seize, lay hold of, either with the hands or with mechanical devices: He *grappled* with the man who had attacked him.

gruff (GRUF) *adj.* rough: His manner was so *gruff* that most of the children feared him.

gyrate (JY rayt) *v.* to revolve around a point, whirl: The tornado *gyrates* around a moving center.

haggard (HAG erd) *adj.* gaunt, careworn, wasted by hardship or terror: After three days of being lost, the *haggard* campers staggered into the village.

haphazard (hap HAZ erd) *adj.* random, without order: He studied in such a *haphazard* way that he learned little.

harrowing (HAYR oh ing) *adj.* severely hurtful or trying, emotionally or physically: The survivors of the crash went through a *harrowing* ordeal before their rescue.

hinder (HIN der) *v.* to retard, slow down, prevent from moving forward: Cold weather has *hindered* the growth of the plants.

holocaust (HAHL uh kawst) *n.* great destruction of living beings, especially by fire: As the fire raged out of control, thousands of lives were lost in the *holocaust*.

hospitable (haw SPIT uh bul) *adj.* welcoming, generous to guests: It was a *hospitable* room, with a soothing color scheme and deep, comfortable chairs.

humility (hyoo MIL uh tee) *n.* humbleness of spirit: The actor accepted the award with *humility*, gratefully acknowledging the talents of his fellow actors.

idiosyncrasy (ih dee oh SING kruh see) *n.* peculiar tendency of an individual: Her *idiosyncrasy* of dropping in on her friends without warning has proved embarrassing on more than one occasion.

illusion (ih LOO zhun) *n.* false, appearance, vision that is misleading: The optical *illusion* made the lines of equal length appear to be unequal.

illusory (ih LOO zer ee) *adj.* unreal, only apparent: Gains from rising stock prices are *illusory* until redemption.

immune (im YOON) *adj.* not susceptible, protected, as from disease: An inoculation for smallpox makes one *immune* to the disease.

impair (im PAYR) *v.* To damage or make worse, especially by lessening, weaken or reducing: Justin *impaired* his department's effectiveness by inciting conflict and ill will among its members.

impartial (im PAR shul) *adj.* not favoring one side or another: The squabbling children appealed to the babysitter for an *impartial* judgment.

impassioned (im PASH und) *adj.* animated, excited, expressive of passion or ardor: The *impassioned* performance of the actor was moving and convincing.

impeccable (im PEK uh bul) *adj.* faultless: Successful comedy depends on *impeccable* timing.

imperative (im PAYR uh tiv) *adj.* of greatest necessity or importance: This is an emergency; it is *imperative* that I reach them at once.

imperil (im PAYR ul) *adj.* to put in danger: The pilot's incompetence *imperiled* the safety of all on board.

impervious (im PER vee us) *adj.* not to be penetrated or passed through: Lead is *impervious* to X-rays.

impetuous (im PECH yoo us) *adj.* impulsive, acting suddenly and without forethought: The *impetuous* boy leaped before he looked.

implement (IM pluh ment) *v.* to put into effect, to realize in practice: When they *implemented* the program, they realized that some of the planned procedures were not practicable and would have to be modified.

imponderable (im PAHN der uh bul) *adj.* not capable of being weighed or measured: The results of the negotiations constitute an *imponderable* at this time.

impoverished (im PAHV er ushd) *v.* poor, lacking, destitute: She was an exceptionally effective manager; the company has been *impoverished* by her loss.

inception (in SEP shun) *n.* beginning: The scheme was harebrained from its *inception;* it was no surprise when it was abandoned.

incidence (IN suh dins) *n.* range of occurrence or effect: The *incidence* of drug use among adults is declining.

incognito (in kahg NEE toh) *adj.* with identity concealed: The prince was traveling *incognito.*

incriminate (in KRIM uh nayt) *v.* to accuse or implicate in a crime or fault: Picked up by the police, the boy *incriminated* his companions by naming them as accomplices in the theft.

indiscriminate (in dis KRIM uh nut) *adj.* not selective: The police made *indiscriminate* arrests, taking into custody scores of people who had broken no law.

induct (in DUKT) *v.* to bring in, initiate a person: A volunteer must pass a physical before being *inducted* into the army.

inept (in EPT) *adj.* incompetent, clumsy, inefficient: The basketball team's center is tall and powerful but so physically *inept* that he frequently loses the ball.

infiltrate (IN ful trayt) *v.* to pass through or into, especially secretly or as an enemy: The radical organization had been *infiltrated* by federal agents who monitored its membership and activities.

inflammatory (in FLAM uh tor ee) *adj.* tending to arouse to anger or violence: An *inflammatory* speech incited the crowd to riot.

inherent (in HAYR unt) *adj.* inborn, existing as a basic or natural characteristic: A cat's need to hunt is *inherent*.

initiate (in ISH ee ayt) *v.* to begin, introduce: The fraternity *initiates* new members every semester.

innuendo (in yoo EN doh) *n.* indirect intimation, hint, especially of something negative: There was an *innuendo* of threat in the phrases she chose.

inquisitive (in KWIZ uh tiv) *adj.* curious, asking questions: Private eyes in detective fiction often get into trouble for being too *inquisitive.*

insatiable (in SAY shee uh bul) *adj.* never satisfied, always greedy: His appetite for wealth was *insatiable;* no matter how rich he became, he always craved more.

instigate (IN stuh gayt) *v.* to urge a bad action: The propaganda was designed to *instigate* an uprising against the government.

instill (in STIL) *v.* to impart gradually: A skillful teacher can *instill* in children a love of learning.

insure (in SHOOR) *v.* to make certain, guarantee: Bail is set to *insure* the defendant's appearance in court.

intangible (in TAN juh bul) *adj.* not able to be touched or easily defined: The company's goodwill among its customers is a genuine but *intangible* asset.

intelligible (in TEL uh juh bul) *adj.* capable of being understood or comprehended; clear: The baby's gibberish is *intelligible* only to its parents.

intent (in TENT) *adj.* firmly directed or fixed; concentrated attention on something or some purpose; act or instance of intending: The tailor was very *intent* at his sewing machine.

irate (y RAYT) *adj.* intensely angry: The *irate* farmer shot the fox in his barnyard.

irreconcilable (ih rek un SY luh bul) *adj.* unable to be harmonized: His statements about liking school were *irreconcilable* with the distaste for reading.

itinerary (y TIN er ayr ee) *n.* plan or schedule of travel: Our *itinerary* includes three days in Florence and a week in Rome.

jargon (JAR gun) *n.* confusing or unintelligible talk, usually a specialized language used by experts: Computer programming *jargon* is rife with acronyms.

judicious (joo DISH us) *adj.* prudent: His policy was *judicious;* he got results without taking great risks.

kindred (KIN drid) *adj.* alike, related: Though from diverse backgrounds, they were *kindred* spirits, alike in intellect and ambition.

knead (NEED) *v.* to mix, squeeze and press with the hands: She *kneaded* the dough before shaping it into four loaves for baking.

labyrinth (LAB er inth) *n.* maze, complex and confusing arrangement: The ancient town within the city walls was a *labyrinth* of narrow, winding streets.

lapse (LAPS) *n.* slip, minor or temporary fault or error: I was embarrassed by a momentary *lapse* of memory when I couldn't recall her name.

lavish (LAV ish) *v.* to give generously or extravagantly: The doting boyfriend *lavished* his girlfriend with gifts.

legacy (LAY guh see) *n.* something inherited: He acquired the house as a *legacy* from his grandmother.

legible (LEJ uh bul) *adj.* written clearly, able to be read: Please print if your handwriting is not easily *legible.*

leisurely (LEE zher lee) *adj.* without haste; slow: The lovers took a *leisurely* stroll around the pond.

leniency (LEE nee un see) *n.* mercy, gentleness, lack of strictness: The *leniency* of the court in suspending the sentence was well repaid by the convicted man's later contribution to the community.

levity (LEV uh tee) *n.* lightness of spirit, frivolity, playfulness: The party toys and silly costumes epitomized the *levity* of the occasion.

lucrative (LOOK ruh tiv) *adj.* profitable: A *lucrative* enterprise is attractive to investors.

ludicrous (LOO duh kris) *adj.* apt to raise laughter, ridiculous: The scene was so *ludicrous* that the audience roared with laughter.

lurid (LOOR id) *adj.* shocking, sensational, tastelessly violent or passionate: The cheap novel told a *lurid* tale of murder and lust.

magisterial (maj uh STEER ee ul) *adj.* authoritative, arrogant, dogmatic: In front of a class the normally humble man assumed a *magisterial* air.

magnitude (MAG nih tood) *n.* size: The apparent *magnitude* of the moon is greater near the horizon than at the zenith.

malpractice (mal PRAK tis) *n.* improper professional conduct: The surgeon was sued for *malpractice* after a sponge was found in his patient's abdomen.

mar (MAR) *v.* to damage: The floor has been *marred* by scratches and scuff marks.

marginal (MAR juh nul) *adj.* Close to a margin or limit, especially a lower limit; limited; minimal: The gains on the stock were *marginal* and did not inspire him to maintain it in his portfolio.

maternal (muh TER nul) *adj.* Of, like, or characteristic of a mother or motherhood: Molly treated her staff in a protecting, almost *maternal* fashion.

matriarch (MAYT ree ark) *n.* mother who rules a family or clan: All important decisions were referred to the *matriarch* of the tribe.

meager (MEE ger) *adj.* deficient in quality and quantity; inadequate: It is impossible to feed a family of four on that *meager* salary.

meddle (MED ul) *v.* to interfere with or take part in other people's affairs without being asked or needed: Justin liked to *meddle* in the projects of other departments.

medicinal (muh DIS uh nul) *adj.* having the property of healing: The plants had a high *medicinal* value.

metamorphose (met uh MOR fohz) *v.* to transform: His travels *metamorphosed* him into a worldly man.

militant (MIL uh tunt) *adj.* defiant, ready to fight, especially for a cause: *Militant* in their political beliefs, they considered any compromise a sellout.

mingle (MING ul) *v.* to mix, join a group: The mayor *mingled* with the crowd at the reception, shaking hands and thanking her supporters.

minuscule (MIN uh skyool) *adj.* tiny, minute: It is impossible to view such *minuscule* particles with an ordinary microscope.

miscellany (MIS uh lay nee) *n.* collection of various or unlike things: The old steamer trunk contained a *miscellany* of papers, clothes and assorted junk.

morale (mor AL) *n.* level of spirits, mental or emotional condition: After a landslide victory at the polls, *morale* in the party was at a peak.

muddle (MUD ul) *v.* to confuse or stupefy: The liquor had gotten him badly *muddled.*

mutilated (MYOO tuh lay tud) *adj.* cut up, damaged severely: The computer's disk drive could not read the *mutilated* diskette.

nauseate (NAW zee ayt) *v.* to cause disgust and nausea to: Any food *nauseates* the patient.

negate (NAY gayt) *v.* to make nothing, undo or make ineffective: The witness's full confession *negated* the need for further questions.

neutralize (NOO truh lyz) *v.* to reduce to a state of indifference, make inactive: The multi-national treaty *neutralized* tensions between the nations.

niche (NICH) *n.* A position or role particularly suitable to the person or thing in it: The convertible model occupied a small but attractive market *niche.*

nonchalant (nahn shuh LAHNT) *adj.* indifferent, cool, unconcerned: The woman acted in a *nonchalant* manner, pretending not to notice the celebrities.

noncompliance (nahn kum PLY uns) *n.* failure to comply: His *noncompliance* with the terms of the contract forced them to sue.

notorious (nuh TOR ee us) *adj.* famous in an unfavorable way: The official was *notorious* among his associates for failing to keep appointments.

novice (NAH vus) *n.* person new to a job or activity, someone inexperienced: A *novice* in the job, she needed more time than an experienced worker to complete the same tasks.

nullify (NUL uh fy) *v.* to make void or without effect: The new contract *nullifies* their previous agreement,

obesity (oh BEE suh tee) *n.* excessive fatness: Her *obesity* was due to her love of rich foods.

obituary (oh BICH yoo ayr ee) *n.* account of the decease of a person: Newspapers keep files on famous people in case they have to run an *obituary.*

obligatory (uh BLIG uh tor ee) *adj.* required, morally or legally binding: He feels nothing for his family, yet he makes an *obligatory* visit to them once or twice a year.

oblique (oh BLEEK) *adj.* Not straight to the point, not straightforward, indirect: At first the witness' answers were rather *oblique*; however, when prompted, she gave a more straightforward response.

obliterate (uh BLIT uh rayt) *v.* to demolish, destroy all trace of: The building had been *obliterated;* we could not even be sure exactly where it had stood.

oblivious (uh BLIV ee us) *adj.* so preoccupied as not to notice: The patron, absorbed in her reading, was *oblivious* to the librarian's question.

obscure (ub SKYOOR) *adj.* dim, murky, not easily seen or understood: Despite attempts at interpretation, the meaning of the passage remains *obscure.*

obsess (ub SES) *v.* to beset, haunt the mind: He was *obsessed* with the idea that he was being followed.

omnipotent (ahm NIP uh tunt) *adj.* all-powerful: By the end of the third match the champion felt *omnipotent.*

optimum (AHP tuh mum) *adj.* best for a purpose, most favorable: Under *optimum* conditions of light and moisture, the plant will grow to over three feet.

orifice (OR uh fus) *n.* opening into a cavity: The surgeon worked through an *orifice* below the ribs.

outcast (OWT kast) *n.* A person or thing cast out or rejected, such as by society: Nick's liberal views made him an *outcast* in politically conservative household.

pacific (puh SIF ik) *adj.* calm, tranquil, placid: The explorer who named the ocean *pacific* found it free from storms and tempests.

pamper (PAM per) *v.* to gratify to the full, coddle, spoil: She *pampered* her pet dog in every possible manner.

panoramic (pan uh RAM ik) *adj.* offering a broad or unlimited view: From the summit of the mountain one has a *panoramic* view of the whole range.

paraphrase (PAYR uh frayz) *v.* to reword: To *paraphrase* someone's work without acknowledging the source of one's information is a form of plagiarism.

pending (PEN ding) *adj.* waiting to be decided: We are waiting for a decision about our *pending* appeal.

per capita (per KAP uh tuh) *adj.* for each person: The *per capita* income of this state is among the highest in the nation.

perforate (PER fer ayt) *v.* to make holes in: The top of the box had been *perforated* to allow air to circulate.

perpetrate (PER puh trayt) *v.* to do something evil, to commit (as a crime): The election committee *perpetrated* the hoax in an attempt to defame the rival candidate.

pertinent (PER tuh nunt) *adj.* relevant, concerning the matter at hand: Since those circumstances were vastly different, that example is not *pertinent* to this case.

perturb (per TERB) *v.* to disturb greatly; to disquiet: We were greatly *perturbed* by strange noises in the night.

petty (PET ee) *adj.* small, trivial, unimportant, small-minded: Don't bother the supervisor with *petty* problems; try to handle them yourself.

picturesque (pik cher ESK) *adj.* having a rough, unfamiliar, or quaint natural beauty: The mountains descending to the lake provide a *picturesque* landscape.

pinnacle (PIN uh kul) *n.* peak, acme: She had reached such a *pinnacle* of fame that everywhere in the country her name was a household word.

placid (PLAS ud) *adj.* peaceful, undisturbed: The drug had relieved her anxiety, leaving her in a *placid* mood.

potent (POH tunt) *adj.* powerful or effective in action: Penicillin is a *potent* medicine that should be administered with care.

preclude (prih KLOOD) *v.* to make impossible: Obeying the speed limit would *preclude* my getting home early.

predatory (PRED uh tor ee) *adj.* plundering, hunting: The hawk is a *predatory* bird.

predecessor (PRED uh ses er) *n.* one who has preceded or gone before another in a position or office: In his inaugural address the new president of the association praised the work of his *predecessor*.

predicament (pruh DIK uh munt) *n.* troublesome or perplexing situation from which escape seems difficult: The new president's promise to balance the budget while cutting taxes put him in a hopeless *predicament*.

prejudiced (PREJ uh dust) *adj.* biased, judging in advance without adequate evidence: Since I have never liked Western movies, I was *prejudiced* against the film before I ever saw it.

preoccupied (pree AHK yoo pyd) *adj.* having one's thoughts elsewhere, inattentive: *Preoccupied* by her dilemma, she missed her stop on the train.

preposterous (prih PAHS ter us) *adj.* very absurd: The idea of the president's visiting our class was *preposterous*.

prescribe (prih SKRYB) *v.* to recommend, especially in a professional capacity: For the headache the physician *prescribed* aspirin.

prevalent (PREV uh lunt) *adj.* current, widely found, common: Golfers are even more *prevalent* among doctors than lawyers.

principal (PRIN suh pul) *adj.* main, most important: The mayor's *principal* concern is for the city's economy.

probation (proh BAY shun) *n.* period of testing or evaluation: After a week's *probation* the employee was hired permanently.

proclaim (proh KLAYM) *v.* to announce loudly, publicly and with conviction: The coach *proclaimed* sure victory when the other team lost its best player.

procrastinate (proh KRAS tuh nayt) *v.* to delay doing something, put off without reason: Since you'll have to get it done eventually, you might as well stop *procrastinating* and get started.

prolong (proh LAWNG) *v.* to draw out to greater length: The treatment *prolongs* life but cannot cure the disease, which is terminal.

prompt (PRAHMPT) *adj.* quick, following immediately: Correspondents appreciate *prompt* replies to their inquiries so they can dispatch news in a timely manner.

proportionate (pruh POR shun ut) *adj.* in correct proportion or relation of amount, fairly distributed: An area's representation in the House of Representatives is *proportionate* to its population.

prosper (PRAH sper) *v.* to thrive, do well, grow richer: In order to *prosper* a fledgling business must strive to draw customers away from its established competitors.

proximity (prahk SIM uh tree) *n.* nearness: The *proximity* of the shopping mall is a great advantage to those residents who don't drive.

punctuality (punk choo AL uh tee) *n.* being on time: The train had an excellent record for *punctuality;* it almost always arrived precisely at eight o'clock.

queasy (KWEE zee) *adj.* causing or affected by nausea; squeamish: The very thought of a visit to the dentist makes some people *queasy.*

quiver (KWIV er) *v.* to shake, tremble, shudder: The dog *quivered* with excitement.

quota (KWOH tuh) *n.* proportional share: The school had a *quota* system that set limits on the proportion of applicants accepted from different geographical areas.

rambunctious (ram BUNK chus) *adj.* wild; marked by uncontrollable exuberance; unruly: The children's *rambunctious* behavior often leaves the room in complete disorder.

rapidity (ruh PID uh tee) *n.* speed: The *rapidity* with which her hands flew over the piano keys was too great for the eyes to follow.

rationale (rash uh NAL) *n.* rational basis, explanation or justification supposedly based on reason: They defended their discrimination with the *rationale* that women were physically incompetent to handle the job.

recede (rih SEED) *v.* to go back or away: The waters *receded* and left the beach covered with seaweed.

reciprocal (rih SIP ruh kul) *adj.* done in return, affecting both sides, mutual: Many nations maintain *reciprocal* trade agreements with other nations.

recuperate (rih KOO per ayt) *v.* to become well, get better: It is best to stay home from work until you fully *recuperate* from your illness.

recur (rih KER) *v.* to happen again: Unless social conditions improve, the riots are bound to *recur.*

redeem (rih DEEM) *v.* to save (as from something), free by buying back: Though the film is boring in parts, it is *redeemed* by a gripping finale.

refinement (rih FYN munt) *n.* fineness or elegance of taste, manners, or language: Full appreciation of the office building's architecture requires a certain *refinement* on the part of its occupants.

refrain (rih FRAYN) *v.* to keep from doing something, to not do: Considerate parents *refrain* from criticizing their children in front of others.

regal (REE gul) *adj.* pertaining to a monarch, royal: He had a *regal* air that impressed even those who knew him as an imposter.

regimen (REJ uh mun) *n.* regular manner of living, routine: The *regimen* of army life stifled the free-spirited young man.

reimburse (ree um BERS) *v.* to refund, pay back: The bankrupt company was unable to *reimburse* its salespeople for their company-related expenses.

relinquish (rih LING quish) *v.* to give up, hand over: The aunt *relinquished* custody of the child to its mother.

renounce (rih NOWNS) *v.* to give up or disown, usually by formal statement: The nation was urged to *renounce* its dependence on oil and to develop alternative fuels.

replenish (rih PLEN ish) *v.* to supply again, to make full or complete again something that has been depleted: Some natural resources, such as lumber, can be *replenished*.

replica (REP lih cuh) *n.* A reproduction or copy of a work of art: Dan couldn't afford the original work of art, but he did own a *replica* of it.

repress (rih PRES) *v.* to subdue, hold back, keep down, keep from expression or consciousness: We could not *repress* our fear as the plane suddenly lost altitude.

reprimand (REP ruh mand) *n.* severe criticism, especially a formal rebuke by someone in authority; *(v.)* to criticize severely: Since it was a first offense, the judge let the teenager off with a *reprimand.* The judge *reprimanded* the teenager.

residue (REZ uh doo) *n.* something left over, remainder: A *residue* of coffee grounds was left at the bottom of the cup.

resilient (rih ZIL yunt) *adj.* able to spring back: The car's shock absorbers were still *resilient* after years of use.

resume (rih ZOOM) *v.* to begin again after an interruption: The courtroom proceedings *resumed* after an hour's recess for lunch.

resuscitate (rih SUS uh tayt) *v.* to bring back to life: The paramedic could not *resuscitate* the drowning victim.

retaliate (rih TAL ee ayt) *v.* To return like for like, especially injury for injury: The boxer *retaliated* for the punch with a stunning blow to the head.

retard (rih TARD) *v.* to slow: Drugs were successfully used to *retard* the progress of the disease.

retroactive (ret roh AK tiv) *adj.* applying to what is past: The law is not *retroactive;* it applies only to future events.

reverence (REV runs) *n.* feeling of deep respect or awe, as for something sacred: The popular novelist was uncomfortable with the *reverence* by which students treated her at the college where she taught classes.

revive (rih VYV) *v.* to come or bring back to life: A cool drink and a bath *revived* her spirits.

robust (roh BUST) *adj.* hardy, strong, healthy: Her *robust* health was apparent in her springy walk and glowing skin.

rouse (ROWZ) *v.* to stir up; to excite or awaken: Let us *rouse* the citizenry to a new era of patriotism.

rupture (RUP cher) *v.* a breaking off, breach; *(n.)* a break or breach: Undue stress on the abdomen can *rupture* its lining. The bungled rescue operation led to a *rupture* in diplomatic relations.

salvage (SAL vij) *v.* to save or recover from disaster, such as shipwreck or fire: Divers *salvaged* gold coins and precious artifacts from the sunken Spanish galleon.

saturate (SACH er ayt) *v.* to fill fully, soak, cause to become completely penetrated: The cloth was thoroughly *saturated* with the soapy water.

schematic (skih MAT ik) *adj.* in the form of an outline or diagram: A *schematic* drawing of the circuitry illustrated how the computer chip worked.

scrupulous (SKROO pyuh lus) *adj.* having scruples (principles or morals), conscientiously honest and upright: That attorney is too *scrupulous* to get involved in racketeering.

simulate (SIM yuh layt) *v.* to pretend, feign, give a false appearance of: To prepare for their space walks astronauts *simulate* the experience under water.

site (SYT) *n.* piece of land considered as a location for something, such as a city: The archeologists began excavations at the *site* of the ancient city.

skepticism (SKEP tuh sih zum) *n.* doubt, partial disbelief: He listened to the fantastic story with patent *skepticism.*

slate (SLAYT) *v.* to put on a list, to schedule: The meeting is *slated* for next Tuesday.

slipshod (SLIP shahd) *adj.* shabby; careless in appearance or workmanship: *Slipshod* work habits tend to lead to faulty products.

smother (SMUH ther) *v.* to destroy life by depriving of air; to suppress expression or knowledge: One way to extinguish a small fire is to *smother* it with thick foam.

spontaneous (spahn TAY nee us) *adj.* coming from natural impulse, having no external cause, unplanned: Oily rags improperly disposed of may cause a fire by *spontaneous* combustion.

stalemate (STAYL mayt) *n.* deadlock, situation in which neither side in a game or contest can make a move: Talks have reached a *stalemate;* neither side is authorized to make the necessary concessions.

stamina (STAM uh nuh) *n.* power of endurance, physical resistance to fatigue or stress: While younger swimmers tend to be faster over short distances, older swimmers often have more *stamina.*

stature (STACH er) *n.* height, elevation (often used figuratively): The professor's contributions to the field of physics afforded him great *stature* among his peers.

status (STAT us) *n.* position, rank, present condition: Her *status* as vice president allows her to take such action without prior approval by the board of directors.

sterile (STAYR ul) *adj.* free from germs, barren, infertile, unproductive, lacking in liveliness or interest: The room was depressingly *sterile* with its drab colors, bare walls, and institutional furniture.

stratagem (STRAT uh jum) *n.* scheme that outwits by cleverness or trickery: His *stratagem* confused his opponent, thereby helping him to win the chess match.

stringent (STRIN junt) *adj.* severe, strict, compelling: The buying and selling of securities is governed by *stringent* government regulations.

suave (SWAHV) *adj.* smoothly polite: His *suave* manner reflected great confidence and poise.

subdue (sub DOO) *v.* to overcome, calm, render less harsh or less intense: The understanding actions of the nurse helped to *subdue* the stubborn and unruly patient.

subsequent (SUB suh kwint) *adj.* following in time, order or place: *Subsequent* to his arrest, the suspect was arraigned before the judge.

successive (suk SES iv) *adj.* following one after another without interruption: Last week it rained on four *successive* days.

successor (suk SES er) *n.* one who follows another, as in an office or job: Retiring from office, the mayor left a budget crisis and a transit strike to his *successor*.

superficial (soo per FISH ul) *adj.* on or concerned with the surface only, shallow: The *superficial* movie review merely gave a synopsis of the movie's plot.

surcharge (SER charj) *n.* an additional tax or cost above the usual: The airline levies a *surcharge* for heavy baggage.

surveillance (ser VAYL uns) *n.* a watching: The suspect was kept under *surveillance*.

susceptible (suh SEP tuh bul) *adj.* easily affected, liable: She is *susceptible* to colds because of her recent illness.

suspend (sus PEND) *v.* to stop or cause to be inactive temporarily; to hang: Service on the train line was *suspended* while the tracks were being repaired. The light fixture was *suspended* from the ceiling.

tabulate (TAB yoo layt) *v.* to arrange data in some order: The bookkeeper *tabulated* expenses one at a time.

tedious (TEE dee us) *adj.* boring, long and tiresome: The film was so *tedious* that we walked out before it was half over.

tentative (TEN tuh tiv) *adj.* done as a test, experiment, or trial: Negotiators have reached a *tentative* agreement, but the details have not yet been worked out.

toxic (TAHK sik) *adj.* poisonous: Alcohol consumed in very large quantity may prove highly *toxic.*

tranquil (TRANK wul) *adj.* quiet, calm, peaceful: The motorboat's wake disturbed the *tranquil* surface of the lake.

transcript (TRAN skript) *n.* written copy: The court reporter read the *transcript* of the witness' testimony.

trauma (TRAH muh) *n.* bodily injury caused by an outside force or agent: Many emotional ailments in adults are related to psychic *traumas* in childhood.

tribulation (trib yoo LAY shun) *n.* great trouble or hardship: The Pilgrims faced many *tribulations* in order to firmly establish their first colony.

truncate (TRUNG kayt) *v.* to shorten by cutting: The shrubs were uniformly *truncated* to form a neat hedge.

turbulent (TERB yuh lunt) *adj.* violent, in wild motion, agitated: The *turbulent* stream claimed many lives.

unaccountable (un uh KOWN tuh bul) *adj.* mysterious, not able to be explained: His *unaccountable* disappearance led his family to contact the police.

unbridled (un BRY duld) *adj.* Not controlled or restrained: Anxious to earn a commission, the sales representative pursued the new account with *unbridled* enthusiasm.

uncouth (un KOOTH) *adj.* unrefined, awkward: The girl was so *uncouth* she could hardly handle a knife and fork and had no notion of table manners.

undermine (UN der myn) *v.* To injure, weaken, or impair, especially by subtle, stealthy, or insidious means: Jan tried to *undermine* Jose's authority at every chance.

uniformity (yoo nuh FOR muh tee) *n.* sameness, lack of variation: Although the temperature is pleasant, the *uniformity* in weather from season to season can become boring.

unilateral (yoo nuh LAT er ul) *adj.* one-sided, coming from or affecting one side only: The decision to separate was *unilateral*; one spouse moved out against the other's wishes.

unprecedented (un PRES uh den tid) *adj.* never before done, without precedent: The movie *Star Wars* was an *unprecedented* feat in the use of special effects for film.

utensil (yoo TEN sul) *n.* implement, tool: Forks and other *utensils* are in the silverware drawer.

utilize (YOO tuh lyz) *v.* to use, put to use: If we fully *utilize* all our firm's resources we'll become profitable.

vacate (VAY kayt) *v.* to leave empty: The court ordered the demonstrators to *vacate* the premises.

vacuous (VAK yoo us) *adj.* empty, without substance: His *vacuous* promises were forgotten as soon as they were uttered.

vain (VAYN) *adj.* unsuccessful, useless: A *vain* rescue attempt only made the situation worse.

valor (VAL er) *n.* worthiness, courage, strength of mind in regard to danger: His *valor* enabled him to encounter the enemy bravely.

vandal (VAN dul) *n.* one who deliberately disfigures or destroys property: *Vandals* broke all the windows in the vacant building.

vanquish (VANG kwish) *v.* to conquer, overcome, overpower: Napoleon *vanquished* the Austrian army.

vengeance (VEN juns) *v.* Revenge on behalf of a person, usually oneself: The victim's brother sought *vengeance* for her death by prosecuting the suspect in her killing.

verbatim (ver BAY tum) *adj.* word for word, in the same words: The lawyer requested the defendant to repeat the speech *verbatim*.

versatile (VER suh tul) *adj.* competent in many things, subjects, fields; flexible: *Versatility* is the hallmark of the good handyman.

vertex (VER teks) *n.* top, highest point, apex: The view from the *vertex* of the hill was breathtaking.

vitality (vy TAL uh tee) *n.* life, energy, liveliness, power to survive: She had been physically active all her life and at the age of eighty still possessed great *vitality*.

vocation (voh KAY shun) *n.* regular occupation or work: My *vocation* is accounting; my avocation (hobby) is hiking.

volatile (VAHL uh tul) *adj.* changing to vapor, quickly changeable, fickle: She had a *volatile* temper easily angered and easily appeased.

vulnerable (VUL ner uh bul) *adj.* open to attack or danger; easily wounded or physically hurt; sensitive: A person with AIDS is very *vulnerable* to infection.

wayward (WAY werd) *adj.* perverse, capricious, willful, erratic: The bat's *wayward* flight was difficult to track.

wily (WY lee) *adj.* artful, cunning: He was *wily* enough to avoid detection.

wince (WINS) *v.* to shrink, as from a blow or from pain, flinch: She *winced* when the dentist touched the tooth.

yearn (YERN) *v.* to feel longing or desire: The busy couple *yearned* for a day when they could retire to a more relaxed life.

zeal (ZEEL) *n.* ardor, fervor, enthusiasm, earnestness: The candidate campaigned with great *zeal* because he truly believed he could serve the electorate more effectively than his opponent.

Level 2

Advanced Quick Vocabulary

The words in Level 2 are more difficult than those in Level 1. Each listing includes the pronunciation, part of speech, definition, and a sample sentence. Note that the parts of speech are general rules since many words can be used in different ways.

abase (uh BAYS) *v.* to cast down or make humble, to reduce in estimation: He refused to *abase* himself by admitting his mistake in front of the crowd.

abate (uh BAYT) *v.* to lessen in intensity or number: After an hour the storm *abated* and the sky began to clear.

aberrant (AB er unt) *adj.* differing from what is right or normal: *Aberrant* behavior is frequently seen as a sign of emotional disturbance.

abeyance (uh BAY uns) *n.* temporary suspension of an action: The strike motion was held in *abeyance* pending contract negotiations.

amicable (AM uh kuh bul) *adj.* friendly: Courts often seek to settle civil suits in an *amicable* manner.

ardent (AR dunt) *adj.* passionately enthusiastic: His *ardent* patriotism led him to risk his life in the underground resistance movement.

attrition (uh TRISH un) *n.* a gradual wearing down: With the armies dug into the trenches, World War I became a war of *attrition.*

autocratic (aw tuh KRAT ik) *adj.* despotic, acting without regard for the rights or opinions of others: An *autocratic* attitude on the part of a supervisor is deeply resented by subordinates.

avuncular (uh VUNG kyoo ler) *adj.* Having traits considered typical of uncles (*e.g.*, jolly, indulgent, stodgy): Walter Cronkite's *avuncular* demeanor endeared him to a generation of Americans.

besmirch (bih SMERCH) *v.* to soil or tarnish, especially a person's honor or reputation: One critical remark about the mayor by the popular local newspaper columnist forever *besmirched* his reputation.

blithe (BLYTH) *adj.* Showing a lighthearted, cheerful disposition: Despite the potential downsizing, Martha remained a *blithe* spirit, unconcerned about how events might affect her future.

candor (KAN der) *n.* unreserved honest or sincere expression: *Candor* and innocence often go hand in hand.

capacious (kuh PAY shus) *adj.* roomy, spacious: The travelers had all their possessions in one *capacious* suitcase.

capricious (kuh PREE shus) *adj.* changing suddenly, willfully erratic: He is so *capricious* in his moods that no one can predict how he will take the news.

cede (SEED) *v.* to yield, assign, transfer: A bill of sale will *cede* title in personal property.

chicanery (shih KAY ner ee) *n.* unethical methods, legal trickery: He accused the winning candidate of *chicanery* in manipulating the election.

chide (CHYD) *v.* to rebuke, scold: The parents *chided* the disobedient child.

circuitous (ser KYOO uh tus) *adj.* Roundabout; indirect; devious: James gave a long, *circuitous* explanation for why the orders had not arrived as expected.

clemency (KLEM un see) *n.* leniency: The governor granted *clemency* to the prisoners.

cogent (KOH junt) *adj.* conclusive, convincing: A debater must present *cogent* arguments to win his point.

commiserate (kuh MIZ er ayt) *v.* to express sympathy for: It is natural to *commiserate* with the innocent victim of an accident.

compunction (kum PUNK shun) *n.* remorse, uneasiness: He showed no *compunction* over his carelessness.

conciliatory (kun SIL ee uh tor ee) *adj.* tending to placate or to gain goodwill: After the quarrel he sent flowers as a *conciliatory* gesture.

condole (kun DOHL) *v.* to express sympathy with a person who is in sorrow: His friends gathered to *condole* him over the loss of his wife.

consign (kun SYN) *v.* to entrust, hand over: The child was *consigned* to the care of her older sister until the court could appoint a guardian.

contrition (kun TRISH un) *n.* sincere remorse: They were overwhelmed by *contrition* when they realized the damage they had caused.

corpulent (KOR pyoo lunt) *adj.* very fat: The *corpulent* individual must choose clothing with great care.

corroborate (ker AH ber ayt) *v.* to provide added proof: Laws of evidence require that testimony on a crime be *corroborated* by other circumstances.

craven (KRAY vun) *adj.* cowardly: His *craven* conduct under stress made him the butt of many jests.

cull (KUL) *v.* to select, pick out from a group: From the pile we *culled* all the mail for local delivery.

culpable (KUL puh bul) *adj.* faulty, blameworthy, guilty: The *culpable* parties should not escape punishment.

de facto (dee FAK toh) *adj.* actual as opposed to legal: Although he holds no official position, he is the *de facto* head of the government.

dearth (DERTH) *n.* scarcity: Deserts are characterized by a *dearth* of water, and thus often a *dearth* of people.

debase (dih BAYS) *v.* to reduce in dignity or value: Inflation has *debased* the currency so that a dollar now buys very little.

decorum (dih KOR um) *n.* that which is suitable or proper: He had gentlemanly notions of *decorum;* he always held doors open for ladies and held their chairs when they sat down to dinner.

deleterious (del uh TEER ee us) *adj.* injurious, harmful: Fluorocarbons have been shown to have a *deleterious* effect on the Earth's ozone layer.

denigrate (DEN uh grayt) *v.* to blacken, defame: The lawyer tried to *denigrate* the character of the witness by implying that he was a liar.

desuetude (DES wih tood) *n.* lack of use: The law, which had never been repealed, had fallen into *desuetude* and was never enforced.

disconcert (dis kun SERT) *v.* to throw into confusion: An apathetic audience may *disconcert* even the most experienced performer.

dissemble (dis SEM bul) *v.* to conceal or misrepresent the true nature of something: He *dissembled* his real motives under a pretence of unselfish concern.

dissuade (dis SWAYD) *v.* to advise against, divert by persuasion: Her friends *dissuaded* her from the unwise plan.

dossier (daw see AY) *n.* file on a subject or person: The French police kept a *dossier* on every person with a criminal record.

duplicity (doo PLIS ih tee) *n.* hypocrisy, double-dealing: The *duplicity* of the marketplace may shock the naive.

ebullient (eh BYOO lee unt) *adj.* overflowing (bubbling over) with excitement, enthusiasm, or fervor: To sell cars salespeople become instantly *ebullient* about whichever model the customer expresses most interest.

efface (ih FAYS) *v.* to obliterate, wipe out: Victims of physical abuse often wish they could *efface* their memories of the abuse.

effigy (EF uh jee) *n.* image of a person, especially of one who is hated: They burned his *effigy* in the public square.

effrontery (eh FRUNT er ee) *n.* audacity, rude boldness: He had the *effrontery* to go up to the distinguished guest and call him by his first name.

egress (EE gres) *n.* a going out, exit: The building code requires that the apartment have at least two means of *egress*.

emendation (em un DAY shun) *n.* change or correction in a text: The author corrected typographical errors and made a few other *emendations* in his manuscripts.

endemic (en DEM ik) *adj.* restricted or peculiar to a particular place or region: The labor shortage is *endemic* to the information technology industry; all other fields are experiencing a labor glut.

enervate (EN er vayt) *v.* to weaken, enfeeble: A poor diet will *enervate* a person.

enmity (EN muh tee) *n.* state of being an enemy, hostility: The *enmity* between China and Vietnam is traditional and unabated.

envenom (en VEN um) *v.* to make poisonous, embitter: Out of jealousy he tried to *envenom* the relationship between his friend and his rival.

equanimity (ek wuh NIM uh tee) *n.* calm temper, evenness of mind: Adversity could not ruffle her *equanimity*.

equivocal (ih KWIV uh kul) *adj.* having more than one possible meaning, deliberately misleading while not literally untrue: His *equivocal* statements left us in doubt as to his real intentions.

eulogize (YOO luh jyz) *v.* to praise highly in speech or writing: The deceased was *eulogized* at his funeral.

exacerbate (ig ZAS er bayt) *v.* to make worse, aggravate: Drinking coffee can *exacerbate* an already upset stomach.

excise (EK syz) *v.* to remove by cutting out: The surgeon will have to *excise* the tumor.

execrable (EK sih kru bul) *adj.* extremely bad: Although her acting was *execrable,* she looked so good on stage that the audience applauded.

exhort (eg ZORT) *v.* to incite by words or advice: The demagogue *exhorted* the crowd to attack the station.

exonerate (eg ZAHN er ayt) *v.* to free from blame: The confession of one prisoner *exonerated* the other suspects.

explicate (EK splih kayt) *v.* to explain, develop a principle: He *explicated* the parts of the text that the students had found confusing.

extenuate (eks TEN yoo ayt) *v.* to partially excuse, seem to lessen: His abrupt rudeness was *extenuated* by his distraught state of mind; no one could blame him for it.

factotum (fak TOH tum) *n.* employee with miscellaneous duties: He was the chief *factotum* of the plant.

gauche (GOHSH) *adj.* without social grace, tactless: It is considered *gauche* to ask acquaintances how much they earn or how much they paid for something.

genial (JEEN yul) *adj.* pleasant, friendly: The president's rotund and *genial* face made him the perfect Santa Claus.

germane (jer MAYN) *adj.* pertinent, on the subject at hand: The point, though true, was not *germane* to the argument.

goad (GOHD) *v.* to drive with a stick, urge on: Although she was naturally lax, she was *goaded* on by her parents' ambitions.

gratuitous (gruh TOO uh tus) *adj.* free, voluntary, unasked for or unnecessary: Her spiteful temper expressed itself in *gratuitous* insults.

gratuity (gruh TOO uh tee) *n.* tip: He left a *gratuity* for the chambermaid.

heinous (HAY nus) *adj.* Outrageously evil or wicked, abominable: The murderer's crime was so *heinous* that the prosecutor asked for the death penalty.

homage (AH mij) *n.* respect, expression of veneration or extreme admiration: She paid *homage* to her mentor by dedicating her book to him.

homily (HAH mu lee) *n.* discourse on a moral problem, sermon: The judge read the boy a *homily* on his conduct before sentencing him.

ignominy (ig NAH nuh mee) *n.* a discrediting, disgrace: After the *ignominy* of the impeachment he retired from public life.

immolate (IM uh layt) *v.* to offer as a sacrifice: The Buddhist monk *immolated* himself in a public square as a gesture of protest against the war.

impel (im PEL) *v.* To push, drive, or move forward; to force or urge: Terrance *impelled* his staff to get the project in gear by threatening them with termination if they didn't.

impalpable (im PAL puh bul) *adj.* not able to be felt: The seismograph can measure tremors in the earth's crust *impalpable* to humans.

impediment (im PED uh munt) *n.* hindrance, something that delays or stops progress: Lack of training may be an *impediment* to advancement.

imperturbable (im per TER buh bul) *adj.* not easily excited: His *imperturbable* expression was a great aid in poker.

importune (im per TOON) *v.* to urge or beg: Do not *importune* me for another loan; you never paid back the last one.

impudence (IM pyoo duns) *n.* shamelessness, want of modesty, assurance accompanied by a disregard for the opinions of others: His *impudence* in denying having made the promise left us flabbergasted.

impunity (im PYOO nuh tee) *n.* exemption from punishment, penalty, injury or loss: No person should be permitted to violate the laws with *impunity.*

impute (im PYOOT) *v.* to attribute, ascribe: The difficulties were *imputed* to the manufacturer's negligence.

inalienable (in AYL ee uh nuh bul) *adj.* not transferable, not able to be taken away: As humans we are endowed with certain *inalienable* rights.

incessant (in SES unt) *adj.* unceasing, uninterrupted, continual: The *incessant* rain kept the children indoors all day.

incorrigible (in KOR uh juh bul) *adj.* That which cannot be corrected, improved, or reformed: After Jimmy's third criminal offense, his parole officer became convinced that he was *incorrigible* and was destined for a career in crime.

ingratiate (in GRAY shee ayt) *v.* to establish (oneself) in the favor or good graces of others: He tried to *ingratiate* himself with his boss by working late.

inopportune (in ah per TOON) *adj.* inconvenient or unseasonable; not appropriate: To suggest a change of itinerary at this time would be *inopportune.*

inquest (IN kwest) *n.* judicial investigation: The state held an *inquest* to examine the cause of the disaster and determine whether charges should be brought against any parties.

insidious (in SID ee us) *adj.* secretly dangerous, tending to entrap: The casino games were *insidious;* before he realized it, he had gambled away all of his savings.

insinuate (in SIN yoo ayt) *v.* to suggest subtly, especially something negative: By her comment that the music was unusual she *insinuated* that she didn't like it.

insolent (IN suh lunt) *adj.* Boldly disrespectful in speech or behavior, defiantly disrespectful: Kevin's *insolent* behavior earned him a trip to the principal's office.

intercede (in ter SEED) *v.* to interpose in behalf of: The young girl asked her minister to *intercede* in the quarrelsome relationship between her two parents.

lacerate (LAS er ayt) *v.* to tear tissue roughly: The baby swallowed the safety pin, which *lacerated* his intestine.

laconic (luh KAH nik) *adj.* terse, pithy: Her *laconic* replies conveyed much in few words.

lament (luh MENT) *v.* to bewail, mourn for: The boy *lamented* the death of his father.

languid (LANG gwid) *adj.* listless, slow, lacking energy: His *languid* walk irritated his companions, who were in a hurry.

lassitude (LAS uh tood) *n.* feeling of weariness, languor: The *lassitude* caused by the intense heat led them to postpone their sightseeing.

laxity (LAK sih tee) *n.* looseness, lack of strictness: In summer, when business was slow, the manager allowed the employees some *laxity* in their hours.

liaison (lee AY zahn) *n.* connection, linking: The diplomat served as a *liaison* between the opposing military forces.

loathe (LOHTH) *v.* to dislike with disgust; to detest; to hate: I *loathe* people who mistreat animals.

lucid (LOO sid) *adj.* clear, transparent: The directions were written in a style so *lucid* that a child could follow them.

lugubrious (luh GOO bree us) *adj.* excessively mournful in a way that seems exaggerated or ridiculous: The bloodhound had an endearingly *lugubrious* look.

machination (mak uh NAY shun) *n.* scheme or secret plot, especially an evil one: The new employee resorted to various *machinations* to obtain a managerial position despite her lack of experience with the firm.

magnate (MAG nayt) *n.* important business person: The steel *magnate* refused to approve the consolidation.

malaise (muh LAYZ) *n.* general bodily weakness: She complained of a *malaise* that caused her to sleep ten hours a day.

malfeasance (mal FEE zuns) *n.* wrongdoing, especially in public office: The governor was accused of acts of *malfeasance*, including taking graft.

malign (muh LYN) *v.* to speak ill of: The students often *maligned* the strict professor.

martinet (mar tuh NET) *n.* rigid, petty disciplinarian: The captain was a *martinet* who considered an unpolished button criminal negligence.

mawkish (MAW kish) *adj.* slightly nauseating, insipidly sentimental: Her constant display of fawning affection .was *mawkish*.

meritorious (mayr uh TOR ee us) *adj.* deserving reward: Medals were awarded for *meritorious* service.

militate (MIL uh tayt) *v.* to operate against or in favor of: Windy conditions result in high ocean surf, which *militates* against swimmers but in favor of surfers.

misappropriation (mis uh proh pree AY shun) *n.* act of using for a wrongful or illegal purpose: The stock broker was charged with *misappropriation* of her clients' funds for her personal use.

misnomer (mis NOH mer) *n.* wrong or inaccurate name: This season Muddy River is a *misnomer*; the river's waters are clear and crystalline.

mitigate (MIT uh gayt) *v.* to lessen, make milder: He sought to *mitigate* their grief with soothing words.

modicum (MAHD ih kum) *n.* a little, a small quantity: Lacking formal musical training, the aspiring pianist had only a *modicum* of success learning to play his favorite classical pieces.

modulation (MAH jyoo LAY shun) *n.* adaptation or variance in pitch, intensity, volume, musical key: The dis-

tinctive *modulations* of Eastern music sound strange to
many Westerners.

morass (muh RAS) *n.* swamp, bog, messy or troublesome
state: The application became mired in a *morass* of pa-
perwork; there was no response for several weeks.

moribund (MOR uh bund) *adj.* dying: The *moribund* tree
put out fewer and fewer leaves each spring.

morose (muh ROHS) *adj.* gloomy, sulking, unreasonably
unhappy: The teenager's failure to obtain tickets to his
favorite band's concert left him *morose* for days.

nascent (NAS unt) *adj.* coming into being; being born;
beginning to develop: As popular as the Internet has
become, it is still a relatively *nascent* phenomenon.

negligible (NAY glih juh bul) *adj.* too small or insignifi-
cant to be worthy of consideration: The difference in
their ages is *negligible.*

node (NOHD) *n.* knot or protuberance: At both ends of
each length of the bridge's rope is a *node* connecting
that length with other rope lengths.

nomenclature (NOH mun klay cher) *n.* names of things
in any art or science, whole vocabulary of technical
terms appropriate to any particular branch of science:
The *nomenclature* used in medical science is almost
entirely derived from Latin.

obsequious (ub SEE kwee us) *adj.* servile, overly willing
to obey: His *obsequious* obedience to the conquerors
turned our stomachs.

obtrusive (ub TROO siv) *adj.* characterized by uninvited
or unwelcome behavior: They considered his *obtrusive*
behavior an invasion of their privacy.

odious (OH dee us) *adj.* deserving hatred or repugnance: Publicly comparing the talents of children is an *odious* habit.

onerous (OH ner us) *adj.* difficult and unpleasant, burdensome: The work was so *onerous* she often thought of quitting.

opportune (ah per TOON) *adj.* suitable or appropriate: Since you have just made an impressive sale, this is an *opportune* time to ask for a raise.

opprobrium (uh PROHB ree um) *n.* reproach for disgraceful conduct, infamy: He deserved all the *opprobrium* he received for turning his back on his friend.

ordure (OR jer) *n.* filth, excrement: Any person near the barnyard can smell the stench of *ordure*.

ostensible (aw STEN suh bul) *adj.* avowed, apparent: Although his *ostensible* purpose for obtaining a loan from his parents was to buy text books, he actually used the money to purchase a new audio system.

palliate (PAL ee ayt) *v.* to make an offense seem less grave: She attempted to *palliate* her error by explaining the extenuating circumstances.

pariah (puh RY uh) *n.* Any person despised or rejected by others: By alienating the entire company's staff Jeff had become a *pariah* at work.

parity (PAYR ih tee) *n.* comparative equality: Municipal employees demanded wage *parity* with workers in the private sector.

parsimonious (par sih MOH nee us) *adj.* frugal or stingy: The extravagant person may consider the average man to be *parsimonious*.

patent (PAT unt) *adj.* obvious, easily seen; *(n.)* exclusive right, as to a product or invention: The promise of tax relief was a *patent* attempt to win last-minute support from the farmers. The company's *patent* on the formula expires after a certain number of years.

pedantic (puh DAN tik) *adj.* making a needless display of learning: The *pedantic* lecturer made several allusions to obscure literary works unknown to his audience.

peevish (PEE vish) *adj.* fretful, hard to please: The girl was unpopular because she was so *peevish;* she was always complaining about something.

peremptory (per EMP ter ee) *adj.* imperative, dictatorial: He announced his opinions in a *peremptory* tone extremely rankling to his listeners.

permeable (PER mee uh bul) *adj.* capable of having fluids pass through: Most clay dishes are *permeable* unless glazed.

perquisite (PERK wuh zut) *n.* incidental compensation: A chauffeured car is one of the *perquisites* of a commissioner's position.

peruse (per OOZ) *v.* to read carefully, study: She *perused* the text, absorbing as much information as she could.

petulance (PECH yoo luns) *n.* petty fretfulness, peevishness: Her *petulance* in demanding her own way reminded me of a two-year-old child.

piquant (PEE kunt) *adj.* stimulating the sense of taste, agreeably pungent: Mustard and chutney are both *piquant* in different ways.

pique (PEEK) *n.* fit of resentment: His *pique* at being scolded lasted all day.

placate (PLAY kayt) *v.* to soothe the anger of, pacify: A quick temper is often easily *placated*.

poignant (POYN yunt) *adj.* having sharp emotional appeal, moving: Reading the *poignant* story, he began to cry.

pontificate (pahn TIF uh kayt) *v.* to speak pompously: He would rise slowly, *pontificate* for half an hour, and sit down without having said a thing we didn't know before.

portentous (por TEN tus) *adj.* foreshadowing future events, especially somber ones: The thunderstorm that broke as we were leaving seemed *portentous* but in fact the weather was lovely for the rest of the trip.

posterity (pah STAYR uh tee) *n.* succeeding generations: Some buildings we construct for the sake of *posterity*, but most we construct for the sake of expediency.

precarious (prih KAYR ee us) *adj.* insecure: The animal had found a *precarious* perch on the window ledge.

precipitous (pruh SIP uh tus) *adj.* steep like a precipice: The road had a *precipitous* drop on the south side.

precursor (prih KERS er) *n.* predecessor, forerunner: The Continental Congress was the *precursor* of our bicameral legislature.

preeminent (pree EM uh nunt) *adj.* most outstanding: She is the *preeminent* authority in her field.

preempt (pree EMPT) *v.* to exclude others by taking first: Regularly scheduled programs were *preempted* by convention coverage.

preponderance (pree PAHN der uns) *adj.* Greater in amount, weight, power, influence, importance, etc.:

The *preponderance* of evidence indicated that Bryce was guilty of the offense.

prerogative (pruh RAH guh tiv) *n.* exclusive privilege or right: As the child's guardian, she had the *prerogative* of deciding whether he would attend private or public school.

primordial (pry MOR dee ul) *adj.* First in time; existing at or from the beginning: The building blocks of life were present in the *primordial* ooze.

proclivity (proh KLIV ih tee) *n.* tendency: The child has a *proclivity* for getting into trouble.

prodigious (proh DIJ us) *adj.* exciting wonder; monumental: The architect's *prodigious* building was awe inspiring and beautiful to behold.

promulgate (PRAH mul gayt) *v.* to announce publicly as a law or doctrine: The revolutionary government *promulgated* some of the promised reforms.

proscribe (proh SKRYB) *v.* to outlaw, forbid by law: Theft is *proscribed* by the laws of every state.

protocol (PROH tuh kahl) *n.* rigid code of correct procedure, especially in diplomacy: *Protocol* demands that we introduce the ambassador before the special envoy; to fail to do so would be interpreted as an affront.

provisional (proh VIZH uh nul) *adj.* temporary, for the time being only: The *provisional* government stepped down after the general elections.

provocation (prah vuh KAY shun) *n.* a provoking, a cause for resentment or attack: The attack, coming without *provocation,* took them by surprise.

putative (PYOO tuh tiv) *adj.* supposed, reputed: The braggart's *putative* wealth amounted to nothing more than a fabrication.

quench (KWENCH) *v.* to extinguish, put out: She *quenched* the flames with water.

query (KWEER ee) *v.* to question: He *queried* the witness about his alibi.

quorum (KWOR um) *n.* minimum number of members that must be present for an assembly to conduct business: No votes may be taken until there are enough representatives present to constitute a *quorum*.

ramification (ram uh fuh KAY shun) *n.* breakdown into subdivisions, a branching out: The *ramifications* of the subject were complex.

raze (RAYZ) *v.* to destroy down to the ground, as a building: Buildings in the path of the highway construction will be *razed*.

rebuff (rih BUF) *n.* a snub, repulse, blunt or impolite refusal; *(v.)* to snub or refuse bluntly: His overtures of friendship were met with *rebuff*. The young girl *rebuffed* the boy's awkward attempt to woo her.

rebuke (rih BYOOK) *v.* to reprimand, criticize sharply: He *rebuked* his son for borrowing the car without permission.

rebuttal (rih BUT ul) *n.* contradiction, reply to a charge or argument: The judge allowed each participant in the debate five minutes for *rebuttal*.

recalcitrant (rih KAL suh trunt) *adj.* stubborn, refusing to obey: A *recalcitrant* child is difficult to teach.

recapitulate (ree kuh PICH yoo layt) *v.* to mention or relate in brief, summarize: The abstract *recapitulated* the main points of the argument.

recondite (REK un dyt) *adj.* profound; obscure; concealed: Anthropologists have put forth various *recondite* theories about why the ancient civilization suddenly vanished.

recriminate (rih KRIM uh nayt) *v.* to return accusation for accusation: The two business partners constantly *recriminated* against each other, each blaming the other whenever anything went wrong.

rectitude (REK tuh tood) *n.* honesty, integrity, strict observance of what is right: Her *rectitude* in business dealings earned her the trust of her associates.

recumbent (rih KUM bunt) *adj.* lying down: The painting depicted the goddess *recumbent* on a sumptuous couch.

redress (rih DRES) *n.* compensation for a wrong done: The petitioners asked the state for a *redress* of grievances for which they had no legal recourse.

reiterate (ree IT er ayt) *v.* to repeat: The instructions were *reiterated* before each new section of the test.

relegate (REL uh gayt) *v.* to transfer to get rid of, assign to an inferior position: He *relegated* the policeman to a suburban beat.

reminisce (rem uh NIS) *v.* to remember, talk about the past: When old friends get together, they love to *reminisce*.

remit (rih MIT) *v.* to pay, to send payment: Payment for services was *remitted* by check.

remuneration (ree myoo ner AY shun) *n.* reward, payment, as for work done: Health benefits are part of the *remuneration* that goes with the position.

reprehensible (rep ree HEN suh bul) *adj.* deserving rebuke or blame: Conduct that selfishly endangers the safety of others is *reprehensible*.

reprove (rih PROOV) *v.* to censure, rebuke, find fault with: The instructor *reproved* the student for failing to hand in the assignments on time.

requisite (REK wih zit) *adj.* required, necessary: No matter when he starts work, an employee may take vacation time as soon as he has worked the *requisite* number of weeks.

requisition (rek wuh ZISH un) *n.* formal written order or request: The office manager sent in a *requisition* for another desk and chair.

resplendent (rih SPLEN dunt) *adj.* very bright, shining: She was *resplendent* in the jewelry and sequined dress.

restitution (res tih TOO shun) *n.* restoration to a rightful owner, reparation for an injury: He agreed to make *restitution* for the money he had stolen.

resurgent (rih SER junt) *adj.* rising again: The *resurgent* spirit of nationalism caused riots in Cyprus.

reticent (RET uh sunt) *adj.* restrained in speech, unwilling to talk: People are *reticent* to confess anxieties for fear of appearing weak.

retrogress (RET roh gres) *v.* to go backward, lose ground: Many social critics charge that content provided by broadcast media continues to *retrogress* in quality while the technology progresses.

rife (RYF) *adj.* Frequently or commonly occurring, widespread, abundant, abounding: Gregory's report was *rife* with error.

rubicund (ROO bih kund) *adj.* ruddy; reddish: The heavy drinker has a bulbous, *rubicund* nose.

rue (ROO) *v.* to be sorry for, regret: He will always *rue* the day he turned down a job offer from the fledgling software company that would have made him a millionaire today.

saccharine (SAK er in) *adj.* pertaining to sugar, having the qualities of sugar, overly sweet: The *saccharine* sentimentality of the film is cloying to any audience over the age of twelve.

sagacious (suh GAY shus) *adj.* wise, discerning: With a *sagacious* nod of his head the father signified his approval of his son's decision to attend college.

salutary (SAL yoo tayr ee) *adj.* promoting health, conducive to good: The preacher's anecdotes provided a *salutary* lesson.

satiate (SAY shee ayt) *v.* to gratify completely, surfeit: Nothing *satiates* a sweet tooth like a bar of chocolate.

scant (SKANT) *adj.* barely or scarcely sufficient; inadequate: They made do with the *scant* rations in the lifeboat for two days.

scintillating (SIN tuh lay ting) *adj.* sparkling, brilliant, witty: Absorbed in the *scintillating* conversation, the guests lost track of the time.

sequester (sih KWES ter) *v.* to seize by authority, set apart in seclusion: The jury was *sequestered* until the members could reach a verdict.

sinecure (SYN ih kyoor) *n.* job requiring little work: The person who is looking for a *sinecure* should avoid working here; this job is very demanding.

slovenly (SLUV un lee) *adj.* untidy in personal and work habits: The *slovenly* housekeeper was of very little use.

solicitude (suh LIS ih tood) *n.* concern, anxiety, uneasiness of mind occasioned by the fear of evil or the desire for good: The teacher had great *solicitude* for the welfare of her students.

sonorous (suh NOR us) *adj.* resonant: His *sonorous* voice helped make him a success as a stage actor.

soporific (sahp uh RIF ik) *adj.* causing sleep: Because of the drug's *soporific* effect, you should not try to drive after taking it.

specious (SPEE shus) *adj.* deceptively plausible: He advanced his cause with *specious* arguments and misinformation.

sporadic (spuh RAD ik) *adj.* occasional, happening at random intervals: He made *sporadic* attempts to see his estranged wife.

spurious (SPYER ee us) *adj.* false, counterfeit, phony: The junta's promise of free elections was *spurious,* a mere sop to world opinion.

stealthy (STEL thee) *adj.* furtive, secret: While their grandfather was distracted by the phone, the children made a *stealthy* raid on the refrigerator.

stigma (STIG muh) *n.* act or trait perceived by others as highly negative, setting the stigmatized person apart from others: The *stigma* caused by gossip lasted long after the accusation had been disproved.

stoical (STOH ih kul) *adj.* showing calm fortitude: She remained *stoical* in the face of great misfortune.

strident (STRY dunt) *adj.* harsh-sounding: The *strident* tone of her voice sent shivers down my back.

stultify (STUL tih fy) *v.* to cause to appear foolish; to impair or to render ineffectual or futile: A good magician should be able to *stultify* any audience member volunteering to assist with a trick.

subterfuge (SUB ter fyooj) *n.* deceitful means of escaping something unpleasant: The lie about a previous engagement was a *subterfuge* by which they avoided a distasteful duty.

subversive (sub VER siv) *adj.* tending to undermine or destroy secretly: The editor was accused of disseminating propaganda *subversive* to national security.

succor (SUK er) *n.* aid, help in distress: Despite the threat of harsh reprisals, many townspeople gave *succor* to the refugees.

succumb (suh KUM) *v.* to yield to superior strength or force; to give in; to die: The reluctant novice *succumbed* to the pleading of the swimming counselor and plunged into the water.

supercilious (soo per SIL ee us) *adj.* proud and haughty: The *supercilious* attitude of old and wealthy families has contributed to many social upheavals.

supersede (soo per SEED) *v.* to take the place of: The administration appointed new department heads to *supersede* the old.

supine (soo PYN) *adj.* lying on the back, passive, inactive: The girls were *supine* on the beach, roasting in the sun.

supplant (suh PLANT) *v.* to take the place of, especially unfairly: The mother accused her sister of deliberately trying to *supplant* herself as the object of her daughter's affections.

supplicate (SUP lih kayt) *v.* to beg: The prisoner of war *supplicated* his capturers to grant him his freedom.

surreptitious (ser ep TIH shus) *adj.* secret, unauthorized, clandestine: A *surreptitious* meeting in the basement of one of the conspirators was arranged for midnight.

symposium (sim POH zee um) *n.* meeting for discussion of a subject: The high school counselor was invited to participate in a *symposium* on the subject of college admission standards.

synthesis (SIN thuh sis) *n.* combination of parts into a whole: The decor was an artful *synthesis* of traditional and contemporary styles.

tacitly (TAS it lee) *adj.* silently, without words, by implication: He *tacitly* assented to his friend's arguments but wouldn't admit to being convinced.

temerity (tuh MER ih tee) *n.* contempt for danger or opposition; recklessness; nerve; audacity: The arsonist had the *temerity* to offer to help fight the fire.

temporize (TEM puh ryz) *v.* to evade immediate action, to stall for time: Rather than doing her homework, the young boy *temporized* by helping prepare dessert.

tenable (TEN uh bul) *adj.* capable of being held or defended: The club had no *tenable* reasons for the exclusion; it was purely a case of prejudice.

tenacity (tuh NAS ih tee) *n.* persistence, quality of holding firmly: His *tenacity* as an investigator earned him the nickname "Bulldog."

tenuous (TEN yoo us) *adj.* held by a thread, flimsy: The company's survival in a competitive business depended on a *tenuous* relationship with only one customer.

timorous (TIM uh rus) *adj.* fearful; timid: The abused child was a *timorous* little waif.

tirade (TY rayd) *n.* vehement speech: He shouted a long *tirade* at the driver who had hit his car from behind.

torrent (TOR unt) *n.* a swift, violent stream of liquid; rash of words or mail; heavy rain: When a dam breaks, it releases a *torrent* of water.

torsion (TOR shun) *n.* twisting or wrenching: Too much bodily *torsion* may lead to backaches.

tractable (TRAK tuh bul) *adj.* easily led: A *tractable* worker is a boon to a supervisor but is not always a good leader.

transcribe (tran SCRYB) *v.* to make a written copy of: These nearly illegible notes must be *transcribed* before anyone else can use them.

transfusion (trans FYOO zhun) *n.* a pouring from one container into another: They gave the victim a blood *transfusion.*

transverse (trans VERS) *adj.* lying across: The ties were placed in a *transverse* fashion on the railroad tracks.

trepidation (trep uh DAY shun) *n.* involuntary trembling, as from fear or terror: The ghost story caused them to feel a certain *trepidation* walking home late at night.

truculent (TRUK yoo lunt) *adj.* ferocious, savage, harsh in manner: The champion affected a *truculent* manner to intimidate the young challenger.

truncheon (TRUN chun) *n.* club: British police are armed with *truncheons.*

turgid (TER jid) *adj.* swollen: The river was *turgid* from the incessant rains.

unkempt (un KEMPT) *adj.* uncombed, not cared for, disorderly: The eccentric artist was well known for his *unkempt* appearance.

unmitigated (un MIT ih gay tid) *adj.* not lessened, not softened in severity or harshness: According to President Eliot of Harvard, inherited wealth is an *unmitigated* curse when divorced from culture.

upbraid (up BRAYD) *v.* to charge with something disgraceful, reproach, reprove with severity: The husband *upbraided* his wife for her extravagance.

urbane (er BAYN) *adj.* smoothly polite, socially poised and sophisticated: His *urbane* demeanor served him well at the exclusive country club.

vacillate (VAS uh layt) *v.* to fluctuate, change back and forth, be inconsistent: The art critic *vacillated* by first praising the work as inspired genius, then later panning it as a banal attempt at art.

vacuity (vuh KYOO ih tee) *n.* dullness of comprehension, lack of intelligence, stupidity: The *vacuity* of her mind was apparent to all who knew her.

variegate (VAYR ee uh gayt) *v.* to diversify in external appearance, mark with different colors: The builder created a *variegated* facade with marble of varied hues.

venal (VEE nul) *adj.* able to be corrupted or bribed: The *venal* judge privately offered to hand down the desired verdict for a price.

venerate (VEN er ayt) *v.* to respect: We should *venerate* those who help others in need, and deprecate those who seek to destroy others.

venial (VEE nee ul) *adj.* forgivable; pardonable; excusable: A *venial* sin stands in marked contrast to a mortal sin, which is extreme, grave and totally unpardonable.

verisimilitude (ver ih sih MIL ih tood) *n.* appearance of truth: The movie set reproduced the ancient city with great *verisimilitude;* every detail seemed correct.

verity (VER ih tee) *n.* truthfulness, honesty, quality of being real or actual: The *verity* of the document could not be questioned.

verve (VERV) *n.* enthusiasm; energy; vitality: The optimist greets each new day with *verve*.

vestige (VES tij) *n.* remnant, remainder, trace: The appendix is a useless *vestige* of an earlier human form.

vicarious (vy KAYR e us) *adj.* experienced secondhand through imagining another's experience: She took *vicarious* pleasure in the achievements of her daughter.

vigilant (VIJ uh lunt) *adj.* watchful, on guard: As a Supreme Court justice he has always been *vigilant* of any attempt to encroach on the freedoms guaranteed by the Bill of Rights.

vilify (VIL ih fy) *v.* to defame, degrade by slander: She was sued for attempting to *vilify* her neighbor.

vindicate (VIN duh kayt) *v.* to uphold, confirm: The book's success *vindicated* the editor's judgment.

vindictive (vin DIK tiv) *adj.* unforgiving, showing a desire for revenge: Stung by the negative reviews of his film, the director made *vindictive* personal remarks about some of his critics.

volition (voh LISH un) *n.* deliberate will: He performed the act of his own *volition*.

voracious (voh RAY shus) *adj.* ravenous, very hungry, eager to devour: The *voracious* appetite of the man startled the other guests.

warrant (WOR unt) *v.* to deserve, justify: The infraction was too minor to *warrant* a formal reprimand.

wield (WEELD) *v.* to use with full command or power: The soldier was skilled at *wielding* his sword.

winnow (WIN oh) *v.* to sift for the purpose of separating bad from good: Her testimony was so convoluted that the jury could not *winnow* falsehood from truth.

wrest (REST) *v.* to take by violence: The child to *wrest* the toy from the hands of his older brother.

Level 3

Synonyms by Triplets

Level 3 contains 100 word groups. In each group a common, everyday word is followed by three synonyms for that word. (The first word in each group is the closest synonym.) Each listing in Level 3 provides pronunciation, part of speech, a definition, and a sample sentence. Learning words by triplets will afford you additional perspective on the words as you learn them.

1. absorbed

engrossed (en GROHSD) *adj.* Taken the entire attention of; occupied wholly. One can be engrossed with something yet not entirely preoccupied—meaning other matters will still be taken care of.

*David was **engrossed** in the latest Stephen King novel; he found it difficult to put down the book.*

immersed (ih MERSD) *adj.* Absorbed deeply. Immersed implies a rapid and intense learning process.
> *Greg **immersed** himself in preparing for his new assignment, poring over reams of research reports and industry analysis.*

inundated (IN un day tud) *adj.* flooded. Inundation might, but does not necessarily, result in either immersion or absorption.
> *When the craze was at its height, the police were **inundated** daily with reports of UFO sightings.*

2. accident

fortuity (for TOO uh tee) *n.* A chance or accidental event. A fortuitous event can be, but need not be, beneficial.
> *The two business rivals relocating to the same town was **fortuitous**; neither one knew of the other's plans.*

happenstance (HAP un stans) *n.* Mere coincidence; a chance meeting having a beneficial outcome.
> *It was only **happenstance** that Marla went to the department store the day that all winter clothing was marked down 40 percent.*

serendipity (sayr un DIP uh tee) *n.* A seeming gift for finding something good accidentally. Serendipity implies a history of or knack for making pleasant discoveries by accident; serendipity is more than just a one-time occurrence.

*Maria was blessed with **serendipity**; the right thing always seemed to happen at the right time for her.*

3. accompanying

collateral (kuh LAT er ul) *adj.* Accompanying or existing in a subordinate, corroborative, or indirect relationship.
*The salesperson left a catalog and some **collateral** materials.*

tangential (tan JEN chul) *adj.* Merely touching a subject, not dealing with it at length. Tangential implies emphasizing only one small part of a larger issue—and not necessarily the most important part.
*The rookie stockbroker collected a voluminous amount of information, most of it only related to the new offering in a **tangential** way.*

auxiliary (awg ZIL er ee) *adj.* Providing additional support or aide; helpful but not essential.
*The **auxiliary** team members were available in case any of the regular team members suffered injury during the game.*

4. addition

supplement (SUP luh munt) *v.* Add to in order to make up for a lack or deficiency. Supplement differs from augment in that the thing added to is initially lacking.

*Bob's eating habits were so poor he needed to
supplement his diet with a daily multivitamin.*

augment (AWG ment) *v.* To make greater, as in
size, quantity, or strength; enlarge. Weak or small
things can be supplemented; anything can be aug-
mented.

*By **augmenting** the band with a horn section,
Clive found the sound he was searching for.*

complement (KAHM pluh munt) *v.* To complete or
bring to perfection. Complement implies making up
what is lacking in one another.

*Judy and Ralph were the perfect team: her way
with words **complemented** his numerical skills.*

5. agreement

accord (uh KORD) *n.* Mutual agreement. Accord
implies a formal agreement, as between countries.

*The two companies reached an **accord** for the
mutual use of the disputed trademark.*

consonant (KAHN suh nint) *adj.* In harmony or
agreement. Consonant suggests a melodious, soothing agreement or an emotional or spiritual attune-
ment.

*Sherry's tastes in music were **consonant** with
Michael's; she could count on him being pleased
with the CD she bought him for his birthday.*

synchronous (SINK ruh nus) *adj.* Happening at the same time; occurring together. Being in synch implies being aligned in some form or fashion.

*The **synchronous** strains emanating from the various sections of the orchestra pleased the conductor.*

6. almost

virtually (VER choo uh lee) *adv.* In effect, although not in fact. Virtually implies being almost but not quite something.

*The twins were **virtually** identical, save for the length of their hair.*

figuratively (FIG yer uh tiv lee) *adv.* Representing one concept in terms of another that may be thought of as analogous with it. In the phrase "screaming headlines," the word "screaming" is used figuratively.

***Figuratively** speaking, the new project was a black hole in terms of funding.*

allegedly (uh LEJ jud lee) *adv.* So declared, but without proof or legal conviction. Allegedly implies a current or forthcoming formal accusation.

*Crane had **allegedly** broken into the records room and stolen the confidential files.*

7. annoy

exasperate (eg ZAS per ayt) *v.* To irritate or annoy very much; make angry. Exasperate implies intense irritation such as exhausts one's patience or makes one lose one's self-control. Exasperate is more extreme than irritate.

> *The combination of the phone ringing and his inability to find the spreadsheet error **exasperated** Randy.*

vex (VEKS) *v.* To give trouble to, especially in a petty or nagging way. Vex implies a more serious source of irritation and greater disturbance than exasperate, along with an often intense worry.

> *The source of the spreadsheet error **vexed** both Randy and his team.*

plague (PLAYG) *v.* To harass; trouble; torment. Plague implies a constant vexation.

> *Over time, Randy realized that the spreadsheet was **plagued** with multiple errors.*

8. approaching

forthcoming (FORTH kum ing) *adj.* About to appear; approaching. Forthcoming implies something about to happen or something available when required or as promised.

> *If my **forthcoming** book sells as well as my last book, I'll be able to buy a new home theater system with the proceeds.*

imminent (IM uh nunt) *adj.* Likely to happen without delay. Imminent implies the anticipation of something threatening.

*From the tense atmosphere at the White House, it was clear that the invasion was **imminent**.*

looming (LOOM ing) *adj.* Appearing, taking shape, or coming in sight indistinctly as through a mist, especially in a large, portentous, or threatening form.
*The grim specter of bankruptcy was **looming** on the horizon for the beleaguered merchant.*

9. approval

kudos (KOO dohz) *n.* Credit or praise for an achievement; glory or fame. Note that kudos is both singular and plural; there is no such word as kudo.
*Marlon received **kudos** from the board for his outstanding presentation at the annual shareholder's meeting.*

commendation (kah mun DAY shun) *n.* Mention of someone or something as worthy of attention; recommendation. An expression of approval of; praise.
*June called Tom into her office to show him the **commendation** she was about to place in his file.*

accolades (AK uh layds) *n.* Anything done or given as a sign of great respect, approval, appreciation, and so on; words of praise.
*George's performance received **accolades** from most of the critics. He became a star overnight.*

10. **arrogant**

imperious (im PEER ee us) *adj*. Arrogant; domineering. Imperious implies an insensitivity to the feelings of others.

> *Kurt's **imperious** behavior alienated his underlings.*

haughty (HAW tee) *adj*. Having or showing great pride in oneself and disdain, contempt, or scorn for others. Haughty implies a pride behind the arrogance.

> *The vice president's wife was **haughty** with the staff, as if she thought she was better than they were.*

dogmatic (dawg MAT ik) *adj*. Doctrinal; asserted without proof; stating opinion in a positive or arrogant manner. Dogmatic suggests the attitude of a religious teacher in asserting certain doctrines as absolute truths not open to dispute.

> *The politician, **dogmatic** in his opposition, refused to consider alternative solutions.*

11. **association**

clique (KLIK) *n*. A small, exclusive circle of people; snobbish or narrow. Clique refers to a small, highly exclusive group, often within a larger one, and implies snobbery, selfishness, or, sometimes, intrigue. A clique's behavior is clannish and exclusionary.

> *Jennifer was excluded from the **clique** because she lived in the wrong part of town.*

coterie (KOH tuh ree) *n.* A close circle of friends who share a common interest or background. Coterie implies a small, intimate, somewhat select group of people associated for social or other reasons.

*Marie was delighted when she was finally invited to be part of the literary **coterie**.*

retinue (RET uh noo) *n.* A group of servants or attendants.

*Surrounding herself with her **retinue** gave the movie star a false sense of security.*

12. attractive

alluring (uh LOOR ing) *adj.* Highly attractive. If something is alluring, it is highly desirable; one wishes to possess a thing or person that is alluring.

*My new convertible car is **alluring**; all my co-workers want to own one just like it.*

enticing (en TY sing) *adj.* That which attracts by offering hope of reward or pleasure. One is allured by the qualities of a thing itself; one is enticed by an end result related to a thing.

*The real-estate agent found the prospect of earning a six-figure commission for the sale was very **enticing**.*

charismatic (kayr uz MAT ik) *adj.* Of, having, or resulting from a special charm that inspires fascination or devotion. Leaders often possess charisma that inspires their followers. A person with charisma is charming.

> *Mr. Xavier had proven himself a **charismatic**
> leader; he was able to charm his way through
> any situation.*

13. avoid

eschew (is CHOO) *v.* To keep away from (something harmful or disliked). Eschew implies deliberately avoiding and staying away from something or someone.

> *Deliberately playing to his frugal image, the
> chairman **eschewed** the use of a private limousine and took a taxi instead.*

abstain (ub STAYN) *v.* To hold oneself back; voluntarily do without; refrain (from).

> *Ronald **abstained** from smoking while his wife
> was pregnant.*

forswear (for SWAYR) *v.* To renounce on oath; promise earnestly to give up.

> *I **forswear** fatty foods for the good of my health.*

14. believable

credible (KRED uh bul) *adj.* That can be believed; believable; reliable. Credible is used for that which is believable because it is supported by evidence, sound logic, etc.

> *The defendant's account of the events, though
> unusual, was entirely **credible**, considering the
> physical evidence.*

plausible (PLAW suh bul) *adj.* Seemingly true, acceptable, etc. Plausible often implies distrust and applies to that which at first glance appears to be true, reasonable, valid, and so on but which may or may not be so, although there is no connotation of deliberate deception.

*Since his clothes were soaked, his story of falling into the creek seemed **plausible**.*

specious (SPEE shus) *adj.* Seeming to be good, sound, correct, logical, and so on without really being so; plausible but not genuine. Specious applies to that which is superficially reasonable, valid, etc. , but is actually not so, and it connotes intention to deceive.

*Burt's logic about why he should get the raise was **specious**, raising Mr. Wetherby's suspicions.*

15. beside

adjacent (uh JAY sunt) *adj.* Near or close (to something). Adjacent things may or may not be in actual contact with each other, but they are not separated by things of the same kind.

*The new office sat **adjacent** to the fast food restaurant.*

contiguous (kun TIG yoo us) *adj.* In physical contact; touching along all or most of one side.

*The four stores were **contiguous** with the main highway.*

juxtapose (JUK stuh pohz) *v.* to place close together.

> *To minimize the amount of dirt and debris that might be tracked through the new house the architect decided to **juxtapose** the garage and laundry room.*

16. brave

intrepid (in TREP ud) *adj.* Not afraid; bold; fearless; very brave. Intrepid implies absolute fearlessness, especially in facing the new or unknown.

> *Sir William's **intrepid** journey to the wilds of Africa captivated his reading audience.*

valiant (VAL yunt) *adj.* Full of or characterized by courage or bravery; resolute or determined. Valiant emphasizes a heroic quality in the courage or fortitude shown.

> *Johnson made a **valiant** effort to save his employees from the downsizing, knowing full well it could cost him the support of the senior management team.*

audacious (aw DAY shus) *adj.* Bold or daring; fearless. Audacious suggests an imprudent or reckless boldness.

> *Joan's **audacious** accusations proved unfounded.*

17. brief

terse (TERS) *adj.* Free of superfluous words; concise in a polished, smooth, way. Terse language is elegantly concise and cleanly written or spoken.

*Joe Friday's **terse** style set the tone for dozens of fictional detectives to follow.*

pithy (PITH ee) *adj.* Terse and full of substance or meaning. Terse is concise; pithy is concise yet full of content.

*Sarah's **pithy** comments spoke volumes.*

succinct (suk SINGKT) *adj.* Clearly and briefly stated. Succinct is characterized by brevity and conciseness of speech.

*Oliver's **succinct** summary of the facts brought everyone up to speed quickly.*

18. cause

engender (en JEN der) *v.* To bring into being; bring about; cause; produce. One can engender anything, conflicts included.

*Winona **engendered** a show of support for her downsized colleagues.*

impetus (IM puh tus) *n.* Anything that stimulates activity; driving force or motive; incentive; impulse. Impetus implies initiative, a pushing forward, or an energetic beginning.

*The Senator gave **impetus** to the school standards movement when he proposed the abolition of social promotion.*

incite (in SYT) *v.* To urge to action; stir up. Incite implies an urging or stimulating to action, either in an favorable or an unfavorable sense.

> *Leaping to the platform, Marvin tried to **incite**
> the crowd to rush the gates.*

19. capability

facility (fuh SIL uh tee) *n*. A ready ability or skill; a
dexterity or fluency at some endeavor. Facility refers
to an ability that comes with special ease or quickness.

> *Rene's **facility** with languages enabled her to
> quickly master the necessary Japanese phrases
> while preparing for the Asian sales meeting.*

faculty (FAK ul tee) *n*. Power or ability to do some
particular thing; a special aptitude or skill. A faculty
is a special ability, often innate.

> *Marcel's **faculty** for problem-solving was present
> at an early age.*

capacity (kuh PAS uh tee) *n*. The ability to contain,
absorb, or receive and hold. Capacity is a measurement of how much you can do.

> *The department had the **capacity** to process 200
> résumés per day.*

20. combine

coalesce (koh uh LES) *v*. To unite or merge into a
single body, group, or mass. Coalesce does not imply
adaptation or adoption; it is a merging rather than an
absorption.

> *Gradually, a consensus of opinion began to
> **coalesce**.*

amalgam (uh MAL gum) *n.* A combination or mixture; blend.

> *The new product was an **amalgam** of the best of the old product with the key features from the chief competitor.*

hybrid (HY brid) *n.* Anything of mixed origin, unlike parts, and so on. Amalgam implies a smooth mixture; hybrid implies a grafting on of disparate parts.

> *Rather than either tearing down the house or leaving it as is, my **hybrid** plan calls for a major restoration during which we'll replace only certain portions of the existing structure.*

21. confuse

obfuscate (AHB fyoo skayt) *v.* To muddle; confuse; purposely make unclear or fuzzy. Obfuscate implies a deliberate attempt to cloud the truth. Someone who obfuscates makes every effort to muddle facts important to someone else's judgment or decision.

> *Smithers attempted to **obfuscate** the situation to draw attention away from his actions.*

bewilder (bih WIL der) *v.* To confuse hopelessly, as by something complicated or involved. Unlike obfuscate, bewilder does not imply any deliberation or ulterior motive.

> *The labyrinth was carefully designed to **bewilder** anyone who attempts to find his or her way through it.*

stupefy (STOO puh fy) *v.* To make numb or dull through confusion or bewilderment. A stupefied person is not only bewildered but also amazed and stunned.

> *Jones was* ***stupefied*** *by the number of options available on the benefits enrollment form.*

22. constant

perpetual (per PECH yoo ul) *adj.* Continuing indefinitely without interruption; constant. Perpetual differs from perennial or periodic in that it never goes away, and it never ends.

> *Although most people consider the Earth's rotating motion about its axis* ***perpetual***, *in fact this rotation will eventually cease as our solar system collapses.*

perennial (per EN ee ul) *adj.* Lasting or continuing for a long time; returning or becoming active again and again. Perennial implies reliability. Sometimes the word evergreen is also used in this fashion.

> *How the Grinch Stole Christmas* *is a* ***perennial*** *favorite with children; it gets high ratings every holiday season.*

immemorial (im muh MOR ee ul) *adj.* Extending back beyond memory or record; ancient.

> *The act of lighting a candle or fire to facilitate prayer or meditation extends back to time* ***immemorial***.

23. **continue**

persevere (per ser VEER) *v.* To progress toward a goal, without Persevering implies active effort rather than passively sustaining or enduring.

*The fledgling company **persevered** toward its long-term goal of profitability.*

protract (proh TRAKT) *v.* To draw out; lengthen in duration. Protract implies being drawn out needlessly or wearisomely.

*The lawyers attempted to **protract** the negotiations in the hopes of wearing down the other side.*

endure (en DOOR) *v.* To continue in existence; last; remain. Endure implies a struggle against some form of hardship.

*Reed made it clear that the company would **endure** the market downturn.*

24. **counselor**

advisor (ad VYZ er) *n.* One who gives advice, opinions, or counsel. An advisor can be retained in an official or an unofficial capacity.

*The president consulted his **advisors** to determine how to respond to the latest union demands.*

consultant (kun SUL tunt) *n.* An expert who is called on for professional or technical advice or opinions. A consultant is an expert advisor.

> *Annabelle hired a **consultant** who was experienced in direct mail.*

confidant (KAHN fih dant) *n.* A close, trusted friend, to whom one confides intimate matters or secrets, especially those relating to affairs of love. Confidant implies a closer and more intimate relationship than does advisor or consultant.

> *Steve was honored to be one of his boss's **confidants**; he knew what was going to happen days before his peers.*

25. co-worker

colleague (KAHL eeg) *n.* A fellow worker in the same profession; associate. An affiliate has to formally belong to an organization; a colleague simply has to work at the same company or in the same profession.

> *Even though they never ran into each other, Daniel and Michelle were **colleagues** at Macro-Tech Corporation.*

cohort (KOH hort) *n.* An associate, colleague, or supporter; a conspirator or accomplice. Cohort implies a behind-the-scenes relationship.

> *Despite his lack of experience, the mayor's **cohort** garnered the appointment.*

affiliate (uh FIL ee ut) *n.* An officially related individual or organization; member. Affiliate implies having joined some overriding organization, club, and so on.

*MarketCorp was an **affiliate** of the International Marketing Cooperative.*

26. decorate

adorn (uh DORN) *v.* To add beauty, splendor, or distinction to. Adorn implies that something had beauty beforehand but has been made even more pleasing or attractive.
> *The Christmas tree was **adorned** with a beautiful glass angel at the top.*

embellish (em BEL ish) *v.* To improve (an account or report) by adding details, often of a fictitious or imaginary kind; touch up. Embellish suggests the addition of something for effect.
> *Walter **embellished** the story by adding some colorful—but fictitious—details.*

accentuate (ak SEN choo ayt) *v.* To emphasize; heighten the effect of. If the right parts of a story are accentuated, no embellishment may be necessary.
> *The President **accentuated** the positive impact of the latest legislation.*

27. dislike

abhor (ub HOR) *v.* To shrink from in disgust, hatred, etc.; detest. Abhor implies an intense physical response to some object, situation, or person.
> *Joyce **abhors** certain types of bugs; the very sight of a spider, for instance, might cause her to cringe or even shriek.*

despise (dih SPYZ) *v.* To regard with dislike or repugnance. Despise implies a strong emotional response toward that which one regards with contempt or aversion; compare with abhor, which is a more intense physical response.

*The exterminator grew to **despise** Joyce's monthly appointment; she wouldn't let him leave until every corner of the house had been inspected.*

begrudge (bih GRUJ) *v.* To regard with displeasure or disapproval. Begrudge is more passive than either despise or abhor; begrudge implies that you allow something to occur even though you don't like it.

*Joyce did her best to manage her phobia and not **begrudge** her son an ant farm in his room.*

28. disprove

refute (rih FYOOT) *v.* To prove a person to be wrong. Refute not only denies something, but also it goes the extra step of trying to prove it wrong.

*Andi **refuted** her supervisor's personal attacks by showing how honest she had been in the past.*

impugn (im PYOON) *v.* To attack by argument or criticism; oppose or challenge as false or questionable. Impugn implies a direct, forceful attack against that which one calls into question.

*Jolanda's supervisor **impugned** her by attacking her character and motivation.*

gainsay (GAYN say) *v.* To deny, refute, or speak against.

*Peter **gainsaid** the company accountant's accusation that he had embezzled from the company; yet Peter made no attempt to disprove the accountant's allegations.*

29. distinctiveness

distinction (dih STINK shun) *n.* Uniqueness. A thing or person of distinction is not necessarily superior, honored, or famous—just different.

*The school's third-grade teacher had the **distinction** among the school's instructors of having never completed a teaching credential program.*

cachet (ka SHAY) *n.* Distinction or prestige. Manufacturers of many high-priced products attempt to create a cachet around their brands, lending them an air of exclusivity that often commands a higher price in the marketplace.

*Among the group of doctors, owning a Mercedes-Benz carried a certain **cachet**.*

notoriety (NOH tuh RY uh tee) *n.* Fame or renown. Notoriety implies widespread recognition, usually for a specific accomplishment. Unlike cachet, notoriety does not necessarily imply honor or prestige.

*The recently indicted Congressman, having gained a large measure of **notoriety**, was asked to appear on several popular national television talk shows.*

30. **doubter**

skeptic (SKEP tik) *n.* A person who habitually doubts or questions matters that are generally accepted. A cynic has predefined negative notions about things. A skeptic's opinions aren't predefined or negative; he or she simply questions everything.

Skeptics doubted whether upstart Econo Corporation could execute the acquisition as planned.

cynic (SIN ik) *n.* A person who believes that people are motivated in their actions only by selfishness, without sincerity. Where a pessimist expects the worst in any given situation, a cynic simply views other people negatively.

Ever a cynic, Marlon viewed the reverend's charitable activities with suspicion.

negativist (NAY guh tiv ist) *n.* A person who ignores, resists, or opposes suggestions or orders from other people. Whereas a skeptic continually questions the status quo, a negativist continually resists the status quo.

Janet grew tired of her boss' being a negativist; he refused to even consider her plans to overhaul the department.

31. **edit**

abridge (uh BRIJ) *v.* Shorten by using fewer words but keeping the main contents; condense. To edit a version of a written work, usually to shorten an overly long work, yet retaining the sense of the original.

> *The magazine's editor asked the author to* ***abridge*** *her short story for publication in the magazine, because the original story's length exceeded the magazine's specifications.*

expurgate (EKS per gayt) *v.* To expunge objectionable material from; delete. An expurgated version of a thing has had parts removed to make it less objectionable.

> *It is the job of television censors to* ***expurgate*** *certain words and phrases from network broadcasts so as not to offend the sensibilities of some viewers.*

censor (SENS ser) *v.* To subject (a book, writer, and so on) to the removal of anything considered obscene, libelous, politically objectionable, etc. Censorship implies a larger agenda behind what is and is not permitted to be viewed by the public.

> *Whole sections of his book were* ***censored*** *by the committee at the public library.*

32. essential

integral (IN tuh grul) *adj.* Necessary for completeness; essential. Integral implies acting as a constituent and essential member of the whole.

> *The woodwind section is an* ***integral*** *part of an orchestra.*

intrinsic (in TRIN sic) *adj.* Belonging to the real nature of a thing; not dependent on external circumstances. Intrinsic implies fundamental in character.
*The international monetary system is based on the **intrinsic** value of gold.*

innate (ih NAYT) *adj.* Existing naturally rather than acquired; that seems to have been in one from birth. Innate describes that which belongs to something as part of its nature or constitution; inborn.
*Beth could always rely on her **innate** sense of right and wrong.*

33. evil

nefarious (nih FAYR ee us) *adj.* Extremely wicked.
The wicked witch in the Wizard of Oz *is one of the most **nefarious** characters in literature.*

malevolent (muh LEV uh lunt) *adj.* Wishing evil or harm to others; having or showing ill will. A malevolent person is not necessarily evil, just someone who wishes evil on others out of spite or malice.
*Rudy's **malevolent** threats disturbed his ex-girlfriend.*

miscreant (MIS kree unt) *n.* A person who behaves criminally or viciously.
*Convicted for his violent crime, the felon was incarcerated along with many other **miscreants**.*

34. experience

seasoning (SEE zun ing) *n*. Refers to the depth and richness of practical experience gained through time or seasons. Savvy can refer to an instant understanding whereas seasoning gives one understanding only through the passage of time.

*Martha's ten years in the business gave her a **seasoning** no new college recruit could match.*

savvy (SAV ee) *n*. Shrewdness or understanding; know-how. It refers to someone who is adept in a specific area due to a keen understanding or experience in that area.

*Barbara's adept handling of the acquisition revealed her **savvy** in new business ventures.*

expertise (eks per TEES) *n*. The skill, knowledge, judgment, and so on of an expert. Anyone can have skills or experience; only an expert at a given endeavor can have expertise.

*Johnson relied on the lawyer's **expertise** in crafting the new contract.*

35. external

extrinsic (eks TRIN sik) *adj*. Not belonging to; coming from outside; not inherent. Extrinsic refers to that which, coming from outside a thing, is not essential to or part of its real nature.

*The amendment was **extrinsic** to the bill to which it was attached, but helped forward the senator's own private agenda.*

extraneous (eks TRAYN ee us) *adj.* Not truly or properly belonging; not essential. Extraneous may connote the possibility of integration of the external object into the thing to which it is added.

The lengthy book report was filled with ***extraneous*** *information about works by other authors .*

irrelevant (ih REL uh vunt) *adj.* Not pertinent; not to the point; not relating to the subject. Irrelevant implies no connection to the subject whatsoever.

Hastings' ***irrelevant*** *comment about real estate investments elicited puzzled looks from those around the table comparing stock mutual funds.*

36. friendly

affable (AF uh bul) *adj.* amiable, pleasant, easy to talk to.

The friendly smile and ***affable*** *manner of the realtor put the potential buyers at ease.*

gregarious (grih GAYR ee us) *adj.* Fond of the company of others. A gregarious person is not necessarily affable (and vice versa).

Phil's ***gregarious*** *nature made him a natural greeter for the company party.*

convivial (kun VIV yul) *adj.* Fond of eating, drinking, and good company.

In spite of her reputation as a homebody, Joan was quite ***convivial*** *when given the opportunity.*

37. flexible

supple (SUP ul) *adj.* Adaptable, as to changes.
Supple implies an ability to bend without breaking, to
adapt rather than to change.

> *Joan possessed a **supple** mind, continually
> adapting to the changing conditions around her.*

malleable (MAL ee uh bul) *adj.* able to be shaped;
adaptable. Malleable suggests a capacity to be re-
shaped more so than supple.

> *Many employees prefer to hire new employees di-
> rectly out of college, because these recent gradu-
> ates are more **malleable** and thus can be trained
> more readily.*

protean (PROH tee un) *adj.* Very changeable; readily taking on different shapes and forms. Protean implies the innate ability to assume multiple forms, to
willingly and proactively change as circumstances
dictate.

> *Willis' **protean** nature allowed him to assume
> multiple roles within the group as conditions
> dictated.*

38. genuine

authentic (aw THEN tik) *adj.* That is in fact as represented; genuine; real. Authentic implies reliability
and trustworthiness, stressing that the thing considered is in agreement with fact or actuality.

> *Included in the collection was an **authentic** copy
> of Fantastic Four #1.*

bona fide (BOH nuh fyd) *adj.* In good faith; made or done without fraud or deceit. Bona fide implies genuine or real and is properly used when a question of good faith is involved. Something that is bona fide is unquestionably authentic.

> *Bobby received a **bona fide** offer to buy his entire collection of old comic books.*

veritable (VAYR uh tuh bul) *adj.* Being such truly or in fact. Veritable implies correspondence with the truth and connotes absolute affirmation.

> *Bobby's comic book collection was worth a **veritable** fortune, at least $100,000.*

39. harmful

pernicious (per NISH us) *adj.* Causing great injury, destruction, or ruin; fatal or deadly; [rare] wicked or evil. Pernicious applies to that which does great harm by insidiously undermining or weakening. The harm done by a pernicious person or action is usually not detectable until it is too late.

> *Maryanne's continued **pernicious** gossip about Roger didn't seem to be affecting his career until it was repeated on the 6 o'clock evening news.*

malignant (muh LIG nunt) *adj.* Having an evil influence; very harmful; causing or likely to cause death. Malignant implies an inevitability, that the situation cannot be reversed or cured.

> *Hastings' very presence was **malignant**; whichever department he visited was inevitably downsized.*

malicious (muh LISH us) *adj.* Having, showing, or caused by active ill will; spiteful; intentionally mischievous or harmful.

*Randy's **malicious** attempt to cause permanent damage to the school's computer network resulted in his suspension from school.*

40. hinder

thwart (THWORT) *v.* To hinder, obstruct, frustrate, or defeat a person, plans, etc. Thwart means to frustrate by blocking (not necessarily in a covert way) someone or something moving toward some objective.

*The lack of proper tools **thwarted** Sam's plan to repair the copy machine before lunch.*

impede (im PEED) *v.* To prevent progress or interfere with the effectiveness of a process. Impeding does not necessarily damage or worsen.

*Justin's laziness **impeded** his department's progress toward meeting its production deadline.*

encumber (en KUM ber) *v.* To burden or weigh down; to hinder the function or activity of. Unlike impede, encumber strongly implies a weight or burden.

*The creditor **encumbered** the homeowner's property by placing a lien on it, rendering a quick sale of the property nearly impossible.*

41. hobbyist

dilettante (DIL uh tahnt) *n.* A person who follows
an art or science only for amusement and in a superficial way; dabbler. Dilettante refers to someone who
appreciates art as distinguished from someone who
creates it. The term is sometimes used disparagingly
of one who dabbles superficially in the arts; dilet-
tantes are less serious than hobbyists.

> *Brenda's amateurish paintings and sporadic at-*
> *tendance branded her a **dilettante** in the eyes of*
> *other members of the art club.*

aficionado (uh fish yuh NAH doh *n.* A devoted
follower of some sport, art, etc. An aficionado is a
somewhat sophisticated fan.

> *Randy was a comic book **aficionado** with a col-*
> *lection dating back to the mid-1960s; he even*
> *owned a near-mint copy of "Flash of Two*
> *Worlds."*

connoisseur (kah nuh SOOR) *n.* A person who has
expert knowledge and keen discrimination in some
field, especially in fine arts or in matters of taste. A
connoisseur often has specific training or skills in his
or her favored area.

> *Martha was a **connoisseur** of French cooking,*
> *having studied under a master chef in Paris.*

42. inactive

dormant (DOR munt) *adj.* As if asleep; inoperative;
inactive.

Perennial flowers such as irises remain **dormant**
every winter and burgeon in the spring.

inert (in ERT) *adj.* Motionless, immobile, or inactive. Inert implies permanent lack of operability.
The chemistry experiment resulted in an **inert**
combination of gases, which were of no danger
to anybody.

latent (LAY tunt) *adj.* Present but invisible or inactive; lying hidden and undeveloped within a person or thing, such as a quality or power.
Tom's **latent** *leadership abilities emerged during*
the crisis.

43. insert

interject (in ter JEKT) *v.* To throw in between; insert or interpose. Interject implies a suddenness that could be perceived as rudeness.
With everyone talking at once, it was hard for
Mary to **interject** *her opinion.*

interpolate (in TER puh layt) *v.* To insert new words into written text, or into conversation.
Adroit politicians often **interpolate** *during*
speeches by adding impromptu remarks to their
prepared scripts.

intersperse (in ter SPERS) *v.* To scatter among other things; put here and there or at intervals.
Laura **interspersed** *cartoons in the text to break*
up the monotony.

44. insult

disparage (dis PAYR uj) *v.* To speak slightingly of; show disrespect for. To disparage is to attempt to lower in esteem, as by insinuation, invidious comparison, faint praise, etc.

> *Samuel's libelous remarks **disparaged** Sally, damaging her pride and reputation.*

belittle (bih LIT ul) *v.* To make seem little, less important, and so on; speak slightingly of; depreciate. Belittle is to lessen (something) in value by implying that it has less worth than is usually attributed to it and implies a contemptuous attitude in the speaker or writer.

> *He **belittled** the actress's talent by suggesting that her beauty, rather than her acting ability, was responsible for her success.*

deride (dih RYD) *v.* To laugh at in contempt or scorn; make fun of; ridicule.

> *Michael's efforts in the negotiations were **derided** as being too little, too late.*

45. keepsake

memento (muh MEN toh) *n.* Anything serving as a reminder or warning; a souvenir. Typically a memento is an object that carries a fond personal remembrance of some past time.

> *Sherry kept Mike's ring as a **memento** of their time together.*

memorabilia (mem uh ruh BEEL yuh) *n.* Things worth remembering or recording, such as a collection of anecdotes, accounts, items, etc. , especially about one subject or event. A memento is a single thing; memorabilia is a collection of things.

> *Mike collected musical **memorabilia**, especially vintage instruments and sheet music.*

memoir (MEM war) *n.* An autobiography, especially one that is objective and anecdotal in emphasis rather than inward and subjective. A memoir can also be a report or record of important events based on the writer's personal observation or knowledge. Unlike a diary, a memoir is usually written with the hope of being read by others.

> *Mike began writing his **memoirs**, starting with his remembrances of high school days.*

46. lie

feign (FAYN) *v.* To give a false appearance or to assert a falsehood as truth. Feign suggests a affirmative falsehood rather than merely an evasion of the truth.

> *Frank **feigned** illness to avoid going to school on the day his book report was due.*

prevaricate (prih VAYR uh kayt) *v.* To evade the truth. A prevarication is not necessarily a lie, just an avoidance of the truth.

> *Carly **prevaricated** about the accident with her father, but the insurance company later revealed her deception.*

ruse (ROOZ) *n.* A stratagem or trick. A ruse is not necessarily a lie; it is a trick, often designed to divert attention away from some point or scenario.

> *Although the planes and tanks looked real enough, it was all a **ruse** to trick the enemy into thinking the allies were invading elsewhere.*

47. luxurious

opulent (AHP yuh lunt) *adj.* Characterized by abundance or profusion; luxuriant. Whereas affluence applies to people, opulence can apply to either people or things.

> *The executive's house was appointed in an **opulent** fashion.*

elegant (EL uh gunt) *adj.* Characterized by dignified richness and grace, as of design, dress, style, and so on; luxurious or opulent in a restrained, tasteful manner. One can be elegant without being affluent; richness is not the same as being rich.

> *The gown was **elegant** and understated.*

affluent (AF loo unt) *adj.* Wealthy; rich. Affluent implies an abundance of money and other possessions.

> *Now that he was making over $100,000 a year, Jameson felt that he could easily afford to associate with the more **affluent** people in town.*

48. model

archetype (ARK uh typ) *n.* The original pattern, or model, from which all other things of the same kind are made; prototype. An archetype infers something that serves as a symbol.

> *The English House of Commons served as an archetype for all representative bodies created thereafter.*

paragon (PAYR uh gahn) *n.* a model of perfection; an ideal. Paragon doesn't necessarily imply that a thing will be imitated, only that it is worthy of being imitated.

> *Ursula was a paragon of efficiency; she accomplished more each morning than any of her coworkers could accomplish in a full day.*

exemplar (ig ZEMP lar) *n.* A person or thing regarded as worthy of imitation. Like paragon, exemplar doesn't necessarily implies only that it is worthy of being imitated.

> *Michael Jordan was an exemplar of success for all would-be basketball stars.*

49. noise

cacophony (kuh KAW fuh nee) *n.* Harsh, jarring sound. Cacophony implies a multitude of sounds (including those from musical instruments) speaking or playing at the same time.

> *During peak work hours a **cacophony** of sounds and voices emanated from the main floor of the factory.*

dissonance (DIS uh nuns) *n.* An inharmonious sound or combination of sounds. Dissonance also suggests any lack of harmony or agreement or an incongruity.

> *While listening to the chirping of a solitary bird can be pure pleasure, when many different types of birds join in together the result can sometimes be characterized as pure **dissonance**.*

babel (BAY bul) *n.* A confusion of sounds, especially voices or languages. From the Biblical city of Babel. Babel implies multiple voices talking at the same time.

> *The meeting deteriorated to a state of **babel** with everyone trying to talk at the same time.*

50. obedient

compliant (kum PLY unt) *adj.* Acting in accordance. Compliant implies a willingness to adhere to a formal or informal rule or code of behavior.

> *The company was **compliant** with the agency's directives.*

complaisant (kum PLAY zunt) *adj.* Willing to please. Complaisant implies yielding too easily to another's request or insistence and is often used in derogatory reference, implying a lack of strong will.

Hastings thought the store personnel were too
complaisant *when it came to customer returns;*
he couldn't believe they'd let customers return
purchases without the original sales receipt.

amenable (uh MEEN uh bul) *adj.* Able to be controlled or influenced. Amenable implies being controlled or influenced by another.
*Quincy was **amenable** to his boss's suggestion*
that he work extra hours on Saturday.

51. obscene

ribald (RY buld) *adj.* Characterized by coarse or
vulgar joking or mocking; dealing with sex in a hu-
morously earthy or direct way. Ribald implies humor
behind the vulgarity.
*Mort told a **ribald** limerick, which offended the*
more puritanical members of the group.

lewd (LOOD) *adj.* Showing, or intended to excite,
lust or sexual desire in an offensive way.
*The prostitute's **lewd** behavior made her a target*
for the vice squad.

profane (proh FAYN) *adj.* Showing disrespect or
contempt for sacred things;. Profane language (pro-
fanity) comprises "swear" words.
Bobby was sent to the principal's office for using
***profane** language in class.*

52. obtain

procure (proh KYOOR) *v.* To get or bring about by some effort; obtain. Suggests active effort or contrivance in getting or bringing to pass.
> *It took some effort, but Joel was able to **procure** the documents from Senator Randolph's safe deposit box.*

appropriate (uh PROH pree ut) *v.* To get or gain possession intentionally. Appropriate implies a taking from someone else, legitimately or not.
> *Carmen **appropriated** her prom dress by foraging through her grandmother's attic.*

secure (sih KYOOR) *v.* To make sure or certain; guarantee; ensure, as with a pledge. To get hold or possession of; obtain. To bring about; cause. Implies difficulty in obtaining something and perhaps in retaining it.
> *Karen talked to each board member individually to further **secure** in writing the acceptance of her radical proposal.*

53. obvious

manifest (AHB vee us) *adj.* Apparent to the senses or to the mind. Manifest applies especially to that which can be perceived by the senses (especially sight) and implies something that is obvious to the understanding, apparent to the mind, or easily apprehensible.

*Joan's eating disorder was **manifest** in her appearance; she had lost considerable weight and now appeared bony and sickly.*

palpable (PAL puh bul) *adj.* Easily perceived by the senses; audible, recognizable, perceptible, noticeable. Palpable applies especially to that which can be perceived through some sense other than that of sight.

*During the negotiations the tension in the meeting room was **palpable**; neither party not their attorneys appeared the least bit at ease.*

apparent (uh PAYR unt) *adj.* Readily understood or perceived. Apparent suggests the use of reasoning.

*Based on his group's poor performance, it was **apparent** that he would take the fall when the downsizing began.*

54. opposition

adversary (AD ver sayr ee) *n.* A person who opposes or fights with another. An adversary is not necessarily an enemy, simply an opposing player. An adversarial relationship is one characterized by opposition, disagreement, and hostility.

*Roy's **adversary** was an overly political animal who tried to circumvent the system at every chance.*

antagonist (an TAG uh nist) *n.* A person who opposes or competes with another. Antagonist implies ill feelings or making an enemy.

> *Rudy became an **antagonist** when he deliberately recruited one of John's key managers.*

nemesis (NEM uh sis) *n.* Anyone or anything that seems to be the inevitable cause of a someone's downfall or defeat.

> *Holmes was Moriarty's **nemesis**, appearing at the most inopportune moments to thwart his schemes.*

55. ordinary

mundane (mun DAYN) worldly, humdrum, ordinary, everyday. Mundane suggests something common and ordinary, but not necessarily something trite.

> *The only jobs currently available at the firm involve **mundane** tasks such as filing, bookkeeping and word processing.*

banal (buh NAHL) *adj.* Dull or uninteresting due to triteness (ordinariness). Banal implies triteness, but not necessarily lifelessness.

> *The film was undistinguished, a **banal** exercise in the use of horror-movie clichés.*

insipid (in SIP ud) *adj.* Not exciting or interesting; dull; lifeless. Insipid does not necessarily imply triteness or even ordinariness.

> *Marie was bored to tears by the **insipid** small talk at the party.*

56. **overcome**

surmount (ser MOWNT) *v.* To overcome or rise superior to, especially an obstacle or hurdle.
   *The physically challenged athlete **surmounted** his disability to not just participate but actually place third in the cycling competition.*

transcend (tran SEND) *v.* To go beyond the limits of; exceed. Transcend suggests a surpassing to an extreme degree.
   *The so-called art exhibit **transcended** all boundaries of good taste.*

surpass (ser PAS) *v.* To excel or be superior to. Surpass implies a going beyond (someone or something specified) in degree, amount, or quality.
   *Kimberly's work **surpassed** her manager's expectations.*

57. **partner**

accomplice (uh KAHM plis) *n.* A person who knowingly participates with another in an unlawful act; partner in crime.
   *Laura was an **accomplice** to Vance's plot to sabotage the packing line; she helped him gain entrance through the back door.*

confederate (kun FED er ut) *n.* A person, group, nation, or state united with another or others for a common purpose. A confederate is an ally.

*Johnson gathered his **confederates** before the big press conference to announce their new project.*

peer (PEER) *n.* A person of the same rank, quality, or ability; an equal.

*Bob and Ray were **peers** in the organization and were compensated equally.*

58. persevering

diligent (DIL uh junt) *adj.* Persevering and careful in work. Diligent implies a careful, steady, painstaking effort applied to some form of work.

*Curt was **diligent** in assembling the details necessary to move forward with the project.*

assiduous (uh SIJ yoo us) *adj.* Done with constant and careful attention. Assiduous implies hardworking, active, and alert and emphasizes an almost fastidious attention to details.

*A less **assiduous** secretary would not have noticed that the wrong form had been submitted.*

tenacious (tuh NAY shus) *adj.* Holding firmly; stubborn.

*The hijackers were **tenacious** in maintaining that their demands be strictly met before they would release their hostages.*

59. picky

fastidious (fas TID ee us) *adj.* Not easy to please, disdainful, squeamish, delicate to a fault. A fastidious person is meticulous, exacting, and sensitive to procedure—sometimes to the point of obsession.

*The **fastidious** home owner disinfected every corner of her kitchen and bathroom each week.*

punctilious (punk TIL ee us) *adj.* Very careful about every detail of behavior, ceremony, and so on. As with fastidious, punctilious conveys an extreme behavior that may not be seen as normal in some quarters.

*Robinson was a **punctilious** host, attending to every detail of the affair.*

meticulous (mih TIK yoo lus) *adj.* Careful and exacting in one's performance of a task, or one's appearance, etc. Unlike fastidiousness or punctiliousness, meticulousness is not generally viewed as abnormal or extreme.

*Jonathan was **meticulous** about how he worded the contract, in order that the other party could find no loophole.*

60. possible

feasible (FEE zuh bul) *adj.* Within reason; likely; able to be performed or executed. Feasible implies the most likely and realistic reason or result.

*Given the facts of the case, Murray had the most **feasible** explanation for what might have happened.*

practicable (PRAK tih kuh bul) *adj.* Something that can be done or put into practice. Applies to that which can readily be affected under the prevailing conditions or by the means available.

*Only a minor remodeling plan seemed **practicable** given the homeowners' tight budget.*

viable (VY uh bul) *adj.* Workable and likely to survive or to have real meaning, pertinence, etc. In the business world, viability implies ongoing profitability.

*After three years of losses, the new unit was on the verge of being a **viable** business.*

61. practical

expedient (ik SPEED ee unt) *adj.* Useful for effecting a desired result; suited to the circumstances or the occasion; advantageous; convenient. Expedient is sometimes used derogatorily in reference to precipitous action meeting immediate needs but not in concert with overarching principles.

*Carter took the **expedient** route to complete his project, even though it ultimately made the results less effective.*

pragmatic (prag MAT ik) *adj.* Concerned with actual practice, everyday affairs, and so on, not with theory or speculation; practical.

*Julie's **pragmatic** concern for meeting her sales quota was nevertheless consistent with her company's long-term commitment to improving the local economy.*

efficacious (ef uh KAY shus) *adj.* Producing or capable of producing the desired effect; having the intended result.

> *Robert believed that the new software would be* ***efficacious*** *in solving the firm's Y2K problems.*

62. predict

prognosticate (prahg NAHS tuh kayt) *v.* To foretell or predict, especially from signs or indications. To prognosticate is to prophesize based on current symptoms or indications.

> *James refused to* ***prognosticate*** *the outcome of the Super Bowl.*

conjecture (kun JEKT shoor) *n.* An inferring, theorizing, or predicting from incomplete or uncertain evidence; guesswork. Conjecture is an educated guess based on available facts.

> *The paper's editorial was full of* ***conjecture*** *based on an incomplete set of facts.*

forecast (FOR kast) *v.* To estimate or calculate in advance; predict or seek to predict. A forecast can also refer to a prediction of future weather conditions.

> *The analyst's* ***forecast*** *was for increasing earnings for the next fiscal quarter.*

63. prediction

foreboding (for BOH ding) *n.* A prediction, portent, or presentiment, especially of something bad or harmful.
*Neil had a sense of **foreboding** that something bad was about to happen.*

foreshadow (for SHAD oh) *v.* To be a sign of something to come; indicate or suggest before hand.
*The high turnover rate **foreshadowed** the labor problems the company would encounter in the coming months.*

harbinger (HAR bin jer) *n.* A person or thing that comes before to announce or give an indication of what follows. A harbinger (person) is a forerunner; a harbinger (thing) is an omen. A harbinger foreshadows a future event or trend.
*Slow business during Thanksgiving weekend was a **harbinger** of a disappointing Christmas sales season just ahead.*

64. preference

predilection (pred uh LEK shun) *n.* A preconceived liking; partiality or preference. Predilection implies a preconceived liking formed as a result of one's background or temperament that inclines one to a particular preference.
*When it came to buying books, Ralph had a **predilection** for murder mysteries.*

penchant (PEN chunt) *n.* A strong liking, taste, or fondness, though not necessarily preconceived.

*Since his trip to Europe Ned's new culinary **penchant** has been for Italian food.*

propensity (pruh PEN suh tee) *n.* A natural inclination or tendency. Propensity implies an inherent inclination, as well as an almost uncontrollable attraction.

*Sue's **propensity** to speak her mind eventually cost her a job promotion; her boss took offense at her candid critique of his managerial style.*

65. productive

prolific (pruh LIF ik) *adj.* Turning out many products of the mind; fruitful; abounding. Prolific implies an above-average volume.

*Asimov was a **prolific** writer, turning out as many as a dozen books in one year.*

fertile (FER tul) *adj.* Fruitful or capable of producing fruit or offspring. Unlike prolific, fertile may imply a *potential* for production.

*The geologist explained that the plot of land was very **fertile** and was well suited for agriculture.*

profuse (pruh FYOOS) *adj.* Giving or pouring forth freely; generous, often to excess. Profuse implies giving to the point of excess.

*After the accident at the dinner party, Kim made **profuse** apologies to the hostess.*

66. proverb

adage (AD uj) *n.* An old saying that has been popularly accepted as a truth.
*As the **adage** says, "A stitch in time saves nine."*

aphorism (AF uh riz um) *n.* A short, pointed sentence expressing a wise or clever observation or a general truth. An aphorism employs cleverness or wit to make an observation.
*"The early bird catches the worm" is a classic **aphorism**.*

maxim (MAK sum) *n.* A concisely expressed principle or rule of conduct or a statement of a general truth. A maxim employs conciseness to state a principle or truth.
*Nicole adhered to the **maxim** "Love is love's reward."*

67. questionable

dubious (DOO bee us) *adj.* Causing doubt; of doubtful quality or integrity. Dubious implies shadiness or a rousing of suspicion.
*He had the **dubious** distinction of being absent more than any other student.*

moot (MOOT) *adj.* Questionable; arguable; easily disputed or contested.
*The lawyer asserted a **moot** argument, which was based on a law that had recently been repealed.*

untenable (un TEN uh bul) *adj.* That cannot be held, defended, or maintained. Untenable implies being put into an unworkable situation in which succeeding in one respect will cause failure in another.

*Thomas found himself in the **untenable** position of trying to increase both sales and profitability in an increasingly competitive market.*

68. quiet

quiescent (kwee ES unt) *adj.* Quiet; still; inactive. Quiescent implies no motive or dislike of talk; it simply describes a quiet state.

*The **quiescent** waters of the lake proved just the tranquilizer the busy executive needed to rejuvenate himself.*

reticent (RET uh sunt) *adj.* Habitually silent or uncommunicative; disinclined to speak readily. Reticent implies a pattern of uncommunicative behavior.

*Everyone noticed that Dennis was **reticent** to speak in public.*

taciturn (TAS uh tern) *adj.* Almost always silent; not liking to talk. Reticent is a disinclination to talk; taciturn is an actual dislike of talk.

*Alex was termed "the great stoneface" for his **taciturn** demeanor at management meetings.*

69. record

archive (AR kyv) *v.* To place or keep records or papers. An archive is a place where public records, or other documents are kept. Archive can also refer to old computer files stored on backup disks or tapes.

> *Randy decided it was time to **archive** all the old cash flow records, so he told his assistant to take the boxes out to the warehouse.*

chronicle (KRAHN uh kul) *v.* To tell or write the history of; put into an historical record or register of facts or events.

> *Donna set out to **chronicle** the events of the past decade.*

catalog (KAT uh lawg) *v.* To make a complete or comprehensive list, usually with descriptive comments.

> *Sean **cataloged** all the forms available from the human resources department.*

70. remove

expunge (ik SPUNJ) *v.* To erase or remove completely; blot out or strike out; delete or cancel. Expunge implies a complete wiping out of something that previously existed.

> *Trying to cover his steps, Robinson sought to **expunge** all evidence of his existence from the computer files.*

invalidate (in VAL uh dayt) *v.* To make null and void; to deprive of legal force. Invalidate implies depriving a formal directive of any impact.

> *The new directive from the home office **invalidated** the local office's standing policy.*

omit (oh MIT) *v.* to leave out, pass by, or neglect. An omission can be either intentional or unintentional.

> *Jan unintentionally **omitted** an important ingredient from her cake recipe, thereby losing any chance of winning the baking contest.*

71. request

plea (PLEE) *v.* To *request* earnestly and urgently.
> *He **pleaded** with the two parties to put aside their differences and help the community in its time of need.*

petition (puh TISH un) *v.* To ask formally or earnestly.
> *She **petitioned** the county council to waive the zoning ordinance for her home business.*

solicit (suh LIS ut) *v.* To ask for or seek earnestly or pleadingly for; appeal to or for.
> *He **solicited** her advice on the new project.*

72. righteous

virtuous (VER chyoo us) *adj.* Having, or characterized by, moral uprightness or righteousness. Virtuous implies a morally excellent character, connoting justice and integrity.
> *The Prince was the most **virtuous** man in the kingdom, leading a pure and righteous life.*

ethical (ETH uh kul) *adj.* Conforming to moral standards; conforming to the standards of conduct of a given profession or group. Ethical implies conformity with an elaborated, ideal code of moral principles, specifically with the code of a particular profession.

*Morrison had **ethical** problems with his company's hiring practices, which bordered on sexual discrimination.*

moral (MOR ul) *adj.* Relating to, dealing with, or capable of making the distinction between right and wrong in conduct. Moral implies conformity with the generally accepted standards of goodness or rightness in conduct, character, or sexual conduct.

*Jeffrey's high **morals** would not allow him to cheat on his wife with another woman?*

73. rude

brusque (BRUSK) *adj.* Rudely abrupt or blunt in speech or manner. Brusque speech is by definition curt (terse or short).

*Busy executives often resort to **brusque** behavior with subordinates in order to manage their own time effectively.*

impudent (IM pyoo dunt) *adj.* Shamelessly bold or disrespectful. Impudent implies a shameless or brazen impertinence.

*Ricky's **impudent** behavior when he talked back to his math teacher earned him detention after school.*

impertinent (im PER tuh nunt) *adj.* Having no connection with a given matter; irrelevant. Impertinent implies a forwardness of speech or action that is disrespectful and oversteps the bounds of propriety or courtesy.

*The young reporter's **impertinent** questions about the Senator's personal habits shocked everybody at the press conference.*

74. settle

arbitrate (AR buh trayt) *v.* To decide a dispute. In collective bargaining negotiations, an arbitrator is named with the consent of both sides. An arbitrator is someone literally put in the middle of a dispute.

*A special judge was appointed to **arbitrate** the long-running dispute between the company and the union.*

mediate (MEE dee ayt) *v.* To bring about by conciliation. In arbitration a neutral third party makes an impartial decision; mediation requires both sides to make concessions.

*Judge Randolph **mediated** an agreement that called for compromises from both the company and the union.*

compromise (KAHM pruh myz) *v.* To settle or adjust by concessions on both sides. Compromise is often the only way to break an impasse in negotiations.

*After long hours of negotiations, management **compromised** by granting a pay increase of half the amount the labor union requested.*

75. showy

grandiose (GRAN dee ohs) *adj.* Seeming or trying to seem very majestic or important; pompous and showy. Grandiose implies taking normal behavior and making it larger.

*Tutwiller made a **grandiose** entrance as he entered the boardroom for his presentation.*

pretentious (prih TEN chus) *adj.* Making claims, explicit or implicit, to some distinction, importance, dignity, or excellence. Pretentious implies creating an appearance of often undeserved importance or distinction; in other words, pretending to be something one is not.

*It was **pretentious** of James to claim credit for the company's success when in fact he was a mid-level employee with no major decision-making power.*

ostentatious (ahs tun TAY shus) *adj.* Putting on a showy display, as of wealth, knowledge, etc. Pretentious involves a claim; ostentatious involves a physical display or act.

*Mrs. Williams' **ostentatious** display of her new ring, by waving her hand incessantly, annoyed everyone.*

76. similar

homogeneous (huh MAJ uh nus) *adj.* Having similarity in structure because of common descent. Homogenous implies overall similarities, for example, over an entire population.

The small island's inhabitants were remarkably ***homogenous*** *in appearance; they had the same color hair and eyes as well as overall body shape.*

fungible (FUN juh bul) *adj.* Easily replaced by something else that is essentially the same.

The temporary workers' skills were so similar that each of them was considered ***fungible****.*

commensurate (kuh MEN ser ut) *adj.* Equal or corresponding in measure—either quantity or quality.

The striking workers demanded compensation ***commensurate*** *with their job duties and performance.*

77. skill

competence (KAHM puh tuns) *n.* Condition or quality of being well qualified, capable, or fit. One who is competent does not necessarily excel but is capable of performing essential functions of a job.

Joan's ***competence*** *at the task was barely enough to win her the job, given the high standards set by the rest of the staff.*

acumen (AK yoo mun) *n.* Keenness and quickness in understanding and dealing with a situation; shrewdness.

> *Robert spent years honing his business **acumen** so that he could respond effectively to any possible business development.*

aptitude (AP tuh tood) *n.* A natural ability or talent; quickness to learn and understand.

> *Florence's **aptitude** for numbers put her in good stead among the other members of the group.*

78. slow

deliberate (duh LIB er ayt) *adj.* Unhurried and methodical. Deliberate implies purposeful, measured, unhurried behavior or decision-making or a thoroughly considered action.

> *Everyone thought Raymond was slow, but he was actually **deliberate**; he made sure everything was right before proceeding.*

indolent (IN duh lunt) *adj.* lazy; averse to exertion; slothful; sluggish. The noun form is *indolence.*

> *My next door neighbor is forty years old and still lives with his parents at their house; this is a sign of either terminal **indolence** or frugality gone amuck.*

lackadaisical (lak uh DAY zih kul) *adj.* Showing lack of interest or spirit. Lackadaisical implies a casual, disinterested attitude, attributed to mental outlook.

*A **lackadaisical** attitude toward deadlines cemented Richard's fate at the bottom of the secretarial pool.*

79. slyness

guile (GYL) *n.* Slyness and cunning in dealing with others; craftiness. Guile implies skill in deception and a wily or duplicitous nature.

*Unscrupulous salespeople often resort to **guile** in order to gain the confidence of potential customers.*

ulterior (ul TEER ee er) *adj.* Further; more remote; especially, beyond what is expressed, implied, or evident; undisclosed. Ulterior implies something that is alternative, less visible or obvious, but is in fact the principal factor or reason.

*In volunteering for cleaning detail, Tony had an **ulterior** motive: he was interested in dating one of the women on the detail.*

suspect (SUS pekt) *adj.* Viewed with suspicion; suspected. Suspect implies a belief that one is guilty of something specified, on little or no evidence.

*Viola's motives have been **suspect** ever since she revealed her former employment with the company's chief competitor.*

80. **split**

bifurcate (BY fer kayt) *v.* To divide into two parts or branches. Bifurcate implies something that was once one breaking into two.

> *To accommodate the bi-level reading program the teacher **bifurcated** her class of students according to reading ability.*

dichotomy (dy KAH tuh mee) *n.* Division into two parts, groups, or classes, especially when they are sharply distinguished or opposed.

> *A **dichotomy** of opinion emerged about the most effective plan for the aging city library; one camp wished to tear down the building, the other wished to add a library annex.*

diametric (dy uh MET rik) *adj.* Designating an opposite, a contrary, or a difference, that is wholly so.

> *In the end, Bob and Janet's **diametric** positions on abortion doomed their marriage to failure.*

81. **spontaneous**

impromptu (im PRAHMP too) *adj.* Without preparation or advanced thought. Impromptu is applied to that which is spoken, made, or done on the spur of the moment to suit the occasion and stresses spontaneity.

> *The candidate's **impromptu** remarks at the press conference told voters more about his real opinions than did any of his carefully edited speeches.*

improvise (IM pruh vyz) *v.* To compose, or simultaneously compose and perform, on the spur of the moment and without any preparation. Improvise suggests the ingenious use of whatever is at hand to fill an unforeseen and immediate need.

*The chef lacked all the proper ingredients for the recipe, so she **improvised** by using those that were on hand instead.*

extemporaneous (ek stem per AY nee us) *adj.* Made, done, or spoken without any formal preparation. Extemporaneous is most often used to describe a speech or performance that has received a small degree of preparation but has not been written out or memorized.

*Kristi gave an **extemporaneous** speech when she accepted the award for best project.*

82. spying

espionage (ES pee uh nahzh) *n.* The act of spying. In a business context, espionage refers to the use of spies in industry or commerce to learn the secrets of other companies.

*The rival firm resorted to industrial **espionage** to find out what products GlobalComp was planning to unveil at the upcoming trade show.*

intelligence (in TEL uh juns) *n.* The gathering of secret information, such as for military or police purposes. Intelligence is commonly used to refer to information of value in a business situation, publicly available or not.

*Higby needed more **intelligence** about what his competitor had planned.*

intrigue (IN treeg) *n.* A secret or underhanded plot, scheme, or machination. Intrigue, implying intricate scheming, suggests furtive, underhanded maneuvering, often of an illicit nature.

*Megan refused to be drawn into Bob's **intrigues**; she hated all the cloak-and-dagger activity.*

83. stubborn

resolute (rez uh LOOT) *adj.* Having or showing a fixed, firm purpose; determined; resolved; unwavering. Resolute implies having a goal and sticking to it.

*Ann was **resolute** that she would purchase a new house by the end of the year.*

steadfast (STED fast) *adj.* Not changing, fickle, or wavering; constant. Steadfast implies stable and unmoving.

*The candidate's **steadfast** support of the anti-abortion plank cost him the nomination.*

entrenched (in TRENCHT) *adj.* Established securely. Entrenched implies a permanence, firmly fixed and not likely to be uprooted. Entrenched is often used pejoratively to refer to a practice or belief that is undesirable and next to impossible to eliminate.

*The inward focus was an **entrenched** part of the company culture in spite of its potentially disastrous effect on marketplace performance.*

84. superiority

elite (ay LEET) *n.* The group or part of a group selected or regarded as the finest, best, most distinguished, most powerful, etc. A group can be regarded as elite based on the amount of money they have, their pedigree, or the magnitude or type of their accomplishments.

*George's prowess in marksmanship made him a potential member of the infantry **elite**.*

intelligentsia (in tel uh JEN see uh) *n.* The people regarded as, or regarding themselves as, the educated and enlightened class; collectively, the learned, intellectuals, or literati.

*The novelist was regarded by the **intelligentsia** as somewhat of a hack—even though her book had been on the bestseller list for six weeks running.*

meritocracy (mayr uh TAHK ruh see) *n.* An intellectual elite, based on academic achievement. A system in which such an elite achieves special status, as in positions of leadership.

*It's too bad that public service doesn't attract more candidates from the **meritocracy** of this country's colleges and universities.*

85. substitute

surrogate (SER uh gut) *n.* A deputy or substitute. A surrogate mother is a woman who substitutes for an-

other unable to become pregnant, such as by undergoing artificial insemination.

> *The company's chief financial officer acted as
> the chief executive officer's **surrogate** for the out-
> of-town meeting.*

proxy (PRAHK see) *n.* authority to act (e.g., to vote)
for another. Proxy is a very specific legal form of
substitution.

> *Shareholders who could not attend the meeting
> could cast votes by **proxy**.*

ersatz (ER zahts) *adj.* Substitute or synthetic. Ersatz
usually suggests inferior quality.

> *The **ersatz** diamonds didn't fool Cavandish; he
> knew the ring was a fake.*

86. supporter

patron (PAYT run) *n.* A person who sponsors and
supports some person or activity, usually financially.

> *Mrs. Gilbride had been a **patron** of the arts for
> twenty years, supporting both the chamber or-
> chestra and the dance troupe.*

benefactor (BEN uh fak ter) *n.* A person who has
given financial help to an individual or organization.
A benefactor typically offers short-term help,
whereas a patron's support is long-term.

> *Ron thanked his **benefactor** for helping him
> through a financially trying time while searching
> for a job.*

mentor (MEN tor) *n.* A wise advisor of a less experienced person. A mentor is typically an older person who informally takes the other person under his or her wing in order to help the person succeed.

*I'm lucky to have Mr. Seligman as my **mentor**; he can help me avoid the day-to-day politics in the accounting department.*

87. surrender

capitulate (kuh PICH yoo layt) *v.* To give up (to an enemy) on prearranged conditions; surrender conditionally. Capitulate comes from the practice of settling or drawing up the heads or chapters of an agreement. (The Latin word caput means "head.")

*The company **capitulated**, conditional on the union agreeing to a new vote in twelve months.*

concede (kun SEED) *v.* To admit as certain or proper.

*The contractor **conceded** to the inspector that his electrical wiring was not in conformance with the building code.*

forfeit (FOR fut) *v.* To lose, give up, or be deprived of as a penalty for some crime or fault. Forfeit implies a loss dictated by a third party or because of a breaking of a rule.

*Agreeing that it had infringed on an existing trademark, CanCorp **forfeited** use of the slogan in the United Kingdom.*

88. temporary

transitory (TRAN suh tor ee) *adj.* Of a passing nature; not enduring or permanent. Transitory refers to that which by its very nature must sooner or later pass or end.

> *As he gazed down into his father's casket, Richard realized that life was **transitory**.*

ephemeral (ih FEE muh rul) *adj.* Short-lived. Ephemeral literally means existing only one day and, by extension, applies to that which is markedly short-lived.

> *The cast of the popular television show knew their fame was **ephemeral** because viewers' tastes quickly change as new shows are aired each season.*

evanescent (ev uh NES unt) *adj.* Tending to fade from sight; vanishing. Evanescent applies to that which appears momentarily and fades quickly away.

> *For however briefly, Sherry cherished the **evanescent** image of his face.*

89. tempt

pander (PAN der) *v.* To provide the means of helping to satisfy the ignoble ambitions or desires, vices, etc. of another. Pandering refers to an almost obsequious willingness to get what someone else wants whether it is illicit, of a sexual nature, or not.

> *Politicians often **pander** to special interest groups in order to obtain campaign financing.*

seduce (suh DOOS) *v.* To persuade someone to do something disloyal, disobedient, etc. In the throes of passion, it is sometimes easy to mistake seduction for romance.

> *Overly leveraged with a substantial mortgage, Don was easily **seduced** by the promise of a higher salary.*

tantalize (TAN tuh lyz) *v.* To tease or disappoint by promising or showing something desirable and then withholding it. Tantalize differs from seduce in that the promise is never realized.

> *Dave **tantalized** the new recruit with stories of rapid promotions—promotions that, unfortunately, were not to come.*

90. trusting

gullible (GUL uh bul) *adj.* easily deceived, tricked, or fooled.

> ***Gullible** consumers can easily by duped by outrageous claims of telemarketers.*

credulous (KREJ yoo lus) *adj.* Tending to believe too readily; easily convinced.

> ***Credulous** co-workers are prime targets for all kinds of practical jokes.*

naïve (ny EEV) *adj.* Unaffectedly or sometimes foolishly simple; not suspicious. Naïve implies an almost foolish lack of worldly wisdom.

*James' **naïve** belief in the kindness of others led him to pick up the two hitchhikers—who later robbed him and stole his car.*

91. uncertain

vacillating (VAS uh lay ting) *adj.* Wavering or tending to waver in motion, opinion, and so on. Actively debating between various options.

*The candidate's **vacillating** stance on affirmative action issues alienated his entire constituency.*

ambivalent (am BIV uh lunt) *adj.* having conflicting feelings.

*I am **ambivalent** about the job; although the atmosphere is pleasant, the work itself is boring.*

mutable (MYOO tuh bul) *adj.* Tending to frequent change; inconstant; fickle; subject to mutation. Mutable refers more to a constant characteristic of going back and forth on issues. A mutable person or thing can be easily changed or swayed.

*The governor was so **mutable** that his inside staffers referred to him secretly as "the chameleon."*

92. unexplainable

inexplicable (in ik SPLIK uh bul) *adj.* That which cannot be explained, understood, or accounted for. Inexplicable implies an element of surprise, as if one thought something could be explained and then it couldn't.

*The background check revealed the **inexplicable** fact that Roy seemed to have no official existence prior to his current job.*

enigmatic (en ig MAT ik) *n.* perplexing, baffling, or seemingly inexplicable. Enigma is synonymous with riddle or puzzle and refers to a person or thing, as opposed to a state or behavior.

*Roy was **enigmatic**; no one knew where he came from or where he went after work.*

abstruse (ub STROOS) *adj.* Hard to understand; deep. Abstruse means not so much puzzling as difficult to understand; implies a depth of content that is not easily mastered.

*Roy attempted to explain that his records had been corrupted by a computer error, but the details were too **abstruse** for his co-workers to understand.*

93. uninterested

apathetic (ap uh THET ik) *adj.* Not interested; unconcerned; feeling little or no emotion. Apathetic stresses an indifference or listlessness from which one cannot easily be stirred to feeling. Apathy is difficult to overcome because it is typically deep-rooted and connotes an extinction of passion, not simply a passing disinterest.

*Due to a lack of real issues, the electorate was **apathetic** about the upcoming election; voter turnout was expected to be at an all-time low.*

indifferent (in DIF runt) *adj.* Having or showing no partiality, bias, or preference; neutral. Indifferent implies a neutrality, especially with reference to choice.
   *James remained **indifferent** about the campaign; neither candidate appealed to him.*

impassive (im PAS iv) *adj.* Not feeling or showing emotion; calm. Although impassive means not having or showing any pain or emotion, it does not necessarily connote an incapability of being affected.
   *He stood by **impassively**, not betraying the anguish he felt by Beatrice's declaration that she was leaving him for another man.*

94. unnecessary

redundant (rih DUN tunt) *adj.* More than enough; overabundant or excessive. To be redundant, you have to go past the point where you should have stopped. Redundant implies that any new thing that could be done has already been done in some other fashion.
   *Bob found his weekly trade journal **redundant** now that he was getting the same information sooner on the Web.*

superfluous (soo PER floo us) *adj.* Not needed; unnecessary. Whereas redundancy implies that something was once necessary but is now in excess, superfluous implies that the thing was never necessary.

*The coach's side-line instructions were **superfluous** because he had already given his players all the instruction they needed to win the game.*

verbose (ver BOHS) *adj.* Using or containing too many words. Verbosity implies long-windedness.

*Mr. Roberts had a reputation for being **verbose**; it took him three sentences to say what most people could say in one.*

95. unpredictable

whimsical (WIM zuh kul) *adj.* Subject to sudden change. Whimsical implies a sudden fancy or humorous or light-hearted intent.

*Feeling **whimsical**, Karen recorded a humorous new message on her answering machine.*

erratic (ih RAT ik) *adj.* Having no fixed course or purpose; random; wandering. Erratic behavior is random, not impulsive, and often refers to one's mental or emotional instability.

*As she became more depressed, Patricia's behavior became more **erratic**.*

precipitate (prih SIP uh tut) *adj.* Acting, happening, or done hastily or rashly; headstrong. Very sudden, unexpected, or abrupt.

*Doug's **precipitate** job resignation in anticipation of his annual review cost him not only his job but a job promotion, because his review was far more complimentary than he had expected.*

96. **useless**

ineffectual (in ih FEK choo ul) *adj.* Not producing or not able to produce the desired effect. Something or someone who is ineffectual can actually cause harm by not being able to stop something bad from happening.

> *Tony's entire division was **ineffectual** in reversing the company's accelerating losses from one quarter to the next.*

unavailing (un uh VAYL ing) *adj.* Ineffectual, pointless, without results, fruitless; to be of no use, help, worth, or advantage (to), as in accomplishing an end. Implies a sense of helplessness or an inability to fix something.

> *All contingency plans were **unavailing**; nothing could restore the politician's reputation.*

innocuous (ih NAHK yoo us) *adj.* That does not injure or harm; not controversial, offensive, or stimulating; dull and uninspiring. Innocuous is sometimes used in a derogatory fashion to imply a person or thing that has no impact or is useless.

> *Mr. Beevis was so **innocuous** as to be unnoticed at the office party.*

97. **verbal**

eloquent (EL uh kwunt) *adj.* Having a vivid, forceful, fluent, graceful, and persuasive speaking style; vividly expressive.

*Mitchell's **eloquent** farewell speech brought many in the audience to tears.*

fluent (FLOO unt) *adj.* Able to write or speak easily, smoothly, and expressively. Often used to describe a facility to speak in a foreign tongue.
*Henderson was **fluent** in both Japanese and Spanish.*

florid (FLOR ud) *adj.* Excessively ornate or flowery, especially in written or spoken expression.
*Brennan's **florid** writing style was better suited for poetry or fictional prose than for news reporting.*

98. waver

fluctuate (FLUK choo ayt) *v.* To be continually changing or varying in an irregular way.
*Speculation over quarterly earnings caused the stock price to **fluctuate** wildly.*

oscillate (AH suh layt) *v.* To swing or move regularly back and forth.
*The high winds caused the bridge to **oscillate** dangerously.*

undulate (UN juh layt) *v.* To move in, or as in, waves.
*The belly dancer's hips began to **undulate**.*

99. widespread

pervasive (per VAY siv) *adj.* Tending to be prevalent or spread throughout.

> *Computitan's products were **pervasive** in most corporate environments.*

rampant (RAM punt) *adj.* Spreading unchecked. Rampant implies a violent and uncontrollable action, manner, speech, and so on, characterized by rage and fury. Something that runs rampant is viewed to be almost unstoppable.

> *The virus ran **rampant** over the entire computer network.*

ambient (AM bee unt) *adj.* Surrounding or pervasive. Ambiance generally refers to a particular atmosphere.

> *The **ambient** sounds at the outdoor cafe, especially the live violin music, were conducive to romantic dinners for two.*

100. wild

fractious (FRAK chus) *adj.* Hard to manage. Fractious implies irritability and stubbornness; a fractious person is quarrelsome and difficult.

> *The boys from the group home were **fractious**, paying no attention to the leader's instructions.*

intractable (in TRAK tuh bul) *adj.* Not easily controlled. An intractable person is by nature unruly and uncontrollable, but not necessarily incapable of being reformed.

> *The **intractable** student was eventually suspended from school for his disruptive behavior in the classroom.*

insubordinate (in suh BOR duh nut) *adj.* Failing to obey. Insubordination implies stubbornness but requires unwillingness to comply with specific orders or commands.

> *Ignoring a direct order is an **insubordinate** act with grave consequences.*

Level 4

Synonyms and Antonyms

Level 4 features both synonyms and antonyms in a thesaurus format. The listings in Level 4 provide pronunciations, parts of speech, and brief definitions, as well as similar and contrary words for you to explore using a dictionary.

abut (uh BUT) *v.* to border upon; adjoin
    similar: contiguous; tangent; adjacent; append; annex; nexus
    contrary: discontiguous; disjointed; disunited

acuity (uh KYOO ih tee) *n.* keenness; sharpness (as in perception)
    similar: perspicacity; astuteness; discernment; acumen
    contrary: imbecility; fatuity; idiocy; obtuseness

addle (AD ul) *v.* to confuse, muddle, or bewilder, so as to annoy or irritate
    similar: befuddle; perturb; obfuscate; confound; perplex; stupefy; pester
    contrary: clarify; elucidate; explicate

adept (uh DEPT) *adj.* skillful; competent
similar: proficient; able; adroit; deft
contrary: incompetent; loutish; inept

adherent (ad HEER unt) *n.* follower; supporter; believer
similar: proselyte; disciple; apostle
contrary: antagonist; adversary; rival

allay (uh LAY) *v.* to calm or pacify
similar: appease; assuage; abate; mitigate
contrary: aggravate; provoke; exacerbate; vex; affront;
    chafe; embitter; envenom

ancillary (AN suh layr ee) *adj.* pertaining or connected to
something but not part of it
similar: auxiliary; peripheral; marginal; tangential; am-
    bient; extrinsic
contrary: primary; nuclear; chief; capital; cardinal; ax-
    ial; definitive; incisive; fundamental; primary; or-
    dinate; axiomatic

antagonistic (an TAG uh nis tik) *adj.* opposed to; hostile
similar: contentious; combative; adverse; contrary;
    belligerent; pugnacious; bellicose
contrary: amiable; amicable; allied; sympathetic; con-
    genial

aperture (AP er cher) *n.* an opening or gap (as in the aperture setting of a camera)
similar: orifice; breach; fissure; chasm
contrary: seal; contiguity; juxtaposition

aplomb (uh PLAHM) *n.* poise; composure
similar: assurance; intrepidity; impassivity; unflappability; imperturbability
contrary: intemperance; irascibility; petulance

apothegm (APP uh them) *n.* a short, pithy, instructive saying
similar: aphorism; epigram; maxim; adage; proverb; axiom

asylum (uh SY lum) *n.* a refuge or sanctuary (especially, for criminals or the insane)
similar: haven; sanitarium

avarice (AV er is) *n.* greed
similar: cupidity; avidity; covetousness; parsimony
contrary: philanthropy; charity; benevolence; munificence; beneficence; altruism

awry (uh RY) *adj.* twisted; gone wrong (as in plans that went awry)
similar: amiss; astray; afield; askew; aslant; tortuous; serpentine; convoluted; vermicular
contrary: true; assiduous; undeviating

balk (BAWK) *v.* to stop short; refuse to continue
similar: demur; spurn; shun; desist; halt; falter; stammer; suspend
contrary: advance; proceed; persevere; persist; endure; pertinacious; dogged; indefatigable

bate (BAYT) *v.* to moderate or restrain; hold back (as in bated breath)
similar: impede; bridle; abate; repress; quell; quash; suppress; curb
contrary: unfetter; emancipate; manumit; discharge; extricate

bauble (BAW bul) *n.* a trinket
similar: trifle; toy; triviality; memento; souvenir

behemoth (buh HEE mith) *n.* a huge creature
similar: leviathan; mammoth; gargantuan; prodigious; titanic; colossal; vast
contrary: dwarf; mannequin; pygmy; diminutive; bantam; lilliputian; minutia

bereaved (buh REEVED) *adj.* the state of having lost something cherished or valuable (as in the death of a family member)
similar: bereft; deprived; denuded; forfeited

bilk (BILK) *v.* to deceive; defraud
similar: dupe; swindle; beguile; delude; cozen; feign

blazon (BLAY zun) *v.* to proclaim or announce publicly or conspicuously
similar: herald; publicize; divulge; promulgate; publish; flaunt
contrary: ensconce; shroud; camouflage

boisterous (BOY ster us) *adj.* loud, rough, or violent
similar: clamorous; tumultuous; obstreperous; rambunctious; riotous; turbulent

> *contrary:* sedate; staid; reconciled; subdued; placid; tranquil

bovine (BOH vyn) *adj.* cowlike; dull or inactive
> *similar:* inert; loutish; slothful; torpid; indolent; languid; phlegmatic; listless
> *contrary:* astir; exuberant; animated; vivacious; effervescent; ebullient

bucolic (byoo KAHL ik) *adj.* rustic; pastoral
> *similar:* idyllic; halcyon; provincial; agrarian; campestral; bucolic; georgic

bungle (BUNG gul) *v.* to mishandle; botch up; make a bad mistake
> *similar:* blunder; bollix; spoil; ruin; impair
> *contrary:* ameliorate; rectify; finesse

caliber (KAL ih ber) *adj.* degree of quality, competence, or merit
> *similar:* import; consequence; esteem; notoriety; gravity

callous (KAL us) *adj.* insensitive; unfeeling
> *similar:* obdurate; indurate
> *contrary:* humane; clement; beneficent; commiserating; benevolent

canard (kuh NARD) *n.* a rumor or false report
> *similar:* hoax; gossip; hearsay; scandal; calumny

candid (CAN did) *adj.* sincere and forthright
> *similar:* frank; ingenuous; guileless; earnest; fervent

contrary: hypocritical; sanctimonious; ingenuous; equivocal; mendacious; devious

cardinal (KAR dih nul) *adj.* chief; most important; primary
similar: capital; principal; pivotal; axial
contrary: subordinate; subsidiary; subservient; auxiliary; ancillary; negligible

cauterize (KAH ter yz) *v.* to burn with a hot iron or with fire, usually to cure or heal
similar: sear; char; singe; scorch; brand; scald; parch

cavil (KAV ul) *v.* to raise irritating and trivial objections
similar: quibble; carp; gripe; snivel; bewail
contrary: concur; accord; cooperate; assent; accede; acquiesce

cloy (KLOY) *v.* to weary by excess or overindulgence, especially of pleasure
similar: glut; surfeit; satiate; superfluity; plethora

comport (kum PORT) *v.* to behave; to conform oneself
similar: comply; accord; acquiesce
contrary: transgress; trespass; balk

cornucopia (kor nyoo KOH pee uh) *n.* abundance; plenty
similar: plenitude; bounty; copiousness; profusion; affluence
contrary: paucity; dearth; scarcity; want

dapper (DAP er) *adj.* neat; trim
similar: spruce; smart; natty; fastidious

contrary: disheveled; unkempt; tousled; slovenly; rumpled; disarrayed; tatterdemalion

debonair (deh buh NAYR) *adj.* courteous; charming; having pleasant manners
  similar: dashing; ambrosial; rakish; genteel; gallant; urbane; amiable; complaisant
  contrary: impudent; impertinent; insolent; flippant; churlish; boorish; unceremonious

deft (DEFT) *adj.* proficient; skilled; competent
  similar: adroit; adept; dexterous
  contrary: maladroit; inept; gauche

deplete (dee PLEET) *v.* to use up entirely; to empty
  similar: exhaust; dissipate; expend
  contrary: replenish

desultory (DES ul tor ee) *adj.* lacking order or consistency; rambling; disjointed; passing randomly from one thing to another.
  similar: discursive; incoherent; incongruous
  contrary: cohesive; cogent; coherent; congruous

dictum (DIK tum) *n.* an authoritative pronouncement, as from a judge
  similar: proclamation; edict; decree; order; behest; dictate; prescription; injunction; canon; mandate

dither (DIH ther) *n.* great excitement; agitation or trembling
  similar: commotion; frenzy; tumult; clamor; turbulence; ado; perturbation
  contrary: tranquillity; armistice

dolt (DOHLT) *n.* a stupid person
  similar: imbecile; simpleton; moron; ignoramus; dullard
  contrary: prodigy; genius; savant; virtuoso; sage; paragon

dour (DOW er) *adj.* sullen; gloomy
  similar: morose; somber; doleful; melancholy; lugubrious; saturnine
  contrary: blithe; jovial; jocund; insouciant; jaunty; roseate; sanguine

dross (DRAHS) *n.* waste matter; refuse
  similar: dregs; debris; rubble; jetsam; flotsam; excrement; remnant; vestige

effete (eh FEET) *adj.* no longer able to bear young; worn out or exhausted
  similar: sterile; infertile; barren
  contrary: fertile; fecund; prolific

emaciated (ee MAY shee ay tid) *adj.* withered, thin, or wasted
  similar: gaunt; haggard; degenerated; atrophied; wan; peaked; ashen; feeble; enervated
  contrary: robust; hardy; hale; brawny; stalwart

emanating (EM uh nay ting) *adj.* flowing from; issuing from
  similar: emitting; effusing; effluent; superfluent; prolix; prolific
  contrary: viscous; glutinous; mucilaginous

embroil (em BROYL) *v.* to involve someone else in a dispute

  similar: entangle; enmesh; implicate; embattle; entrap
  contrary: extricate; exculpate; exonerate; absolve; dissociate; sunder

emollient (ih MAHL ee unt) *n.* a softening ointment or other agent (*adj.* having the ability to soften or relax living tissues)

  similar: unguent; salve; balm; liniment; cerate; unction; slacken; pliant; supple; malleable
  contrary: callous; frangible; calcifying; ossifying; petrifying; fossilizing

emolument (ih MAWL yuh munt) *n.* salary or other compensation for employment

  similar: (earned) remuneration; stipend; honorarium; recompense
  contrary: (gifts) perquisite; gratuity; largess

emulate (EM uh nayt) *v.* to imitate in order to equal or surpass

  similar: model; mimic; simulate; ape; parrot; impersonate
  contrary (imitate to criticize or make fun of): mock; parody; satirize

enthrall (en THRAWL) *v.* to captivate; hold under a spell; fascinate

  similar: mesmerize; bewitch; stupefy; enamor; enrapture; enchant; engross
  contrary: bore; weary

equestrian (eh KWES tree un) *n.* a rider on horseback (*adj.* pertaining to horseback riding)
    similar: jockey; cavalry; dragoon
    contrary: pedestrian; afoot

esprit (eh SPREE) *n.* sprightliness of spirit or wit
    similar: enthusiasm; vitality; morale; energy; verve; vim; vigor; zest; zeal; ebullience

exemplary (eg ZEMP luh ree) *adj.* outstanding; suitable as a model (either good or bad)
    similar: ideal; consummate; paragon; archetypal; quintessential; epitome; egregious; extant

exhort (eg ZORT) *v.* to urge by words; to caution or advise strongly
    similar: admonish; spur; incite; counsel; entreat; beseech; implore; induce

exorbitant (eg ZOR buh dent) *adj.* beyond what is reasonable excessive; extravagant
    similar: inordinate; immoderate; plethoric; lavish; superfluous; turgid
    contrary: insufficient; wanting; bereft; depleted

extol (ek STOHL) *v.* to praise
    similar: laud; commend; acclaim; hail; eulogize; panegyrize; esteem; venerate; adulate; revere
    contrary: inveigh; censure; fulminate

exuberant (eg ZOO ber unt) *adj.* excited; enthusiastic
    similar: astir; animated; vivacious; effervescent; ebullient; reveling; frolicsome

    contrary: inert; loutish; slothful; torpid; indolent; languid; phlegmatic; listless

facilitate (fuh SIL uh tayt) *v.* to make easier (less difficult)
    similar: assist; expedite; further; succor; dispatch; precipitate
    contrary: impede; hamper; hinder; arrest

fathom (FATH um) *v.* to understand thoroughly; literally, to reach the bottom of something
    similar: discern; conceive; assimilate

fetid (FET ud) *adj.* having an offensive smell
    similar: malodorous; putrid; noisome; rank; noxious; mephitic
    contrary: aromatic; odoriferous; redolent; fragrant

fetter (FET er) *v.* to bind; chain
    similar: bridle; muzzle; lash; encumber; adjure; manacle; batten; gird; fob; indenture; enslave
    contrary: unfetter; emancipate; disencumber; extricate; exculpate; manumit

filch (FILCH) *v.* to steal
    similar: pilfer; purloin; misappropriate; abscond; peculate; embezzle

fledgling (FLEJ ling) *adj.* inexperienced (literally, a young bird)
    similar: neophyte; novice; apprentice; proselyte; callow; green
    contrary: seasoned; veteran

flippant (FLIP unt) *adj.* disrespectful; rude
    similar: impertinent; impudent; insolent; audacious;
      impudent; churlish; unceremonious
    contrary: debonair; chivalrous; duteous

flout (FLOWT) *v.* to show disrespect
    similar: mock; jeer; affront; snub; disdain; scorn; gibe
    contrary: laud; hail; eulogize; panegyrize; venerate;
      defer

flux (FLUKS) *n.* a continuous moving on or passing by;
constant succession or change
    similar: instability; transmutation; metamorphosis;
      transfiguration; influx; efflux
    contrary: stagnancy; stationary; inert; dormancy; stasis

foible (FOY bul) *n.* a small character weakness
    similar: frailty; flaw

foist (FOYST) *v.* to force upon or impose upon fraudu-
lently
    similar: palm; swindle; dupe; chicane

gaffe (GAF) *n.* a social blunder
    similar: oversight; bungle; tactlessness; peccadillo

gall (GAWL) *n.* bitterness; nerve (*v* annoy)
    similar: effrontery; temerity; insolence; audacity;
      brashness; impertinence

gambit (GAM but) *n.* any move by which one seeks to gain an advantage; an opening move in chess in which a piece is sacrificed
> *similar:* stratagem; coven; machination; ruse; tactic; ploy; chicanery; arbitrage; subterfuge; artifice

gamut (GAM ut) *n.* entire range
> *similar:* spectrum; breadth; scope; purview; panoply

garish (GAYR ish) *adj.* gaudy; overly showy
> *similar:* meretricious; ostentatious; tawdry; pretentious; florid; baroque; unbecoming
> *contrary:* seemly; unadorned; unobtrusive

garner (GAR ner) *v.* to gather; store up; collect; accumulate
> *similar:* glean; amass; hoard; cumulate; agglomerate; accrue; compile; anthologize
> *contrary:* distribute; issue; parcel; disseminate; dispense

gesticulate (juh STIK yoo layt) *v.* to gesture or motion
> *similar:* beckon; signal; wave

glower (GLOW er) *v.* to scowl or frown
> *similar:* grimace; glare; smirk
> *contrary:* beam; grin

gluttonous (GLUT un us) *adj.* excessive (immoderate) in engaging in an activity, especially in the partaking of food and strong drink
> *similar:* intemperate; immoderate; veracious; surfeit; cloy

contrary: abstemious; abstinent; abstentious; moderate; temperate

gnome (NOHM) *n.* dwarf
  similar: elf; mannequin; pygmy; lilliputian; bantam; sylph; goblin; gremlin
  contrary: leviathan; mammoth; colossus

grovel (GRAH vul) *v.* to behave in a servile fashion (literally, to crawl on the ground)
  similar: cower; wallow; fawn
  contrary: condescend; deign; patronize

guise (GYZ) *n.* appearance
  similar: countenance; mien; demeanor; facade; semblance

hackneyed (HAK need) *adj.* commonplace; trite; overused
  similar: banal; insipid; prosaic
  contrary: distinctive; singular; unique

hap (HAP) *n.* chance or luck
  similar: fortuitousness; serendipity; happenstance; coincidence

harass (huh RAS) *v.* to annoy by accosting or attacking repeatedly
  similar: badger; harry; heckle; abrade; irk; chafe; vex; perturb

harp (HARP) *v.* to dwell on a subject to the point of being tiresome or annoying
  similar: brood; ruminate; sulk; muse; deliberate

hebetic (hih BET ik) *adj.* dull; fatigued (*n.* hebetude)
   similar: lethargic; torpid; listless; phlegmatic; languid
   contrary: vivacious; effervescent; ebullient; zealous;
      ardent; fervent; fervid

hedonist (HEE dun ist) *n.* a seeker of pleasure
   similar: epicurean; debauchee; sensualist; libertine

heedless (HEED lis) *adj.* careless; unmindful
   similar: remiss; negligent; oblivious; reckless; slack;
      lax
   contrary: circumspect; wakeful; wary; rapt; vigilant;
      punctilious

herald (HAYR uld) *v.* to announce or foretell
   similar: proclaim; divulge; blazon; promulgate; fore-
      shadow; portend; presage

hermetic (her MET ik) *adj.* sealed to be airtight; mysterious
   similar: impervious; impermeable; inscrutable; caulked
   contrary: pervious; permeable; porous; pregnable

heterodox (HET er uh dahks) *adj.* unconventional; unorthodox
   similar: eccentric; maverick; deviant; nonconforming;
      contrary; idiosyncratic; outlandish
   contrary: generic; cognate; doctrinal; sanctioned; ko-
      sher; homogeneous

hew (HYOO) *v.* to cut into pieces with an ax or sword
   similar: hack; rent; lacerate; cleave; dissever

hoary (HOR ee) *adj.* having white hair; very old
    similar: grizzled; ancient; ripened; antique; decrepit;
       doddering
    contrary: callow; nubile; fledgling; puerile; pubescent;
       juvenile; green

horary (HOR er ee) *adj.* occurring once an hour; hourly
    similar: iterative; quotidian; tertian

imbue (im BYOO) *v.* to inspire; to impregnate, or fill
(especially with a quality or characteristic)
    similar: inculcate; instill; indoctrinate; permeate; for-
      tify; admonish; inspirit

impale (im PAYL) *v.* to pierce (as with a sword)
    similar: skewer; lance; skiver; crucify; spike

impasse (IM pass) *n.* a predicament from which there is
no escape; a path with no outlet
    similar: dilemma; quandary; straight; plight; mire

impious (IMP yuss) *adj.* irreverent (*n* impiety)
    similar: sacrilegious; blasphemous; flippant; impudent
    contrary: reverent; pious; respectful; courteous

improvident (im PRAHV uh dunt) *adj.* wasteful; ne-
glectful
    similar: imprudent; negligent; remiss; heedless; prodi-
      gal; profligate; inadvertent
    contrary: prudent; provident; politic; mindful; punc-
      tilious

incongruous (in KAHN groo us) *adj.* out of place; lacking in harmony (among parts)
> *similar:* inconsonant; inapt; unfitting; aberrant; anachronistic; enigmatic
> *contrary:* consonant; befitting; seemly; harmonious

inculcate (IN kul kayt) *v.* to teach persistently and earnestly
> *similar:* indoctrinate; admonish; ingrain; infix; brainwash

indelible (in DEL uh bul) *adj.* incapable of being erased or eradicated
> *similar:* permanent; ineffaceable; ineradicable; immutable
> *contrary:* eradicable; temporary; revocable; evanescent; temporal

ineluctable (in uh LUK tuh bul) *adj.* inevitable; inescapable; irresistible
> *similar:* ineludible; inevasible; inexorable

inscrutable (in SKROO tuh bul) *adj.* impenetrable; not readily understood; mysterious
> *similar:* impervious; impermeable; hermetic; enigmatic; cryptic; abstruse; recondite
> *contrary:* pervious; permeable; porous; pregnable; fathomable; ascertainable

inveterate (in VET er ut) *adj.* deep-rooted; longstanding
> *similar:* habitual; entrenched; ensconced; ingrained; inbred; innate

contrary: nascent; incipient; transient; transitory;
ephemeral; evanescent

iota (y OH tuh) *n.* a very small quantity
similar: shred; trace; fleck; scintilla
contrary: surfeit; surplus; profusion; plenitude; cornucopia; bounty; plethora

jaded (JAY did) *adj.* fatigued; exhausted; weary from
overuse
similar: enervated; spent; cloyed; depleted
contrary: invigorated; revitalized; enlivened

jaunt (JAWNT) *n.* a leisurely trip
similar: excursion; stroll; amble; saunter; promenade
contrary: dash; sprint; gallop; spurt

jaunty (JAWN tee) *adj.* carefree; lighthearted
similar: insouciant; jocund; jocose; jovial; blithe
contrary: dour; sullen; morose; somber; doleful; melancholy; lugubrious; saturnine

jeer (JEER) *v.* to deride, taunt, or ridicule
similar: sneer; flout; gibe; mock; affront; scorn

jeopardy (JEP er dee) *n.* exposure to danger or treachery
similar: peril; risk; vulnerability
contrary: invulnerability; impregnability; sanctuary;
asylum; refuge; haven

jocose (joh KOHS) *adj.* given to joking; playful; light-
hearted
similar: jocular; jocund; waggish; jovial; facetious;
blithe; trifling; buoyant; halcyon

contrary: somber; demure; staid; sedate; stern; grim;
lugubrious; pensive; saturnine

jostle (JAH sul) *v.* to shove or bump
similar: jar; collide; jolt; impact; nudge; propel

jubilant (JOO buh lunt) *adj.* characterized by great joy;
rejoicing; joyful (especially due to a triumph or other joy-
ous event)
similar: elated; exuberant; exultant; reveling; frolic-
some
contrary: despondent; morose; dolorous; melancholy;
somber; grim; lugubrious; pensive; saturnine

juncture (JUNG cher) *n.* an intersection; a crisis
similar: crossroads; concourse; junction; confluence;
bifurcation; exigency; dilemma; quandary

jut (JUT) *v.* to extend out; protrude
similar: extrude; distend; bloat; bastion; cantilever
contrary: recede; atrophy; cringe; recoil

kaleidoscope (kuh LY duh skohp) *n.* anything characterized by dazzling variety, complexity, or change
similar: variegation; matrix; array; mosaic; aurora;
chameleon; protean; mutation

kindle (KIN dul) *v.* to spark, inspire, or fuel
similar: incite; impel; foment; spur
contrary: stifle; quell; douse; quash; extinguish;
squelch; curb

knell (NEL) *n.* the sound of a bell rung to signal or signify something (as in death knell)
   similar: tocsin; summons; proclamation

knoll (NOHL) *n.* a small, grassy hill
   similar: hummock; hillock; promontory; kame

knurled (NERLD) *adj.* knotty; gnarled
   similar: contorted; serpentine

kraft (KRAFT) *n.* strong paper (usually brown in color) used for making bags and for wrapping

lackey (LAK ee) *n.* a servile follower; yes-man; hanger-on
   similar: acolyte; toady; minion; entourage; retinue

lethargic (luh THAR jik) *adj.* sluggish or inactive; indifferent
   similar: torpid; listless; languid; phlegmatic; apathetic
   contrary: vivacious; effervescent; ebullient; zealous;
     ardent; fervent; fervid

libelous (LY buh lus) *adj.* defamatory; slanderous
   similar: derogatory; opprobrious; calumnious; maligning; vilifying
   contrary: laudatory; acclamatory; commendatory;
     eulogistic; adulatory; edifying

libidinous (lih BIH duh nus) *adj.* lustful
   similar: licentious; prurient; lecherous; salacious; lascivious

licit (LIH sit) *adj.* legal; lawful; permitted
　similar: sanctioned; legitimate; mandated; decreed; warranted; empowered; ratified
　contrary: illicit; nefarious; spurious; interdicted; contraband; taboo

lineaments (LIN ee uh mins) *n.* features (especially, facial features)
　similar: visage; countenance; physiognomy; profile; guise

lionize (LY uh nyz) *v.* to treat as a celebrity
　similar: exalt; revere; venerate; idolize; dote; esteem
　contrary: slight; deign

lissome (LIH sum) *adj.* limber or pliable (see lithe, below)

lithe (LYTH) *adj.* flexible; supple
　similar: pliable; pliant; lissome; compliant; resilient; malleable; ductile
　contrary: inelastic; frangible; intractable; refractory; implacable

loiter (LOY ter) *v.* to linger or "hang around"
　similar: tarry; dally; sojourn; abide; dawdle; lag; loll
　contrary: dispatch; scurry; advance

lope (LOHP) *v.* to run slowly (especially, as a horse)
　similar: canter; jog; trot; saunter; amble
　contrary: gallop; sprint; scurry; hasten

lout (LOWT) *n.* a clumsy or stupid person
　similar: boor; oaf; maladroit; bungler

lumber (LUM ber) *v.* to move heavily or clumsily
   similar: trudge; plod; march; drudge

maim (MAYM) *v.* to mutilate or injure severely
   similar: mangle; deface; dismember
   contrary: ameliorate; remedy; alleviate

manumit (man yuh MIT) *v.* to release from slavery or servitude; emancipate
   similar: liberate; discharge; unfetter; disencumber; exculpate; extricate; disenthrall
   contrary: enslave; indenture; fetter; bridle; muzzle; lash; encumber; manacle; adjure

masochism (MAS uh kiz um) *n.* intentional infliction of pain on oneself
   contrary: sadism (intentional infliction of pain on *another*)

mendacity (men DAS ih tee) *n.* deceit; fraud (*adj.* mendacious)
   similar: chicanery; duplicity; disingenuousness; guile; artifice; sham; ruse
   contrary: candor; rectitude; probity; forthrightness; frankness; ingenuousness; guileless; earnestness

mephitic (muh FIT ik) *adj.* offensive to the smell; noxious or poisonous
   similar: fetid; malodorous; putrid; noisome; rank; deleterious
   contrary: aromatic; odoriferous; redolent; fragrant; salubrious; salutary

mete (MEET) *v.* to measure; to distribute (as in mete out rations)
  similar: allot; parcel; allocate; apportion; ration; divvy; dole; dispense; issue

mettle (MET ul) *n.* character of a person
  similar: constitution; spirit; composition; fabric

mien (MEEN) *n.* demeanor, appearance, or character
  similar: air; comportment; mettle

minion (MIN yun) *n.* a servile dependent; a servant or slave
  similar: lackey; acolyte; proselyte; hireling; deputy; subordinate; peon; ensign

misconstrue (mis kun STROO) *v.* to misunderstand or misinterpret
  similar: distort; pervert; err
  contrary: discern; fathom; conceive; assimilate

mollify (MAH lih fy) *v.* to pacify, soothe or put at ease
  similar: placate; appease; allay; alleviate; assuage
  contrary: vex; perturb; peeve; irk; chafe; abrade; exasperate

motile (MOH tul) *adj.* capable of moving spontaneously
  similar: ambulatory; mobile; transportable; migratory; transient
  contrary: stationary; dormant; static; anchored; inert; sluggish; phlegmatic; entrenched; ingrained

motley (MAHT lee) *adj.* consisting of many colors; composed of many elements
>*similar:* variegated; dappled; polychromatic; kaleidoscopic; psychedelic; prismatic; heterogeneous; sundry; commingled; multiform; manifold
>*contrary:* monochromatic; homogenous; uniform; monolithic

mulct (MULKT) *v.* to punish by fine or forfeiture; to deprive another of possession by fraud
>*similar:* penalize; amerce; exact; sanction; confiscate; expropriate

myriad (MEER ee ad) *n.* a great (large) number
>*similar:* legion; multitude
>*contrary:* paucity; scarcity; dearth; deficit

natty (NAT ee) *adj.* neatly or smartly dressed
>*similar:* dapper; chic; spruce; smart; foppish; fastidious
>*contrary:* disheveled; slovenly; unkempt; tatterdemalion

necromancy (NEK ruh mun see) *n.* magic that involves the dead
>*similar:* witchcraft; sorcery; sortilege; wizardry; thaumaturgy; shamanism; conjuration; occultism; alchemy; legerdemain

nettle (NET ul) *v.* to annoy or irritate
>*similar:* vex; perturb; peeve; irk; chafe; abrade; exasperate
>*contrary:* allay; ease; alleviate; pacify; mollify; placate; assuage

niggling (NIG ling) *adj.* tending to dwell on minor or trivial points
  similar: picayune; pedantic; petty; carping; belaboring; quibbling; trifling

nonplus (non PLUS) *v.* to bring to a halt by confusion; perplex
  similar: stupefy; bewilder; confound; baffle; addle; befuddle
  contrary: clarify; elucidate; explicate

nostalgic (nuh STAHL jik) *adj.* longing for the past
  similar: homesick; yearning; sentimental; mawkish; maudlin

noxious (NAHK shyus) *adj.* harmful to health; injurious
  similar: toxic; deleterious; baneful; virulent; pernicious; pestiferous; lethal; malignant
  contrary: salubrious; salutary; healthful; hygienic; tonic

nubile (NOO byl) *adj.* suitable for marriage (referring to a young woman), especially in physical development
  similar: eligible; maturated; ripe; precocious
  contrary: juvenile; pubescent; puerile

oblivion (uh BLIV ee un) *n.* the state of being forgotten (especially by the public)
  similar: vacuity; obsolescence
  contrary: remembrance; amanuensis; reminiscence; nostalgia; memoir

obsolete (ahb suh LEET) *adj.* out of date; no longer useful
  similar: outmoded; antiquated; archaic; anachronistic; vintage
  contrary: contemporary; prevailing; serviceable; utilitarian

obtuse (ahb TOOS) *adj.* slow to understand; insensitive (literally, blunt)
  similar: undiscerning; doltish; dull; dimwitted; moronic
  contrary: perspicacious; keen; astute; discerning

odyssey (AH duh see) *n.* a long, eventful journey
  similar: trek; peregrination; excursion; pilgrimage; junket; safari; transhumance; migration

ogle (AW gul) *v.* to glance flirtatiously at
  similar: eye; stare; leer; gape

onus (OH nus) *n.* burden or responsibility
  similar: accountability; liability; culpability

opulence (AHP yoo luns) *n.* wealth; luxury
  similar: affluence; prosperity; privilege; indulgence; extravagance
  contrary: destitution; pauperism; mendicancy; indigence

ordinate (OR dih nit) *adj.* fundamental; primary
  similar: rudimentary; basal; inchoate; axiomatic; chief; capital; cardinal; axial; definitive; incisive
  contrary: subordinate; subsidiary; subservient; auxiliary; ancillary

oust (OWST) *v.* to force out or expel
    similar: banish; evict; exile; ostracize; extradite

overt (oh VERT) *adj.* out in the open; not hidden
    similar: perceptible; apparent; manifest; evident; palpable
    contrary: covert; camouflaged; shrouded; veiled; clandestine; surreptitious

pall (PAWL) *n.* something that covers over, especially in darkness or gloom; *v.* to become wearisome, tiresome, or unpleasant
    similar: shroud; cloy; surfeit; glut; oppress

pallid (PAL id) *n.* pale or deficient in color (as from fear or ill health)
    similar: sallow; wan; ashen; anemic; waxen; blanched
    contrary: flushed; ruddy; rosy; cerise; rubicund; sanguine

pan (PAN) *v.* to criticize harshly
    similar: censure; reprove; chastise; reprimand; reproach; remonstrate; inveigh; disapprobate; reprobate
    contrary: acclaim; extol; plaudit; laud; hail; adulate; commend; approbate; panegyrize; eulogize

parley (PAR lee) *n.* a conference
    similar: council; intercourse; dialogue; rendezvous; tryst

parochial (puh ROH kee ul) *adj.* narrow or limited in scope
    similar: provincial; insular; sectarian

contrary: pandemic; universal; rife; epidemic

peripheral (per IF er ul) *adj.* pertaining to the outer region of something (as opposed to the core or center)
  similar: marginal; ambient; extraneous; extrinsic; auxiliary; ancillary
  contrary: nuclear; chief; capital; cardinal; axial; definitive; incisive; fundamental; primary; ordinate; axiomatic

platitude (PLAT ih tood) *n.* a trite remark; hackneyed statement
  similar: banality; truism; inanity; apothegm; maxim; adage; proverb; aphorism

poseur (poh ZER) *n.* a person who pretends to be sophisticated or elegant in order to impress others
  similar: feigner; parvenu; upstart

prattle (PRAT ul) *v.* to speak in a childish manner; babble
  similar: jabber; twaddle; chatter; drivel; gibberish

puerile (PYOOR yl) *adj.* pertaining to a child
  similar: callow; nubile; fledgling; pubescent; juvenile; green
  contrary: hoary; grizzled; ancient; ripened; antique; decrepit; doddering

purloin (per LOYN) *v.* to steal or take dishonestly
  similar: pilfer; misappropriate; abscond; peculate; embezzle; foist

quaff (KWAHF) *v.* to drink with relish
similar: guzzle; swig; imbibe; swill; ingurgitate; partake

quail (KWAYL) *v.* to shrink with fear
similar: cower; recoil; cringe; shudder; flinch; wince

quaint (KWAYNT) *adj.* unusual in a charming way
similar: curious; peculiar; eccentric

qualms (KWAWLMS) *n.* misgivings; doubts
similar: scruples; hesitance; skepticism; leeriness;
wariness; reluctance; mistrust; trepidation; dread;
circumspection

quarry (KWOR ee) *n.* a hunt or the object of a hunt; *v.* to
extract stone from the earth's surface
similar: pursuit; chase; prey; excavate

quash (KWAHSH) *v.* to put down or suppress
similar: quell (see below)

quaver (KWAY ver) *v.* to shake tremulously
similar: tremble; shiver; shudder; quiver

quell (KWEL) *v.* to put down or suppress
similar: quash; subdue; squelch; allay; stifle; quench;
vanquish
contrary: spur; induce; promote; facilitate; provoke;
goad; incite; foment; instigate

quibble (KWIH bul) *v.* to nit-pick; to evade an issue by making irrelevant points
   similar: carp; cavil; gripe; elude; parry; muddle; obfuscate

quip (KWIP) *n.* a witty or sarcastic remark
   similar: mockery; insult; gibe; jeer; satire; banter; ridicule; derision

rabid (RAB id) *adj.* irritatingly extreme in opinion; raging violently
   similar: fanatic; frenzied; ultraistic; maniacal; fervent; fervid; ardent

raiment (RAY munt) *n.* clothing; attire
   similar: vestments; garb; garments; apparel; habits; accouterments; ensemble; finery; regalia; trimmings; frippery

rampart (RAM part) *n.* a small mound of earth used defensively in battle
   similar: barrier; fortification; impediment; barricade; bar; blockade; bastion; escarpment; barbican; hummock; hillock

rarefied (RAYR ih fyd) *adj.* lofty; made less dense (as in rarefied gases)
   similar: exalted; esoteric; diffused; thinned; ethereal; vaporous

recourse (REE kors) *n.* access to assistance in time of trouble
   similar: resort; aid; relief; succor; avail; remedy

rejuvenate (rih JOO vuh nayt) *v.* to make fresh or young again
　　similar: refresh; revitalize; reinvigorate; revive; reanimate; enliven; exhilarate; resuscitate

relent (rih LENT) *v.* to surrender or give in
　　similar: yield; capitulate; relinquish; cede; abdicate; succumb; acquiesce

relic (REL ik) *n.* a surviving memorial from the past
　　similar: artifact; curio; vestige; remnant; bibelot; antique; memento

reprieve (ruh PREEV) *v.* to delay punishment
　　similar: suspend; defer; adjourn; pardon

reprisal (rih PRY zul) *n.* the infliction of an injury in return for an injury done
　　similar: revenge; recompense; vengeance; vendetta

requite (ruh QUYT) *v.* to repay; pay back
　　similar: recompense; remunerate; reimburse; rebate; vindicate; avenge
　　contrary: (be in) arrears; owe; withhold

retribution (ret rih BYOO shun) *n.* vengeance
　　similar: revenge; vindication; requital; recompense; retaliation

rift (RIFT) *n.* a break or opening
　　similar: chasm; fissure; breach; crevice; cranny; cleft; aperture; orifice

ruffian (RUF yun) *n.* a bully
similar: scoundrel; miscreant; hooligan; thug

saga (SAH guh) *n.* a myth or legend
similar: tale; epic; fable; allegory; parable

sartor (SAR ter) *n.* a tailor
similar: couturier

scabbard (SKAB erd) *n.* a case for a sword or other blade
similar: sheath; quiver; holster

scathed (SKAYTHD) *adj.* harmed; injured
similar: wounded; damaged; aggrieved; impaired

scotch (SKAHCH) *v.* to injure so as to make harmless; to stamp out
similar: foil; hinder; thwart; arrest; impede; forestall; preclude; interdict; sabotage; undermine; maim

scourge (SKORJ) *v.* to whip (especially, as punishment)
similar: lash; switch; cane; chastise; castigate; discipline

scruple (SKROO pul) *n.* a moral or ethical consideration giving rise to hesitancy or doubt
similar: qualms; misgivings; demurral; conscience; unwillingness; leeriness; wariness; reluctance

scurrilous (SKER uh lis) *adj.* obscene; indecent
similar: lewd; vulgar; uncouth; indecorous; lascivious; licentious; unsavory; libertine; bawdy; ribald
contrary: seemly; decorous; befitting; scrupulous; genteel; courtly

seine (SAYN) *n.* a type of fishing net
similar: snare; lure; trap

shun (SHUN) *v.* to stay away from; avoid
similar: eschew; avert; abstain; evade; elude; spurn;
    snub
contrary: embrace; enfold; welcome

shunt (SHUNT) *v.* to shove out of the way; turn aside
similar: reject; jettison; shed; discard

spartan (SPAR tun) *adj.* characterized by a plain, simple
lifestyle; undaunted and disciplined
similar: ascetic; severe; harsh; rigorous; unadorned;
    austere; stern
contrary: luxurious; opulent; lavish; elegant; indulgent;
    epicurean

squalid (SKWAH lid) *adj.* neglected, dirty, or poor (especially, living conditions)
similar: seedy; ramshackle; shabby
contrary: tidy; immaculate

stentorian (sten TOR ee un) *adj.* extremely loud
similar: clamorous; boisterous; obstreperous; strident;
    plangent; tumultuous; forte; rambunctious; riotous;
    turbulent
contrary: quiescent; mute; tacit; placid; serene; sedate;
    staid; subdued; tranquil

sundry (SUN dree) *adj.* various; diverse
similar: variegated; myriad; multifarious
contrary: homogeneous; uniform

svelte (SVELT) *adj.* gracefully slender
    similar: lithe; willowy; lissome
    contrary: obese; corpulent

sybarite (SIB uh ryt) *n.* a person devoted to luxury or pleasure
    similar: epicurean; voluptuary; hedonist; debauchee
    contrary: ascetic; austere; spartan

taper (TAY per) *v.* to become narrower; *n.* a candle
    similar: cramp; contract; squeeze; compress; constrict; obelisk; pyramid; carafe
    contrary: distend; widen; splay; flare; flute

tedium (TEE dee um) *n.* boredom; weariness
    similar: ennui; monotony; fatigue; pall; apathy; dullness; repetitiveness
    contrary: scintillation; exuberance; titillation; jubilation; ado; melodrama

tepid (TEP id) *adj.* luke-warm (neither cold nor hot)
    similar: indifferent; apathetic; nonchalant; impassive; sedate

tether (TEH ther) *v.* to tie with a rope
    similar: leash; fetter; manacle; moor; berth; anchor
    contrary: unfetter; disencumber; extricate

throng (THRAWNG) *n.* a large crowd
    similar: horde; swarm; host; multitude

tithe (TYTH) *n.* a tax of one tenth (*v.* to give one tenth as a tax or donation)
    similar: levy; tariff; toll; duty; assessment

toady (TOH dee) *n.* a fawning flatterer; a "yes-man"
  similar: acolyte; lackey; minion; entourage; retinue

tocsin (TAHK sin) *n.* an alarm, bell, or other signal
  similar: knell; portent; foretoken; omen

travail (truh VAYL) *n.* laborious, arduous work
  similar: drudgery; toil; labor; turmoil
  contrary: mirth; gaiety; joviality; caprice

tryst (TRIST) *n.* an appointment for a meeting (especially, a secretive meeting of lovers)
  similar: rendezvous; engagement; parley

tutelage (TOO tuh lij) *n.* training under the guidance and protection of another
  similar: apprenticeship; guardianship; conservatorship; custody

tyro (TY roh) *n.* a beginner
  similar: novice; neophyte; apprentice; amateur; rookie; greenhorn; proselyte

uncanny (un KAN ee) *adj.* mysterious; weird
  similar: eerie; bizarre; peculiar; inexplicable; aberrant; deviant; anomalous

unconscionable (un KAHN shun uh bul) *adj.* in violation of one's conscience
  similar: unscrupulous; corrupt; unethical; amoral; venal; sordid
  contrary: conscionable; just; equitable

ungainly (un GAYN lee) *adj.* clumsy; awkward
  similar: inept; maladroit; oafish; gauche; bungling;
    loutish

unguent (UN gwent) *n.* ointment
  similar: liniment; emollient; salve; balm; cerate; unc-
    tion

unrequited (un ruh KWY tid) *adj.* not reciprocated
  similar: unilateral; unrecompensed; delinquent; owing;
    due
  contrary: reciprocated; recompensed; remunerated;
    reimbursed; rebated; avenged; vindicated

unwieldy (un WEEL dee) *adj.* cumbersome or awkward
  similar: unmanageable; bulky; clumsy
  contrary: manageable; controllable; yielding; compli-
    ant; cooperative; acquiescent

unwitting (un WIT een) *adj.* unknowing; unaware; unintentional
  similar: ignorant; oblivious; inadvertent; involuntary
  contrary: witting; cognizant; deliberate; willful; vol-
    untary; intentional

upstart (UP start) *n.* a person who has become arrogant as
a result of a sudden rise to a position of importance
  similar: parvenu; elitist; snob; opportunist

utopia (yoo TOH pee uh) *n.* an imaginary place of political and social perfection
  similar: paradise; consummation; nirvana; millennium

uxorious (uk SOR ee us) *adj.* overly devoted or submissive to one's wife
    similar: doting; fawning; indulgent

vainglorious (vayn GLOR ee us) *adj.* excessively proud of one's accomplishments
    similar: vain; boastful; conceited; egotistical; haughty; pompous; arrogant
    contrary: retiring; unpretentious; unobtrusive; decorous

vantage (VAN tij) *n.* an advantageous position or condition
    similar: benefit; boon; privilege

vapid (VAP id) *adj.* lacking liveliness, spirit, or flavor
    similar: insipid; stale; banal; mundane; prosaic; phlegmatic; insouciant
    contrary: effervescent; ebullient; vivacious; savory

variegated (VAYR ee uh gay tid) *adj.* varied in appearance, especially in color
    similar: kaleidoscopic; polychromatic; dappled; motley; prismatic; mottled; mosaic; multifarious

vaunt (VAWNT) *v.* to speak boastfully (vaingloriously) of
    similar: brag; flaunt; gloat; tout; brandish; publicize

venturesome (VEN cher sum) *adj.* daring; hazardous
    similar: venturous; audacious; intrepid; treacherous; perilous; jeopardous
    contrary: circumspect; solicitous; wary

verge (VERJ) *n.* edge; border; *(v.)* to be on the border or edge
    similar: threshold; brink; precipice; brim

vespertine (VES per teen) *adj.* pertaining to or occurring during the evening
    similar: crepuscular; nocturnal
    contrary: diurnal

victuals (VIK chyools) *n.* food; meals
    similar: fare; comestibles; pabulum; pap; fodder; viand

vie (VY) *v.* to compete
    similar: contend; contest; rival; endeavor; clash; spar

vitriolic (vit ree AH lik) *adj.* severely sarcastic or caustic
    similar: scathing; sardonic; acerbic; mordant; trenchant; acrimonious; pungent

vouchsafe (VOWCH sayf) *v.* to grant condescendingly; to guarantee
    similar: bestow; endow; ensure; pledge; warrant

waffle (WAH ful) *v.* to straddle an issue or refuse to commit oneself to a position
    similar: equivocate; waver; vacillate

waif (WAYF) *n.* a person (especially a child) or animal without a home
    similar: stray; orphan; urchin; rogue; foundling; ragamuffin; tatterdemalion

warble (WOR bul) *v.* to sing in a birdlike manner
    similar: cheep; twitter; coo; chirrup; whistle

wastrel (WAY strul) *adj.* extremely or lavishly wasteful, especially with money
  similar: prodigal; spendthrift; squanderer; profligate
  contrary: frugal; penurious; sparing; provident; thrifty; parsimonious; miserly; illiberal

wean (WEEN) *v.* to break away from a dependency (especially, a baby's dependency on its mother)
  similar: disengage; disentangle

welter (WEL ter) *v.* to roll, heave, or writhe
  similar: flounder; wallow

wheedle (WEE dul) *v.* to deceive or persuade by flattery
  similar: cajole; coax; entice; inveigle; lure; seduce; beguile; hoax

whit (WIT) *n.* a tiny particle
  similar: scintilla; bit; morsel; iota; shred; trace; minutia

wistful (WIST ful) *adj.* characterized by a sad longing or yearning
  similar: nostalgic; sentimental; melancholy; plaintive; lugubrious; pensive

woe (WOH) *n.* misery; sorrow; grief
  similar: affliction; distress; wretchedness; torment; melancholy
  contrary: elation; mirth; glee

wry (RY) *adj.* distorted, twisted, or devious (especially, a sense of humor)
  similar: sly; insidious; crafty; vulpine; askew; awry; aslant; tortuous; serpentine; convoluted; vermicular

xyloid (ZY loyd) *adj.* resembling wood; woodlike
  similar: ligneous

yelp (YELP) *v.* to cry sharply (as a dog)
  similar: bark; shriek; yap; squeal; bellow

yield (YEELD) *v.* to surrender, give in, or submit
  similar: relent; capitulate; defer; relinquish; cede; abdicate; succumb; acquiesce; comply; assent; accede
  contrary: contravene; impede; thwart

yoke (YOHK) *n.* a device for joining (linking) two things together; oppression, domination, or harnessing
  similar: bridle; fetter; cinch; muzzle; halter

yokel (YOH kul) *n.* a country bumpkin
  similar: boor; churl; rustic; peasant; curmudgeon
  contrary: urbanite; bourgeois

yore (YOR) *n.* time past
  similar: ancient; antiquity; bygone; quondam; antecedent; anterior; erstwhile; antediluvian

zenithal (ZEE nuh thul) *adj.* upright or erect; pertaining to the highest vertical point
  similar: vertical; perpendicular; plumb

zodiacal (ZOH dee ak ul) *adj.* pertaining to the heavens (esp., to an imaginary belt over which celestial bodies pass)
  similar: cosmic; astrologic; astronomic; universal; celestial; sidereal

zoophagous (ZOO fih gus) *adj.* meat-eating
  similar: carnivorous; predatory

Level 5

Vocabulary Focus

Level 5 features more difficult words, longer definitions and more detailed contextual material. Each listing provides detailed information about the word, related meanings, multiple usages and at least one sample sentence or quotation. Many sample sentences contain other difficult words as well, for you to explore using a dictionary.

acolyte (AK uh lyt) *n.* a servile attendant; assistant; helper.

> *"The faith of sophisticates goes to large electronic machines with computer printouts on cathode-ray tube terminals, attended by white-coated **acolytes**."*
> —Adam Smith, *Esquire*

Similar words, which refer to servile followers, include *lackey, proselyte, minion, retinue,* and *entourage.*

acquiesce (ak wee ES) *v.* to comply with or assent to passively, by one's lack of objection or opposition.

The word is properly accompanied by the preposition *in*, not *with* or *to*.

> *"I had to **acquiesce** in the situation and accept the fact that no major reorganization, reform, or voluntary fiscal restraint would come from Congress during my first term."* —Richard Nixon, *R.N.*

The noun form is *acquiescence*.

> *Our next-door neighbors have tacitly sanctioned our use of their driveway by their **acquiescence** in our using it during the past several months.*

A *timorous*, *reticent*, or *taciturn* person (one who is shy or reluctant to speak) might *acquiesce* in a situation which he actually finds repugnant.

A closely related word is *accede*: to agree or surrender to.

ameliorate (uh MEEL yuh rayt) *v.* to make better or improve.

The word is commonly confused with three related words: *mitigate*, *alleviate*, and *abate*, all of which refer to a lessening in harshness, severity, or amount (as opposed to making better or improving). This distinction is illustrated in the following trilogy of sentences:

> *Beachfront parking is inadequate to accommodate the influx of weekend tourists; the city can **ameliorate** its tourist appeal by constructing a new parking lot.*

> *The city can **mitigate** (or **alleviate**) the beachfront parking problem by constructing a new parking lot.*

> *The parking problem will not **abate** until the influx of tourists becomes an efflux at the conclusion of the holiday weekend.*

amorphous (uh MOR fus) *adj.* having no definite form or character; shapeless or characterless.

> *The baggy look favored by many young gang members gives them an **amorphous** appearance as well as allowing them to conceal weapons.*

The word is derived from the Latin word *morph* (form). Although the word is now used broadly (as in the sentence above), it was initially used in geology and chemistry, as defined here:

> (geology) occurring in an unstratified and un-crystalline mass
> (chemistry) not crystalline in structure

anathema (uh NATH uh muh) *n.* a person or thing condemned, accused, damned, cursed, or generally loathed.

> *The adulteress Hester Prynne, the main character in* The Scarlet Letter, *is probably the best known example of an **anathema** (adulteress and anathema both begin with the letter "A").*

A similar word is *pariah*: an outcast.
Do not confuse *anathema* with *anesthesia*: any drug that dulls the senses.

anomaly (uh NAH muh lee) *n.* deviation from the norm; abnormality; peculiar or unusual event or phenomenon.

> *Anomaly* is a favorite word among *Star Trek* screen-writers:

>> *"I've completed my analysis of the **anomaly**. It appears to be a multiphasic temporal convergence in the space-time continuum. ...It is, in essence, an eruption of anti-time."* —Data, *Star Trek: The Next Generation* (final episode)

>> *"Poverty is an **anomaly** to rich people. It is very difficult to make out why people who want dinner do not ring the bell."* —Walter Bagehot

> The adjective form is *anomalous.*
> A closely related word is *aberration*: a deviation from what is normal, common, or morally right.

assuage (uh SWAYJ) *v.* to pacify or soothe; to lessen another's fear, distress, or pain.

>> *A skydiving instructor might attempt to **assuage** a student's fears by citing statistics showing that skydiving mishaps occur very rarely.*

> It is the fear or distress that is assuaged, not the person himself or herself.
> Do not confuse *assuage* with *appease*. Both acts serve to calm or pacify; however, assuaging calms fear or distress, while appeasing calms or satisfies a demanding person. (A good synonym of *appease* is *placate.*)

auspice (AW spis) *n.* a favorable sign or omen; (*auspices*) sponsorship or patronage; an emblem or symbol.

> *High scores on standardized tests might be an **auspice** of future academic success.*

The adjective form is *auspicious*.

> *Being accepted by the college of your choice is an **auspicious** occasion—one that portends a favorable or promising future.*

As indicated above and illustrated in the following sentences, the word also has two other meanings:

> *Under the **auspices** of the local art guild, the widely touted and celebrated sculptor created a masterpiece for the town square. The laudatory sculpture, patterned after the colorful state **auspice**, was met with accolades from all.*

austere (aw STEER) *adj.* rigorous; difficult; severe; forbidding.

The word is usually used to characterize abstract ideas, as in this sentence:

> *"Too **austere** a philosophy makes few wise men."*
> —Seigneur de Saint-Evremend

Two similar words are *recondite* and *abstruse*. Do not confuse *abstruse* with *obtuse*: dull or slow-minded.

An *obtuse* person might have trouble grasping *austere* and *abstruse* ideas.

behoove (bih HOOV) *v.* to be incumbent upon, suited to, or proper for.

>This unusual but frequently used word comes to us form the Old English word *beholf* (to need).

>>*It **behooves** us to get out of the rain before our clothes become soaking wet.*

>>*"I believe it would **behoove** divorce-ridden America to learn of the devotion to family that exists amongst the primitive people."* —Thomas A. Dooley, *The Edge of Tomorrow*

bane (BAYN) *n.* any cause of ruin or destruction, lasting harm or injury, or woe

>>*The woman grew to abhor her vituperative husband; among friends she would refer to him hyperbolically as "the **bane** of my existence."*

>>*Money, thou **bane** of bliss, and source of woe."* —Herbert

>The adjective form is *baneful*. A synonym of *baneful* is *pernicious*.

>Do not confuse *bane* with *banal*: trite; hackneyed. The two words are unrelated.

bilious (BIL ee us) *adj.* irritable or irascible; unpleasant or distasteful.

>The word was originally used in medicine to describe the indigestion caused by an excess secretion of bile by the liver.

The word is now used figuratively as well. Did poet
Ogden Nash use the word literally or figuratively in
the following couplet?

> *"A good deal of **superciliousness** Is based on bil-*
> *iousness."* —Ogden Nash

Similar words include *peevish* and *boorish*.

burgeon (BER jun) *v.* to begin to grow or develop, especially suddenly; bloom; sprout; thrive.

The adjective form is *burgeoning*, as illustrated in this
sentence:

> *A relatively young but **burgeoning** high-tech com-*
> *pany could pose a threat to its larger and more*
> *established rivals.*

The word is usually used with an *-ing*, either as a verb
or an adjective (as in the sentence above). It can
also be used as a noun to refer to a bud or sprout of
a plant.

Two similar words include:

> *effloresce*: to bloom or flower, or blossom
> *luxuriate*: to prosper, grow, or produce pro-
> fusely

Do not confuse *burgeon* with *bourgeois*: belonging to
the social middle class.

cajole (kuh JOHL) *adj.* to persuade by flattery or by
promises; entice; taunt.

> *Car salesmen typically **cajole** customers into buy-*
> *ing cars with hackneyed and insipid one-liners*
> *such as: "My boss is going to fire me for practi-*
> *cally giving this car away to you, but I like you, so*

*I'm going to do it anyway." The best place to
watch people **cajole** one another, however, is at a
singles bar.*

Similar words include *wheedle, coax, inveigle,* and
lure.

The word bear no relation to *Cajun:* a French dialect
and subculture of Louisiana.

callow (KAL oh) *adj.* inexperienced; immature.

*The **callow** teenager's voice trembled as he asked
the girl he had a crush on to accompany him to the
prom.*

Although the word suggests youth, an older person can
also fittingly be described as callow:

*My parents are quite **callow** in the ways of the
World Wide Web.*

Do not confuse *callow* with *fallow:* agricultural land
left idle in order to restore productivity.

A person who is callow in a particular endeavor might
be referred to as a *neophyte* or *novice.*

cant (KANT) *n.* any special language used by a particular
group, class, or profession; slang; jargon

Consult a computer hackers' dictionary to explore the
hacker's own distinct *cant.* Ebonics—the distinct
African-American English form—is another form
of *cant.*

The word also refers to insincere, pious, or sanctimonious statements and platitudes. The following sentence seems to use the word in both senses:

> *Of all the **cants** in this **canting** world, though the*
> ***cant** of hypocrites may be the worst, the **cant** of*
> *criticism is the most tormenting."* —Lawrence
> Stone

Similar words include *lingo*, *vernacular*, and *argot*.

censure (SEN sher) *n.* severe criticism, scolding, or fault-finding.

> *"All **censure** of a man's self is oblique praise. It is*
> *in order to show how much he can spare. It has all*
> *the invidiousness of self-praise and all the re-*
> *proach of falsehood."* —Dr. Samuel Johnson

Aside from criticism, *censure* does not involve pun-ishment.

The word is also used as a verb, but there is no adjec-tive form of the word.

Similar words include *reproach*, *reproof*, *stricture*, and *pan*.

Another closely related word is *censor*: to criticize, object to, and possibly delete (from a broadcast or publication), especially on moral grounds. How-ever, censure involves vehement disapproval and thus is a slightly stronger word than censor.

chagrin (shuh GRIN) *n.* irritation marked by disappoint-ment or humiliation

> *His favorite team lost the big game, much to his*
> ***chagrin** since he had bet a large sum of money that*
> *his team would win.*

The word is often improperly used to refer simply to sadness; while disappointment does tend to suggest sadness, chagrin requires humiliation, irritation, or annoyance.

A closely related word is *vexation* (irritation, annoyance, or provocation), as illustrated in this sentence:

After the spelling bee, the winner's facetious and **vexing** *remark comparing the loser's performance to Dan Quayle's misspelling of "potato" exacerbated the loser's* **chagrin**.

chauvinism (SHOH vuh nih zum) *n.* unreasonable devotion to one's race, country, or sex.

During the 1960's, the term "male **chauvinist** *pig" became the mantra for the burgeoning feminist movement.*

"Patriotism has reappeared, along with its scruffy half brothers, xenophobia and **chauvinism**.*"
—Lance Morrow, *Time*

A related word is *jingoism*: excessive patriotism.

chimerical (kih MAYR ih kul) *adj.* imaginary; wildly fanciful; unreal; impossible.

Professional athletes past their prime sometimes attempt to realize their **chimerical** *dream of once again being the best in the world at their sport. Olympic swimmer Mark Spitz and boxer Sugar Ray Leonard are two notable examples.*

The related word *impracticable* refers not to something impossible or imaginary but rather to a goal or action that is unfeasible or unrealistic.

Similar words include *illusory* and *phantasmal*.

churlish (CHER lish) *adj.* peasantlike or rustic; crude, crass, or vulgar

The noun form is *churl*.

The word has two related but distinct meanings, as illustrated by these two sentences:

*The Dark Ages were **churlish** and difficult times in which to live.*

*His **churlish** and uncivilized demeanor seems more befitting the Dark Ages than this age; I want nothing to do with the **churl**.*

Similar words include *boorish*, *impudent*, and *insolent*.

cipher (SY fer) *n.* nothing, zero, or null; a worthless person or thing; a secret code (of numbers or letters); a distinctive emblem, monogram, or colophon; *v.* to use numbers arithmetically.

As suggested above, *cipher* is a very flexible word. In terms of the first meaning, similar words include *naught*, *null*, *nihil*, *nonentity*, *void*, and *vacuum*.

To *decipher* a secret code is to determine or "crack" the code.

The word's flexibility is illustrated in this anecdote:

The jilted husband's incipient autonomy was precipitated by his wife's "Dear John" letter, which she scribbled on her company's letterhead (with

*the company's **cipher** printed at the top). Although
he had trouble **deciphering** her writing, he could
discern that she referred to him throughout the
letter as a "**cipher**."*

Do not confuse *cipher* with *siphon*: to withdraw liquid
by suction.

circumspect (SER kum spekt) *adj.* cautious; wary;
watchful; leery

The word's literal meaning is "to look around"—derived from the Latin words *circ* (round) and *spec*
(see).

*Wild animals should be **circumspect** about drinking alone at their favorite watering hole; if they do
so, it behooves them to constantly look around for
predators.*

*"Be very **circumspect** in the choice of thy company....To be the best in the company is the way to
grow worse; the best means to grow better is to be
the worst there."* —Francis Quarles

A related word is *qualms*: doubts; misgivings.
A circumspect person might have qualms about engaging in a capricious course of action.

coquettish (koh KET ish) *adj.* alluring; enticing; coy
(feigned shyness).

*The young girl's **coquettish** ways lured many suit-
ors and broke many hearts.*

The word *coquette* is usually used in referring to an attractive young lady. A coquette need not cajole in order to get what she wants.

Other words used to refer to an attractive or alluring person or thing include *prepossessing*, *winsome*, *voluptuous*, *comely*, and *fetching*.

Another word which describes a *coy* person (one who pretends to be shy) is *demure*.

A genuinely shy person would also be described as *diffident*.

cynosure (sih NOH zher) *n.* the center of attention or interest; a celebrity.

> *The English professor's current cynosure are the writers of the American Renaissance.*

> *From her first encounter with the Prince of Wales to her tragic death, Princess Diana was the cynosure of the paparazzi.*

A similar word is *luminary*; a prominent person. *Luminary* is derived from the Latin word *lumin* (light). A *luminous* object catches a person's attention for its brightness.

demagogue (DEM uh gahg) *n.* a political agitator and charismatic orator who appeals to emotions and prejudice.

> *Hitler was the epitome of demagoguery; this quintessential demagogue ingratiated himself with the masses by inciting passions, quashing and quelling reason, and rewarding jingoism and chauvinism.*

> *"The secret of the demagogue is to make himself as stupid as his audience so that they believe they are as clever as he."* —Karl Kraus

A demagogue engages in *demagogy* or *demagoguery*.
The adjective form is *demagogic*.

Demagogue is sometimes confused with *demigod* (a deified mortal), understandably since an effective demagogue might be viewed almost as a god by his or her followers.

Do not confuse *demagogue* with *pedagogue*: a teacher.

A similar word is *proselytizer*.

deprecate (DEP ruh kayt) *v.* to express disapproval of.

> *"The friends of humanity will **deprecate** war, wheresoever it may appear."* —George Washington

The noun form is *deprecation*.

The adjective form is *deprecatory*.

Similar words include *reprove, reprimand, rebuke,* and *reprobate*.

Synonyms of deprecation include *disapprobation* and *reprobation*.

Deprecation does not necessarily involve blame, criticism, or punishment. Here are similar words which do carry one or more of these meanings:

> *castigate:* to punish in order to correct or reform
>
> *censure:* to strongly disapprove, criticize, or blame
>
> *reproach*: to find fault with; blame; criticize

diffidence (DIF ih duns) *n.* lack of self confidence or faith in one's own ability; timidity or shyness.

> *Diffident people may go to great lengths to extricate themselves from public speaking obligations, which can be tumultuous ordeals for them.*

A diffident person might be described as retiring and self-effacing, but not necessarily as pusillanimous, timorous, or craven (fearful or cowardly).

The word is unrelated to *different* (not similar) and *indifferent* (unconcerned, disinterested).

dilatory (DIL uh tor ee) *adj.* delaying or procrastinating; designed or intended to bring about delay

> *I apologize for being **dilatory** in my duties, but I assure you that there are exigent circumstances to justify the delay.*

The word is used commonly in law to refer to tactics and strategies used by lawyers to delay court proceedings, as in this sentence:

> *To expedite the legal proceedings, the no-nonsense judge admonished the overzealous advocates to refrain from employing their arsenal of **dilatory** tactics.*

discursive (dis KER siv) *adj.* rambling from subject to subject; digressive or disjointed.

> *The two vagrants' conversations were **discursive**; they ranted about anything and everything, but ranted nothing intelligible.*

A similar word is *desultory:* lacking order, disjointed.

Another related word is *cursory*: performed quickly and superficially (as in a cursory reading of a magazine article)

A contrary word is *cursive*: flowing handwriting in which the letters of words are joined together.

In rhetoric and philosophy, the word has a more particular meaning: proceeding from reason rather than intuition. This definition is derived from the noun *discourse*: communication, discussion, or exchange of ideas, through conversation.

dupe (DOOP) *n.* a person who is easily fooled.

> *"If [a man] pretends to be [your **dupe**], who is the biggest **dupe**—he or you?"* —Jean de La Bruyére

A dupe may be described as *credulous* and *gullible* (overly trusting or believing).

A dupe might be duped by a *charlatan, rogue* or *mountebank* (a fraud).

A person who has been duped has been *beguiled* or *cozened* (fooled, defrauded or deceived).

egregious (uh GREE jyus) *adj.* shocking, extraordinary, or outstanding in a bad way.

> *Introducing the venerable and eminent guest speaker by a derogatory epithet was an **egregious** error.*

> *"There is no more **egregious** fallacy than the belief that order requires central direction."* —Milton Friedman, *Newsweek*

Two similar word are *flagrant* and *glaring*.

enigma (eh NIG muh) *n.* a mystery or puzzle; a perplexing or baffling situation, occurrence, or person

The adjective form is *enigmatic*.

The word is often used to describe a person with a self-contradictory character.

The famous mogul Howard Hughes was perhaps the ultimate enigma, secreting himself away from society for the last dozen years of his life, yet still able to conduct business with the outside world.

It might be redundant to describe a person as an "enigmatic conundrum" or an "anomalous enigma."

The word is also used more particularly to describe a fable or other brief story that contains a hidden meaning or that poses a riddle.

ennui (ahn WEE) *n.* a feeling of discontent or weariness; boredom.

*"Necessity is the constant scourge of the lower classes, **ennui** of the higher ones."* —Arthur Schopenhauer

Similar words include *tedium* and *pall*.

To enliven and rejuvenate a person suffering from *ennui*, one might prescribe a dose of scintillation, titillation, or jubilation.

erudite (AYR yoo dyt) *adj.* scholarly; learned.

The word does not refer to intelligence but rather to knowledge learned

*"... he sat formally and talked to her in his stiff, pedantic way on cold and **erudite** subjects for two hours."* —William Faulkner, *Sartoris*

As suggested by the sentence above, a related word is
　pedantic: showing off one's learning or overem-
　phasizing trivial rules or knowledge

Do not confuse *erudite* with *arrogant*. An erudite pro-
　fessor might seem arrogant in his her knowledge,
　but the two words are unrelated in meaning.

espouse (eh SPOWZ) *v.* to advocate, support, promote,
or argue for.

> *"...we must continue to perfect here at home the
> rights and the values which we **espouse** around the
> world. —Jimmy Carter*

The word is related, albeit in an archaic way, to *spouse*
　(marriage partner). A person who espouses is a de-
　fender, as a man might be viewed as a defender of
　his spouse (wife).

Similar verbs are *vindicate* and *champion*.

exculpate (eks KUL payt) *v.* to free from blame; clear
from a charge of fault or guilt; vindicate.

> *Not so much as a scintilla of evidence has been
> found which might **exculpate** the defendant from
> guilt.*

An *exculpatory* clause in a contract releases one party
　from fault for specified events which may occur
　during performance of the contract.

A contrary word is *culpable*: at fault; blameworthy; re-
　sponsible.

facetious (fuh SEE shus) *adj.* frivolously comical; funny; witty; amusing.

> *In a eulogy at a funeral, facetious remarks about the decedent might be considered indecorous or even insolent.*

The word is often misused to refer to a sarcastic remark in which the speaker says one thing but means the opposite. A facetious remark might be sarcastic, but is not necessarily so.

Two synonyms of facetious are *droll* and *jocular*.

fodder (FAH der) *n.* coarse food, especially for livestock.
The word is widely used figuratively to refer to any source of fuel for human thought or endeavor.

> *The indiscretions of celebrities and other public figures are fodder for tabloid journalists.*

> " *[Our country's military draft deferment tests] are reminiscent of Hitler's twin system of eugenics and education—weed out the intellectually deprived by conscripting them for cannon fodder.*" —Adam Clayton Powell

A similar word is *provender*.
Another related word is *pabulum*: any nourishment for animals or plants.

glib (GLIB) *adj.* fluent in speech or writing, but without thought, restraint, or sincerity.
The word pertains to substance, not quantity; hence, a glib person is not necessarily loquacious or garrulous (talkative).

Certain people, including salespeople and politicians, are notoriously glib.

> *"The more gross the fraud, the more glibly will it go down and the more greedily will it be swallowed...."* —Christian Nestell Bovee

hyperbole (hy PER buh lee) *n.* an obvious exaggeration, intentionally used for emphasis and not to be taken literally

> *A facetious example of hyperbole: "If I've told you once, I've told you a thousand times: don't ever use hyperbolic language with me!"*

> *The speaking in perpetual hyperbole is comely in nothing but in love."* —Francis Bacon

The opposite of hyperbole is *litotes*: an understatement made for emphasis.

idyllic (y DIL ik) *adj.* charmingly simple and carefree.
The word is usually used to describe a lifestyle or culture rather than a personal disposition.
The word is derived from *idyll*: a poem describing pastoral scenes or simple carefree episodes.

> *"...life in these rural towns was never as idyllic as our poets remember it."* —Bill Moyers, *Listening to America*

A charmingly simple and carefree life might seem ideal (perfect). Nevertheless, do not confuse *idyllic* with *ideal*.
Two similar words are *pastoral* and *bucolic*.

incumbent (in KUM bint) *adj.* pressed or emphatically urged; currently in office.

> In the first definition above, the word is always used in the idiomatic expression "it is incumbent upon (on)...," as in this sentence:

>> *"Care of the poor is **incumbent** on society as a whole."* —Benedict Spinoza

> *Incumbent* is also used to refer to a current holder of an office or position (usually political), especially in the context of a race for election against a challenger.

>> *The **incumbent** and popular senator will have no trouble defeating her little-known challenger in the next election.*

indigent (IN dih junt) *adj.* poor; destitute; impoverished.

> An indigent person is sometimes referred to as a pauper.

> A synonym of indigent is *impecunious* (*pecuniary*: pertaining to money).

> The noun form is *indigence* (poverty; destitution; impoverishment; penury).

> A closely related but distinct word is *mendicancy*: begging or living off alms (charity) of another. Some would view mendicancy merely as feigned indigence.

>> *Without a patron or a "day job" the young artist soon became **indigent**, and eventually resorted to **mendicancy** by moving back in with his parents.*

> Do not confuse *indigent* with these words:

indigenous: native to or characterizing a particular region

indulgent: permissive; tolerating

inexorable (in EK sor uh bul) *adj.* relentless; unyielding; merciless.

> *No B-rated science fiction "epic" is complete without the **inexorable** attack of the grotesque monster, impervious to bullets and bombs but capitulating to the charms of a pretty girl.*

> *"What other dungeon is so dark as one's own heart! What jailer so **inexorable** as one's self!"*
> —Nathaniel Hawthorne

A similar word is *implacable*: incapable of being pacified or appeased; stubbornly unyielding (*placate*: to appease or pacify).

Do not confuse *inexorable* with *inevitable*: unavoidable; certain.

ingenuous (in JEN yoo us) *adj.* acting or speaking in a candid manner; innocent, naive, or unsophisticated.

> *Naive in the ways of office politics, the **ingenuous** young employee continually transmitted sensitive information, tacitly understood by others to be confidential, among various departments. The contagion was finally quelled when he quit his job to return to college.*

> *"The officers, however, were quite entranced with the **ingenuous** simplicity of the islanders, their pi-*

> *ety...and their anxiety not to offend."* —H.E.
> Traude, *History of Pitcairn Island*

An ingenuous young girl is an *ingenue* (the word is not
    used to describe ingenuous males).
The noun form is *ingenuousness* (not *ingenuity*).
Do not confuse *ingenuous* with *ingenious*: inventive (*n
    ingenuity*).

intransigent (in TRAN si junt) *adj.* stubborn; unwilling
to compromise; inflexible.

> *During the corporation's policy-making confer-
> ence, the **intransigent** board member did not in-
> gratiate himself among the other members of the
> board of directors.*

The antonym *transigent* is not commonly used.
Similar words include *intractable*, *refractory*, and
    contumacious.
Related but distinct words are *importunate*, *pertina-
    cious*, and *inexorable*, all of which involve unflag-
    ging (unwavering) persistence.

invective (in VEK tiv) *n.* vehement protest, attack, or
abuse with words.

> *Overreacting to his colleague's remarks about the
> efficacy of Senator Burns' plan to balance the
> budget, Burns launched into an **invective** tanta-
> mount to character assassination.*

The word can also be used as an adjective. It is no fun
    being at the receiving end of an *invective* harangue.

A related word, *vexation*, refers either to an irritation or
annoyance or to the state of being irritated or annoyed.

invidious (in VID ee us) *adj.* likely to create ill will, animosity, or envy.

> *By his **invidious** remarks about who he thought
> were the best and worst athletes on the team, the
> impertinent outfielder threatened the collegial re-
> lationship among all the team members.*

Do not confuse *invidious* with *insidious*: wily; crafty;
sly; treacherous.

itinerant (y TIN er unt) *adj.* traveling from place to place,
especially for work.

> *An **itinerant** construction worker moves from place
> to place depending on where work is available.*

The word *itinerary* refers to a travel schedule or plans.
Itinerant can also be used as a noun.
The adjective *itinerate* can be used instead of *itinerant*.
Similar words include *nomadic* and *peripatetic*.
Another related word is *peregrinations*: journeys or
travels.

> *With a laptop computer, modem, and a little help
> from satellite communications technology, the itin-
> erant account executive was able to review her
> **itinerary** as well as send and receive e-mail during
> her peregrinations.*

jocular (JAHK yuh ler) *adj.* not serious; joking; facetious; jesting.

> *Many of the party guests left early, annoyed by the host's incessantly **jocular** and ribald banter that soon grew repugnant.*

A closely related word is *jocose*: given to joking; playful; lighthearted.

Do not confuse *jocular* and *jocose* with *jocund*, which carries a somewhat different meaning: cheerful, merry.

> *"Night's candles are burnt out, and **jocund** day Stands tiptoe on the misty mountaintops."*
> —Shakespeare

languish (LANG gwish) *v.* to lose strength or vitality; weaken; become feeble, droop; fade.

The noun form is *languor*, and the adjective form is *languid*.

> *The Scandinavian tourists **languished** in the summer Mediterranean heat.*

A person who is *languishing* has been *enervated* (deprived of strength and vitality).

Another word with a related but distinct meaning is *wizened*: shriveled or withered.

laudable (LOWD uh bul) *adj.* praiseworthy; commendable.

A related adjective is *laudatory*: expressive of praise. Here's a sentence using both words:

> *According to theater critics, the leading actress gave a **laudable** performance as the recalcitrant and incorrigible Kate in the repertory's recent production of* The Taming of the Shrew. *The critics' reviews of the overall production have also been **laudatory**.*

The verb form is *laud*. The noun form is *laudation*, as illustrated in this sentence:

> *"Self-**laudation** abounds among the unpolished, but nothing can stamp a man more sharply as ill-bred."* —Charles Buxton

The word is unrelated to *loud* (volume).

loquacious (luh KWAY shus) *adj.* talkative; chatty.

A loquacious but vacuous person might be considered inane (foolish or silly) or fatuous (flighty), as in the following sentence:

> *My **loquacious** daughter tends to run up large telephone bills by calling her girlfriends at other colleges. Were her friends not so vacuous, I might agree that her costly conversations are worthwhile.*

Synonyms of loquacious include *garrulous, verbose,* and *voluble*.

The noun form is *loquacity*.

Related *loqu-* and *loc-* words include:

  eloquent: fluent in speech or writing
  elocution: the art of public speaking
  grandiloquent: pompous or bombastic in speech or language
  circumlocution: talk that is not to the point

magnanimous (mag NAN uh mus) *adj.* noble or elevated in mind; generous.

> A magnanimous person typically puts the needs of others before his or her own needs.
>
> The noun form is *magnanimity*.
>
> A magnanimous person may be generous with his or her time, money, or talents.
>
> A similar word is *munificent*, which describes a generous person, but not necessarily a noble person, as illustrated in this sentence:
>
> > *"Everyone, even the richest and most munificent of men, pays much by check more lightheartedly than he pays little in specie."* —Sir Max Beerbohm
>
> Similar words include *altruistic, benevolent, philanthropic,* and *beneficent.*

maladroit (mal uh DROYT) *adj.* bungling; awkward; clumsy.

> A maladroit person would properly be described as a *lout, oaf,* or *boor* (or as *loutish, oafish,* or *boorish*).
>
> A person might be maladroit either in social or physical lack of grace. The waiter in the following sentence is twice maladroit:
>
> > *Our neophyte waiter spilled soup on us, then dismissed his clumsy act by thanking us for wearing cheap blouses.*
>
> Two similar words are *gauche* and *ungainly.*
>
> The opposite of *maladroit* is *adroit*: graceful; skillful; tactful.

maudlin (MAWD lin) *adj.* overly sentimental; foolishly tearful.

> Maudlin people are sometimes labeled "romantic fools" or "hopelessly romantic."
>
> People can be maudlin, but so can songs, stories, and the like.
>
> A related word is *lachrymose*: easily brought to tears (though not necessarily for sentimental reasons).
>
> *The raconteur brought his **lachrymose** audience to tears with his maudlin story about the little boy who ran away from home with his dog.*

mercurial (mer KYER ee ul) *adj.* volatile; given to changing moods suddenly.

> Mercury, the winged Greek god of commerce, possessed a number of characteristic traits; however, his volatile temper was the only trait that endured linguistically, as the definition above suggests.
>
> ***Mercurial** young men with a low center of gravity are particularly suited for the sport of hockey, where assault with a deadly weapon is not only sanctioned but is part of the job description.*
>
> Similar words include *capricious*, *fickle*, and *whimsical*.

miasma (my AZ muh) *n.* noxious, dangerous, or unwholesome emissions, atmosphere, or influence.

> *By the end of a typical Saturday evening, the popular night club becomes a **miasma** of smoke, licentiousness and, most noxious of all, disco music.*

The adjective form is *miasmic*.

> *Environmentalists are fighting for the abatement of the **miasmic** conditions created by the local pharmaceutical factory.*

Because of its adverse effects on health, a miasma might be described as *deleterious*, *pestiferous*, or *virulent*.

An offensive smelling miasma or effluent might be described as *malodorous*, *noisome*, *rank*, or *mephitic*.

misanthrope (MIS un throhp) *n.* a person who hates or distrusts humankind

> *The neighbors came to know her as "Cat Woman"; some saw her as an enigma, while others viewed her as a **misanthrope**—morose and aloof around other people, yet jocund and carefree around her menagerie of felines.*

The word is derived from the Greek word *anthro* (mankind).

A misanthrope (or *misanthropist*) engages in *misanthropy*.

> *[M]isanthropes...are so sure that the world is going to ruin that they resent every attempt to comfort them as an insult to their sagacity."* —Edwin Percy Whipple

mordant (MOR dint) *adj.* biting or stinging (as in a remark or expression).

A mordant remark has a sharp, cutting effect on the listener and is often scornful and derisive.

Similar words include *caustic*, *trenchant*, *petulant*, and *acrimonious*.

A related word is *sarcastic*. A sarcastic remark is usually mordant in tone and effect but may carry some irony as well.

Another related word is *facetious*, which is often misused as a synonym for sarcastic. In fact, a facetious remark is one that is light-hearted or frivolous (although it may also be sarcastic as well).

Each of the following remarks might be interpreted as either mordant or facetious, depending on whether they were spoken in seriousness or in jest:

> *"You look like hell today,"* Naomi remarked.
> *"You sure know how to hurt a guy,"* retorted Roger.

nebulous (NEB yoo lus) *adj.* vague and indistinct, without definite form; cloudy or hazy.

The word is often used to describe ideas or expressions, as in this sentence:

> *The written manual for the computer program was so **nebulous** and confusing that I had to call for help to perform the most basic tasks.*

The noun form is *nebula*: a cloudlike, gaseous mass (a word often overheard on the bridge of *Star Trek's* Enterprise).

Related words include:

> *turbid* and *muddled*, both of which essentially mean "cloudy or muddy"
> *fuliginous*: smoky; sooty

ostracize (AHS truh syz) *v.* to banish, exile, or exclude by general consent.

> *Ostracism* usually results from an adverse judgment against a person and is a demonstration or means of *reproof, reproach, reprobation,* or *censure.*
>
> *Widely **ostracized** for the deaths of his wife and her friend, O.J. Simpson became an expatriate of sorts, a "victim" of pandemic censure.*
>
> *For his acquiescence in Hitler's heinous crimes, the once venerable German dignitary was **ostracized** from his homeland for life.*

panacea (pan uh SEE uh) *n.* a universal remedy for all ills; cure-all.

> The word is used in relation to health problems as well as to other problems or difficulties, as illustrated in this sentence:
>
> *" [George Washington] advocated no sure cure for all the sorrows of the world, and doubted that such a **panacea** existed."* —H.L. Mencken, *Pater Patriae*
>
> The meaning of the word comes from *Panacea,* the Greek goddess of healing.
>
> Do not confuse *panacea* with the unrelated word *panoply*: a complete array (from the Greek word *pan,* meaning "flock").
>
> *Our local health-food store stocks a **panoply** of **panaceas**.*

paradigm (PAYR uh dym) *n.* a model; standard; pattern; example.

> *The research methodology used to discover a cure for a certain virus might become a **paradigm** for future research of similar diseases.*

The adjective form is *paradigmatic*.

A closely related word is *paragon*: a model of perfection; an ideal. The distinction is illustrated in this sentence:

> *My secretary is a **paragon** of organization and efficiency; her filing system should be **paradigmatic** for our entire office staff.*

Another closely related word is *archetype*: anything that serves as a model for (example of) all other similar things.

pejorative (puh JOR uh tiv) *adj.* negative in connotation; belittling.

> *The other students often refer **pejoratively** to the brightest student in the class by the epithet "teacher's pet."*

A personal assistant whose job is to follow orders and blindly serve another person might be referred to in a pejorative manner as a "yes-man" or "bootlick."

Similar words include *deprecatory*, *derisive*, and *opprobrious*.

perfunctory (per FUNG ter ee) *adj.* performed without care, interest, or enthusiasm.

> *Unpleasant tasks which are part of a daily routine are typically discharged (performed) in a perfunctory manner.*

A perfunctory act is not necessarily performed quickly, although haste does suggest indifference or lack of care.

Other words suggesting carelessness include *remiss* and *negligent*.

A stronger word—*wanton*—suggests recklessness.

Other words suggesting lack of interest include *diffidence*, *apathy*, and *insouciance*.

perspicacious (per spih KAY shus) *adj.* insightful; astute; discerning; keen in mental perception.

A perspicacious person may recognize subtle distinctions, fine points, and deeper meanings.

The noun form is *perspicacity*.

Do not confuse *perspicacious* (or *perspicacity*) with *perspicuous* (or *perspicuity*): plain to the understanding.

> *"**Perspicuity** is the framework of profound thoughts."* —Marquis de Vauvenargues

A closely related word is *percipient*: able to see or perceive things clearly or easily.

Two similar words are *incisive* and *trenchant*.

Do not confuse either *perspicacious* or *percipient* with *perspicuous*: clear in expression; lucid (*n. perspicuousness*).

plenary (PLEE nuh ree) *adj.* absolute, complete, or full.

A despot or dictator is said to have *plenary* political power over his domain.

An assistant store manager might be given *plenary* decision-making power while the manager is away.

The word also has a related but distinct meaning in business and politics: attended by all qualified members.

> *The President's "State of the Union" address is one notable example of a **plenary** session of Congress—it is attended by all qualified members of Congress.*

plethora (PLETH er uh) *n.* overabundance; excess; surplus.

> *"Consumption of the **plethora** of consumer goods churned out by affluent economies is itself a time-absorbing activity." —*E.J. Mishan, *The Economic Growth Debate*

The word is often misused to refer merely to a large quantity or an abundance, a meaning properly conveyed by the words *cornucopia, copiousness, plenitude,* and *bounty.*

Synonyms of the word include *surfeit, glut,* and *superfluity.*

Antonyms of the word include *dearth, paucity,* and *want,* all of which mean "insufficiency" or "scarcity."

portend (por TEND) *v.* to indicate in advance; foretell; predict.

> The adjective form is *portentous*, as illustrated in this sentence:
>
>> *"I was thirty. Before me stretched the **portentous**, menacing road of a new future."* —F. Scott Fitzgerald, *The Great Gatsby*
>
> Similar words include *bode*, *forebode*, *presage* and *prophesy*. Grammatically, however, these words are used in different ways, as illustrated by these sentences:
>
>> ***Foreboding** storm clouds do not **bode** well for the camping trip; they **portend** an unpleasant weekend.*
>>
>> *The campers would be foolish to ignore another **presage**: thunder and lightning to the east. Besides, the meteorologist has **prophesied** that a storm is coming.*
>
> The noun form is *portent*: an omen or prophetic sign, especially of something momentous or wonderful.

precocious (prih KOH shus) *adj.* showing maturity beyond one's age, especially in children.

> A child mature beyond his or her age typically will engage in mischief; accordingly, the word is usually used narrowly to describe a mischievous child.
>
> The word is also commonly applied too broadly to describe mischievous behavior by any person. The word is used properly here:
>
>> *"For **precocity** some great price is always demanded sooner or later in life."* —Margaret Fuller

pristine (pris TEEN) *adj.* pertaining to the earliest period or state; pure or unspoiled

The two definitions above are closely related, since the "earliest period" was indeed "pure" and "unspoiled" compared to civilization today.

*We bathed in the **pristine** waters of the mountain springs, and imagined how the valley below, now a bustling city, appeared in its **pristine** state.*

Other words also referring to earlier times include *archaic*, *antediluvian*, and *primeval*.

Other words that refer to something pure or unspoiled include *undefiled*, *unsullied*, *uncultivated*, *virginal*, and *chaste*.

prodigal (PRAH duh gul) *adj.* extremely wasteful, especially with money.

*A person who has struggled through financial difficulties and worked long and hard to build wealth is less prone to becoming **prodigal** than one who comes into a large sum of money suddenly and without sacrifice.*

A similar word is *profligate*: recklessly extravagant or wasteful, shamelessly immoral.

A prodigal person could be referred to as a *wastrel* or *spendthrift*.

A good antonym is *frugal*.

propitious (proh PISH us) *adj.* favorable to; advantageous.

Conditions or circumstances are propitious if they tend to promote, facilitate, or work to one's advantage.

*A tailwind is **propitious** in an airplane's reaching its destination in as short a time as possible.*

*A youthful electorate might be **propitious** for the liberal candidate in the upcoming election.*

A similar word is *auspicious* (promoting success; favorable)

Do not confuse *propitious* with *propiteous*: pitiful.

proselytize (PRAH suh luh tyz) *v.* to convert (or attempt to convert) another to a belief system, ideology, or sect

A *proselyte* is a convert—a person who has been proselytized, typically by a demagogue or other persuasive, charismatic person.

*Ambition sufficiently plagues her **proselytes** by keeping them always in show and in public, like a statue in the street." —Dr. Thomas Fuller*

Proselytes to religious cults and extreme ideologies are often insular (narrow-minded), overzealous, and ardently fervent.

pundit (PUN dit) *n.* an expert or authority.

The word is also used to describe a person who makes comments or judgments with an air of authority, regardless of actual knowledge or expertise. This type of pundit might come across as *bombastic*, *pompous*, or *consequential*.

*During election years, candidates try their best to ignore the plethora of political **pundits**—those journalistic "talking heads," each claiming to*

> *know the real reason for every development and the true intentions of every candidate.*

pusillanimous (pyoo sih LAN ih mus) *adj.* cowardly; faint-hearted; timid.

The following passage employs the word's noun form, *pusillanimity*, as well as two antonyms:

> *The cowardly lion in* The Wizard of Oz *was the embodiment of **pusillanimity**. However, his award for bravery, bestowed by the Wizard, lionized him, transforming him into an intrepid and stalwart "king of the jungle." The epithet befit the beast who saved Dorothy from the wicked witch.*

Similar words are *craven* and *timorous*.

quandary (KWAHN duh ree) *n.* a perplexing or difficult situation; dilemma; predicament; "catch-22".

> *The bride-to-be was in a **quandary** as to how to marshal her bridesmaids, family members, and future in-laws at the wedding so as to avoid indignation or ill will.*

A similar word is *imbroglio*.
A word with a similar but distinct meaning is *conundrum*: a puzzle or mystery.

quintessence (quin TES uhns) *n.* the pure and concentrated essence of a substance.

> *"I have found in Mozart's music the **quintessence** of all that I feel keenly in mind and in emotion."*
> —Marcia Davenport, *Mozart*

The adjective form is *quintessential*. Leonardo de Vinci was the *quintessential* "Renaissance Man." Bill Clinton is the *quintessential* politician. Alan Alda is the *quintessential* nice guy.

The word is derived from the Latin term meaning "the fifth essence." In ancient and medieval philosophy, the five elements (essences) included air, fire, earth, water, and ether (the heavens), ether being the fifth element.

A similar word is *epitome*: a person or thing that is typical of or characterizes a whole class; a summary of a topic or work.

Other similar words are *paradigm*, *paragon*, and *archetype*.

renege (rih NIG) *v.* to go back on one's promise or word; to deny or renounce.

> *The world abounds with **renegers**: spouses **reneging** on their wedding vows, politicians **reneging** on their campaign promises, and dieters **reneging** on their pledge to cut calories.*

> *"Nations don't literally **renege** on their debts; they either postpone them indefinitely...or else pay them off in depreciated currency."* —Roger Bridwell

A *renegade* (traitor or deserter) is a person who reneges on his or her loyalty.

risible (RIH zuh bul) *adj.* laughable, comical, or ludicrous; given to or easily aroused to laughter
Risible is a flexible word, as suggested by the two different meanings above.

> *Popular fashions among teenagers often appear* ***risible*** *to adults.*

> *After a few drinks, she becomes quite* ***risible,*** *giggling and laughing at anything anyone says.*

Another word referring to something ludicrous is *farcical* (a *farce* is a literary form involving *risible* situations).

Other literary forms and approaches to a subject that could be described as risible include *parody*, *lampoon*, *satire*, and *travesty*.

salient (SAY lee unt) *adj.* prominent or conspicuous; notable or significant.

> The word is usually used to describe features or characteristics.

> Note the two related but distinct meanings of the word, as underscored by these two sentences:

> *The most* ***salient*** *feature of my house is its orange color.*

> *At the end of his sermon, the preacher reiterated what he considered to be the most* ***salient*** *points for the congregation to remember.*

> In this sentence, the word might carry either meaning:

> *The "Women Seeking Men" personal ads were resplendent with such* ***salient*** *words as: "adventurous," "petite," "spiritual," and, perhaps most* ***salient*** *of all, "single."*

sanction (SANK shun) *v.* to authoritatively or officially approve, authorize, permit, or support.

> *The motor vehicle code **sanctions** stopping on a freeway shoulder only in the event of an emergency.*

> *A parent **sanctions** a child's delinquency by failing to chastise the child.*

The word is also used as a noun (see below).
In law, the word has a slightly different meaning: official (court) reward for obedience or, more commonly, a penalty for disobedience.

> *A lawyer failing to comply with proper court procedure might be **sanctioned** by way of fine or imprisonment.*

In international politics, the word has yet a different meaning: an action by a nation (or nations) designed to force another nation into compliance with a treaty or other agreement.

> *Joint **sanctions** against Iraq failed to dissuade Saddam Hussein from his oppressive acts against the Kurdish rebels.*

sanguine (SANG gwin) *adj.* hopeful; confident; optimistic; cheerful.

> *"The **sanguine** hopes, which I had not shared, that Germany would collapse before the end of the year, failed."* —Winston Churchill, *Triumph and Tragedy*

A similar but stronger word is *ardent*: eager, zealous, fervent.

The word also has another meaning: ruddy or reddish, as in skin complexion.

sardonic (sar DAH nik) *adj.* disdainful; scornful.

> *"The mood was **sardonic**, fatalistic, and melancholy. I could hear it in our black jokes: "Hey, Bill, you're going on patrol today. If you get your legs blown off can I have your boots?"* —Philip Caputo, *A Rumor of War*

The word is derived from and refers to the Sardinian plant, whose ingestion purportedly resulted in uncontrollable laughter ending in sure death.

A sardonic remark might also be sarcastic or cynical.

Similar words include *mordant* and *trenchant*.

Two words referring to biting or stinging statements are *caustic* and *acrimonious*.

saturnine (SAT er neen) *adj.* characterized by a gloomy, dark, or sluggish disposition.

> ***Saturnine*** *on school days, the children suddenly turn ebullient every Saturday morning.*

The word refers to the planet Saturn; specifically, to the astrological belief that bodily temperaments correspond to the positions of the planets.

Other words suggesting a gloomy disposition are *sullen*, *despondent*, *melancholy*, and *lugubrious*.

Other words suggesting sluggishness are *lethargic*, *indolent*, and *torpid*.

scintilla (sin TIL uh) *n.* a spark or trace; shred; small particle; tiny bit.

> *The investigator has not found a **scintilla** of evidence to implicate the accused as an accomplice in last week's chicanery.*

A related but distinct word is *scintillate*: to emit sparks; to flash, sparkle, or twinkle.

> *Some people find a good book of fiction as **scintillating** as others find skydiving or racing down a ski slope.*

Similar words include *iota*, *mite*, and *whit*.

surfeit (SER fit) *n.* excess; overindulgence, especially in eating or drinking.

> *"Sensual delights soon end in loathing, quickly bring a glutting **surfeit**, and degenerate into torments when they are continued and unintermitted."*
> —John Howe

> *After the **surfeit** of surfing music which inundated the air waves during the mid-1960s, the Beach Boys and their progeny were left behind in the musical "wake" of the Monterey Pop Music Festival.*

Similar words include *nimiety*, *glut*, and *plethora*.
The word is also used as a verb: to satiate; indulge in to excess; fill completely; stuff; cloy.

tortuous (TOR choo us) *adj.* twisting; curving; winding; not direct or straight.

The word is used literally (as in a *tortuous* hiking trail) as well as figuratively (deceitfulness or trickery).

> *"The **tortuous** road which has led from Montgom-*
> *ery to Oslo is a road over which millions of Ne-*
> *groes are traveling to find a new sense of dignity."*
> —Martin Luther King, Jr.

Similar words include *serpentine* and *sinuous*.

A related word is *tort*, a legal term denoting a non-criminal wrongful act (other than breach of contract); a *tortious* act may give rise to a civil law suit in which the victim seeks compensation for damages resulting from the offense.

Do not confuse tortuous with the unrelated word *torturous* (excruciatingly painful).

travesty (TRAV es tee) *n.* a comical and ludicrous parody or imitation; portraying something as ridiculous.

The word is used in literature to describe a burlesque imitation of a serious literary work.

Outside the literary world, *travesty* is heard most commonly in characterizing legal proceedings, as in the sentence at the top of page 83:

> *The defendant's acquittal was a **travesty** of justice,*
> *in view overwhelming evidence of his culpability.*

turpitude (TER pih tood) *n.* depravity; wickedness.

> *While some would label the rancorous acts of vio-*
> *lence by young gang members as incorrigible **tur-***
> ***pitude**, the sociologist would see those acts as a*
> *manifestation of an inner-city social quagmire.*

There is no adjective or verb form of the word.

A person exhibiting turpitude might be described as *dissolute*, *base*, *sordid*, *amoral*, or *vile*.

ubiquitous (yoo BIK wih tus) *adj.* being everywhere, especially at the same time.

> *The fulminating volcano known as Cyclops to the islanders created a **ubiquitous** cloud of black ash that resulted in what has become known as "the year without a summer."*

> *"Today's software, he argues, is too complicated and loaded with gizmos no one ever uses.... 'PCs should be more like pencils,' by which he means cheap, user-friendly and, above all, **ubiquitous**."*
> —*Time*, quoting Larry Ellison, CEO of Oracle Corporation

Similar words include *omnipresent*, *pandemic*, and *pervasive*.

Two words that are contrary in meaning are *insular* and *parochial*, both of which mean narrow in scope.

umbrage (UM brij) *n.* anger; resentment; sense of having been maligned or insulted.

The word is derived from the astronomical term *umbra*, which refers to the darkest shadow formed by an eclipse. Accordingly, a person with *umbrage* is ensconced in a dark shadow of resentment.

> *"The patient who sees 'SOB' on his chart should not take **umbrage**, as it is usually intended to mean 'short of breath.'"* —William Safire, *New York Times Magazine*

Similar words include *vexation*, *animosity*, and *spite*.

unctuous (UNK choo us) *adj.* oily; fervently and overly pious or moralistic; having a suave but insincere manner.

The word is used in the tactile sense as well as to describe a person's disposition or behavior, as illustrated in the first sentence below:

> *The motivational speaker's **unctuous** exhortations were matched only by his **unctuous** head of hair.*

> *"... his voice had changed from rasping efficiency to an **unctuous** familiarity with sin and with the Almighty."* —Sinclair Lewis, *Babbitt*

The word is derived from *unction*: the act of anointing with oil in religious ceremonies or primitive medical treatments.

venerable (VEN er uh bul) *adj.* worthy of or commanding reverence, respect or admiration, especially because of great age.

> *"Corruption...takes away every shadow of authority and credit from the most **venerable** parts of our [nation's] constitution."* —Edmund Burke

The noun form (meaning "reverence") is *veneration*.

The verb form (meaning "to revere") is *venerate*.

An outward demonstration of one's veneration is referred to as *obeisance*: bowing or other physical gesture of honor or respect.

A similar word is *esteemed*: considered as having worth or value.

Do not confuse *venerable* with *veritable*: truly; very much so; genuine.

vicissitude (vih SIS ih tood) *n.* change or variation in the course of something (*esp.* circumstance or fortune in life).

> *"Happy is the man who can endure the highest and lowest fortune. He who has endured such **vicissitudes** with equanimity has deprived misfortune of its power."* —Seneca

> *Many a Hollywood movie, including* Trading Places *and* Reversal of Fortune, *has been predicated on the notion of **vicissitude**.*

wanton (WAHN tun) *adj.* without regard for what is morally right; reckless; unjustifiable.

In criminal law, the prosecution must prove that a defendant accused of first-degree murder acted with *wanton* disregard for human life.

> *"If you suppress the exorbitant love of pleasure and money, idle curiosity, iniquitous purpose, and **wanton** mirth, what a stillness there would be in the greatest cities."* —Jean de La Bruyére

A closely related word is *want*: lack or scarcity. A wanton person possesses a want of scruples, probity, and moral rectitude.

Level 6

Vocabulary of Academia

Level 6 features 31 advanced academic and professional topics—with words and definitions related to each. The words are grouped into subject areas, to help you remember them and to use them properly. (For a list of the subject areas, see page *vi* of this book's *Introduction*.)

Anatomy (the Human Body)

ablation (uh BLAY shun) *n.* destruction of part of the body (especially, part of the brain)

ambulatory (AM byoo luh tor ee) *adj.* able to walk or move about

aspire (uh SPYR) *v.* to breathe

aural (AH rul) *adj.* pertaining to the ear or to the sense of hearing

deglutition (dee gloo TIH shun) *n.* the act or process of swallowing food

hypertrophy (hy PER truh fee) *n.* abnormally large growth of a bodily organ

incontinence (in KAHN tih nuns) *n.* the inability to control one's bodily urges and functions

lacuna (luh KYOO nuh) *n.* a cavity, hole, or gap in a bone (or in a plant's cellular tissue or a rock)

mandible (MAN duh bul) *n.* the principal bone of the lower jaw

myopic (my AH pik) *adj.* nearsighted; unable to see clearly in the distance

nape *n.* back of the neck.

ocular (AHK yuh ler) *adj.* pertaining to the eye

olfactory (ahl FAK tuh ree) *adj.* pertaining to the sense of smell

palate (PAL it) *n.* the roof of the mouth

peristalsis (payr ih STAWL sis) *n.* involuntary contractions that move food through the digestive system

sentient (SEN shunt) *adj.* having the power of one's senses

somatic (suh MAT ik) *adj.* pertaining to the body

surdity (SER dih tee) *n.* deafness

tactile (TAK tul) *adj.* pertaining to the sense of touch

vesicle (VES uh kul) *n.* any fluid-filled sac in the body

visceral (VIS er ul) *adj.* physiological

Anthropology

aboriginal (ab uh RIJ uh nul) *adj.* native to a region; indigenous

antediluvian (an tee dih LOO vee un) *adj.* anything ancient, primitive, or outdated (literally, "before the flood")

artifact (AR tuh fakt) *n.* man-made object, typically found by an archeologist

bibelot (BIB loh) *n.* a small item of rarity, beauty, or curiosity; relic; artifact

conjugal (KAHN joo gul) *adj.* referring to the relationship between two married persons

consanguinity (kahn sang GWIN ih tee) *n.* relationship by blood

dowry (DOW ree) *n.* money or property given by the bride's family to the bridegroom at marriage

ethos (EE thus) *n.* the fundamental (underlying) character of a culture or spirit

genealogy (jee nee AHL uh jee) *n.* history of family descent, a family tree.

husbandry (HUZ bin dree) *n.* exploitation of domesticated animals for consumption, load carrying, etc.

midden (MID un) *n.* a dunghill or refuse heap

nomad (NOH mad) *n.* a person who moves about in a seasonal pattern, especially in search of work and usually without a fixed home

nuptial (NUP shul) *adj.* pertaining to a marriage ceremony or to a marriage

238 Vocabulary of Academia

petroglyph (PET roh glif) *n.* a prehistoric carving or
    drawing on stone

philistine (FIL ih steen) *n.* a person who is extremely
    indifferent to culture or aesthetic refinement

phylogenic (fy loh JEN ik) *adj.* pertaining to a race (or
    species, in biology)

primogeniture (pry moh JEN ih ter) *n.* the condition or
    fact of being firstborn of the same parents; seniority by
    birth among children of the same parents

rite (RYT) *n.* a formal ceremonial act or procedure, often
    part of solemn religious occasions

runic (ROO nik) *adj.* pertaining to the characters of any
    ancient alphabet

sept (SEPT) *n.* a division of a tribe or clan

sepulcher (SEP uhl ker) *n.* a burial tomb or receptacle for
    sacred relics

shibboleth (SHIB uh luth) password, identifying phrase
    of a group or attitude

totem (TOH tum) *n.* an object or animal with which a
    tribe, clan or group of people identify in its rituals

vendetta (ven DET uh) *n.* a private feud in which kin are
    obliged to seek revenge for wrongs done to relatives

Architecture

annulet (AN yoo lut) *n.* a ring-shaped molding or ridge

bastille (bas TEEL) *n.* a fortification or castle, typically
    used as a prison

bastion (BAS chyun) *n.* a projection from an outer wall of a fortification designed to defend the adjacent perimeter

bulwark (BUL werk) *n.* a strong defensive wall structure

buttress (BUT rus) *n.* an extra thickness or projection in a wall designed to strengthen it

cantilever (KAN tuh lee ver) *n.* a structure that projects out beyond its supporting wall

concourse (KAHN kors) *n.* an open space where several paths meet

cusp (KUSP) *n.* the point where two curves meet (e.g., the apex of a vaulted arch)

edifice (ED uh fis) *n.* a monument

facade (fuh SAHD) *n.* the exterior front or face of a building

fenestration (fen uh STRAY shun) *n.* the scheme or pattern of windows in the design of a building

hermitage (HER mih tij) *n.* a private or secluded retreat; a hideaway

hovel (HUH vul) *n.* a shed or poorly constructed or ill-kept house

imbricate (IM brih kit) *adj.* overlapping in a regular, orderly pattern

kiosk (KEE ahsk) *n.* an open summer house or pavilion; a small structure, with one or more open sides, used to vend merchandise

marquee (mar KEE) *n.* roof projecting from a building over the sidewalk

mausoleum (mah zuh LEE um) *n.* a monumental tomb (for a dead person)

mezzanine (MEZ uh neen) *n.* a low balcony above the
   ground floor of a building

obelisk (AH buh lisk) *n.* a tapering (narrowing) column
   that forms a pyramid at the top

oculus (AHK yoo lus) *n.* a round window

peristyle (PER ih styl) *n.* a colonnade or row of piers
   surrounding a building or courtyard

portal (POR tul) *n.* an impressive or monumental entrance
   or gate

refectory (ruh FEK ter ee) *n.* a large dining hall at a
   church, college, or other institution

rococo (ruh KOH koh) *adj.* ornate; highly decorative

rotunda (roh TUN duh) *n.* a dome-covered circular hall or
   building

vestibule (VES tih byool) *n.* an inner or middle room in a
   building

voussoir (voo SWAH) *n.* a wedge-shaped stone used in
   making an arch or vault

Astronomy

aurora (uh ROR uh) *n.* a display of changing colored light
   high in the atmosphere

azimuth (AZ uh muth) *n.* a measurement of direction,
   expressed as an angle and measured clockwise from a
   celestial reference point

corona (kuh ROH nuh) *n.* the faint halo-like outer portion
   of the sun's atmosphere

cosmogony (kahz MAH jun ee) *n.* the study of the ultimate origins of physical systems

facula (FAK yoo luh) *n.* a small, bright spot on the sun's surface

nadir (NAY der) *n.* the point on the celestial sphere directly below the observer

nebula (NEB yoo luh) *n.* an irregular, diffuse interstellar cloud

occultation (ah kuhl TAY shun) *n.* passage of one celestial object in front of another

penumbra (puh NUM bruh) *n.* the region of semi-shadow in an eclipse; the less dark outer region of a sunspot

perturbation (per ter BAY shun) *n.* disturbance in regular motion (usually orbiting) of a celestial body

pulsar (PUL sar) *n.* a collapsed star of extremely high density

sidereal (sy DEER ee ul) *adj.* having to do with the stars

syzygy (SIH zih jee) *n.* straight alignment of three celestial bodies

umbra (UM bruh) *n.* the region of total shadow in an eclipse; the dark center of a sunspot

zenith (ZEE nith) *n.* the point on the celestial sphere directly overhead

Biochemistry

abiosis (ay bee OH sis) *n.* absence of life

antigen (AN tih jin) *n.* a foreign substance (such as a virus) that enters the body, thereby stimulating the production of an antibody

atrophy (AT ruh fee) *n.* a wasting away; diminution in the size of a cell, tissue or part

carcinogen (kar SIN oh jin) *n.* any cancer-causing substance

catalyst (KAT uh list) *n.* any substance which creates or increases the rate of a (chemical) change without itself being affected

clastic (KLAS tik) *adj.* causing or undergoing division into parts

cytology (sih TAHL uh jee) *n.* the study of cells

desiccant (DES ih kint) *n.* any drying agent

detritus (dih TRY tus) *n.* decaying organic matter lying just below the surface

enzyme (EN zym) *n.* a protein which acts as a biological catalyst

immiscible (ih MIS ih bul) *adj.* not capable of being mixed

ionization (y un uh ZAY shun) *n.* the process of charging an electrically neutral atomic configuration by heat, electrical discharge, radiation or chemical reaction

isotopes (Y suh tohp) *n.* chemical elements differing in atomic weight but having the same atomic number

lipid (LIP id) *n.* a fatlike substance that cannot be dissolved in water

osmosis (ahs MOH sis) *n.* diffusion of a substance in a liquid solution across a membrane

polymer (PAHL uh mer) *n.* compound of high molecular weight; polymers are basic to the creation of plastics

substrate (SUB strayt) *n.* any substance which is acted on or altered by an enzyme

symbiosis (sim bee OH sis) *n.* the living together of two dissimilar organisms in a mutually beneficial relationship

synapse (SIN aps) *n.* the junction, usually a tiny gap, between two neurons or nerve cells

synergy (SIN er jee) *n.* coordination of different elements to achieve a common end

systemic (sis TEM ik) *adj.* referring to or distributed throughout an entire organism

zygote (ZY goht) *n.* a fertilized egg

Botany

ambiparous (am BIH per us) *adj.* having both leaves and flowers

aphyllous (ay FIL us) *adj.* without leaves

arboreal (ar BOR ee ul) *adj.* pertaining to trees

autonomic (aw toh NAH mik) *adj.* referring to movements produced by some internal stimulus

biennial (by EN ee ul) *n.* any plant that blossoms or sprouts every two years

conifer (KAHN ih fer) *n.* a cone-bearing tree

cuticle (KYOO tih kul) *n.* the waxy outer layer of a plant (or animal)

deciduous (dih SIH jyoo us) *adj.* shedding all leaves at a certain season of the year

defoliate (dih FOHL ee ayt) *v.* to strip of leaves

epidermis (ep uh DER mis) *n.* the outermost layer of a plant (or animal)

flora (FLOR uh) *n.* the plant population of a given region or period

foliage (FOHL yij) *n.* leaves of a plant or tree

frond (FRAHND) *n.* the leaf of a fern, palm tree, or banana tree

fruticose (FROO tih kohs) *adj.* shrublike

guttation (guh TAY shun) *n.* exudation (sweating) of water droplets from plants in a humid atmosphere

herbarium (er BAYR ee um) *n.* a collection of dried or preserved plants

hermaphrodite (her MAF ruh dyt) *n.* having both male and female organs

hirsute (HER soot) *adj.* covered with very long, soft hairs

hydrophyte (HY droh fyt) *n.* a plant normally growing in water or damp places

ligneous (LIG nee us) *adj.* like wood; having woodlike qualities

perennial (per EN ee ul) *adj.* in botany, a plant that lives for two or more years; generally, continuing through the year; continuing without cessation or intermission; perpetual

pubescent (pyoo BES int) *adj.* covered with a soft down; arriving at puberty

scandent (SKAN dint) *adj.* characterized by a climbing growth

sedge (SEJ) *n.* grasslike herbaceous plant, growing in wet areas

sylvan (SIL vun) *adj.* living in the forest or woods; sylvestrine

tendril (TEN drul) *n.* a thin, modified stem used for climbing by twining or adhesion

terrarium (ter AYR ee um) *n.* a small glass enclosure for plants

tropism (TROH pih zum) *n.* involuntary response—e.g., a stem's bending movement—to some external stimulus (such as water, sun or gravity)

ventral (VEN trul) *adj.* pertaining to the lower or inner surface (of a leaf, petal, etc.)

verdant (VER dunt) *adj.* lush in vegetation (literally, green)

viable (VY uh bul) *adj.* able to live, develop, or thrive

Business, Economics, and Finance

accrue (uh KROO) *v.* to accumulate over time (e.g., interest or money owing)

actuary (AK choo ayr ee) *n.* a specialist or expert on statistics, especially in the area of insurance

amortize (AM or tyz) *v.* to account for the reduction in the value of an asset over the period of ownership of the asset

annuity (uh NOO ih tee) *n.* a contract to pay a sum of money yearly or at regular intervals

appraise (uh PRAYZ) *v.* to assess the market value of an asset

arbitrage (AR bih trahzh) *v.* to take advantage of differing prices for the same security or commodity

arrears (uh REERS) *n.* a debt due but unpaid

boycott (BOY kaht) *v.* to refuse to do business with or to use another's product or service

contraband (KAHN truh band) *n.* goods illegally transported across a border (e.g., to avoid payment of taxes)

debenture (duh BEN cher) *n.* a note by a company promising to pay a debt, backed by the general credit of the company

embargo (em BAR goh) *n.* an official prohibition or restriction of foreign trade by one nation against another

entrepreneur (ahn truh pruh ner) *n.* someone who takes a risk in a business venture, usually as the business owner

escrow (ES kroh) *n.* a temporary account established to hold funds pending the completion of an investment or purchase transaction

exchequer (EKS chuh kur) *n.* the treasury of a state or nation

fiscal (FIS kul) *adj.* pertaining to the finances of a government or business

hedge (HEJ) *v.* to offset the risk of loss (e.g., from market price fluctuations)

insolvent (in SAWL vunt) *adj.* where one's financial liabilities exceed one's assets

inventory (IN vun tor ee) *n.* the stock or goods of a business, list of stock or property

negotiable (nuh GOH shee uh bul) *adj.* transferable (from one party to another)

invoice (IN voys) *n.* a bill, itemized list of goods sent to a buyer

pecuniary (puh KYOO nee ayr ee) *adj.* financial; monetary

mortgage (MOR guj) *v.* to pledge property (usually real estate) as security for a loan

pension (PEN shun) *n.* regular payments to someone who has fulfilled certain requirements, usually involving employment duration

peonage (PEE uh nij) *n.* a system of forced labor based upon debts incurred by workers

prospectus (pruh SPEK tus) *n.* a descriptive circular used in soliciting orders (e.g., for the purchase of stock or other securities)

repatriation (re pay tree AY shun) *n.* return of financial assets deposited in a foreign bank to a home country

scrivener (SKRIV ner) *n.* a professional or public copyist, scribe, or notary

specie (SPEE shee) *n.* money in the form of coins

spendthrift (SPEND thrift) *n.* a person who is overly free or undisciplined in spending money

subsidy (SUB sih dee) *n.* financial grant or aid, especially by a government

surety (SHOOR tee) *n.* one who guarantees the performance (e.g., payment) on behalf of another

syndicate (SIN dih kit) *n.* a group of persons or businesses joined together in a cooperative effort to reduce risk and increase efficiency

underwrite (UN der ryt) *v.* to access, select and reject risks, usually for the purpose of determining insurability and insurance rates

usurious (yoo ZHOOR ee us) *adj.* referring to an extremely high or unlawful rate of interest

voucher (VOWCH sayf) *n.* legally acceptable evidence of debt repayment; written evidence of authorization to make a purchase

warrant (WOR int) *n.* a certificate giving the holder the right to purchase securities at a specified price for a specified time period

yield (YEELD) *n.* the return on an investment (e.g., dividends or interest)

Civil Law

affidavit (af ih DAY vid) *n.* written declaration of fact, made under oath (or affirmation) of the party making it

agency (AY jun see) *n.* a relationship in which one party is legally authorized to act on behalf of another

annul (uh NUHL) *v.* to make or declare invalid or void

arbitration (ar buh TRAY shun) *n.* settling of a legal dispute by deferring to the decision of a third party

attest (uh TEST) *v.* to state a fact in writing and swear to its truthfulness

barrister (BAYR ih ster) *n.* a counselor-at-law; attorney; lawyer

bequeath (buh KWEETH) *v.* to make a posthumous gift by one's will

breach (BREECH) *v.* to break a contractual promise

caveat (KAH vee aht) *n.* legal notice preventing some action; a warning

chattel (CHAT ul) *n.* any movable property (not attached to land)

codicil (KAH dih sul) *n.* a legal document which adds to or changes the provisions of a will

conservator (kun SER vuh tor) *n.* one who is authorized to handle the property and/or personal affairs of another who is incapable of doing so for himself or herself

decedent (dih SEE dunt) *n.* a deceased person

de jure (de JOOR ee) *n.* according to law

demur (duh MER) *v.* to claim that even if another party's facts are true there is no legitimate claim or legal recourse

deposition (dep uh ZISH un) *n.* written testimony taken outside court

easement (EEZ munt) *n.* an interest in land giving the holder the right of access to or a particular use of the land

fiduciary (fuh DOO shee ayr ee) *n.* one charged with the legal responsibility for administering and/or managing another's assets

foreclose (for KLOHZ) *v.* to rescind a mortgage for failure to make payments as promised

franchise (FRAN chyz) *n.* a right or privilege granted by authority (especially, suffrage—the right to vote)

impeach (im PEECH) *v.* to discredit; to detract from a person's credibility or believability

indemnify (in DEM nuh fy) *v.* to restore a victim of a loss to the same position as before the loss occurred

jurisdiction (joor us DIK shun) *n.* the authority (usually of a court) to hear and decide legal disputes

jurisprudence (joor us PROOD uns) *n.* philosophy or theory of law

liable (LY uh bul) *adj.* legally responsible

libel (LY bul) *n.* written defamation, anything tending to lower reputation

lien (LEE un) *n.* a formal claim against property that has been pledged or mortgaged to secure the performance of an obligation

litigation (lit uh GAY shun) *n.* lawsuit, process of carrying on a lawsuit

notary (NOH tuh ree) *n.* a person who is officially authorized to authenticate legal documents (contracts, deeds, etc.)

novation (noh VAY shun) *n.* substitution of a new contract or obligation for an existing one

quitclaim (KWIT klaym) *v.* to transfer or relinquish title in property to another without any representation as to one's legal authority to do so

rescind (ree SIND) *v.* to cancel, nullify, revoke; retract; annul; to invalidate by subsequent action

revocable (ruh VOH kuh bul) *adj.* capable of being revoked, canceled, or rescinded

slander (SLAN der) *n.* spoken false statement damaging to a person's reputation

stipulate (STIP yoo layt) *v.* to specify, require, or set forth a particular fact as a condition of an agreement

subpoena (suh PEE nuh) *n.* a court order compelling a witness to provide information or to be present at a court hearing

subrogate (SUB ruh gayt) *v.* to substitute one party (e.g., a creditor) for another

tort (TORT) *n.* a non-criminal and non-contractual wrongful act committed against another

vest (VEST) *v.* to attain a right or interest without possibility of losing it

waive (WAYV) *v.* to voluntarily give up or surrender a right or privilege

Engineering and Construction

auger (AW ger) *n.* a tool for boring holes in wood

banister (BAN ih ster) *n.* a vertical member used to support a handrail

barb (BARB) *n.* sharp point on a tool projecting in the opposite direction from the main point(s)

batten (BAT un) *v.* to reinforce (a slatted wall or door) with a cross-member

berm (BERM) *n.* a bank of earth piled up alongside a road or wall

bevel (BEV ul) *n.* a non-right angle which one surface makes against another surface

bushing (BUH shing) *n.* a sleeve or fitting used to connect two pipes or cables

caliper (KAL uh per) *n.* a two-pronged instrument used to measure diameter or thickness of an object

conduit (KAHN doo it) *n.* a tube, pipe or channel for conveying a flowing substance, usually water

crampon (KRAM pahn) *n.* a hooked device used to lift heavy weights

crimp (KRIMP) *v.* to bend or warp an object (e.g., metal or wood)

dowel (DOW ul) *n.* a round peg used to join wooden parts together

flange (FLANJ) *n.* a projecting rim, edge, collar or ring on a pipe or shaft

glazier (GLAY zher) *n.* one who cuts and fits glass panes for windows

laminate (LAM ih nayt) *v.* to build up material in layers

lash (LASH) *v.* to bind or fasten with a rope or cord; to whip

lathe (LAYTH) *n.* a machine for shaping circular forms (especially, pieces of wood)

masonry (MAY sun ree) *n.* stonework

nib (NIB) *n.* any projecting piece or part

pitch (PICH) *n.* a dark, sticky substance used for roofing and paving

piton (PEE tahn) *n.* a spike hammered into rock fissures or ice to aid in climbing

rasp (RASP) *n.* an abrading tool made of steel

rout (ROWT) *v.* to groove or hollow out

shear (SHEER) *v.* to cut metal with blades

siphon (SY fun) *v.* to withdraw liquid by suction

slag (SLAG) *n.* the residue of a blast furnace, used for roofing surfaces

solder (SAH der) *v.* to join together or patch metal parts with a melted metal alloy

splayed (SPLAYD) *adj.* fanned apart

strut (STRUT) *n.* a type of structural brace

tachometer (tak AH muh ter) *n.* instrument for measuring rotational speed

weld (WELD) *v.* to join pieces of metal by compression and great heat

winch (WINCH) *n.* a machine used to pull up heavy weights

Criminology (Crimes and Criminal Procedure)

abduct (ab DUKT) *v.* to carry off a person by force

abet (uh BET) *v.* to encourage or countenance the commission of an offense

abscond (ub SKAHND) *v.* to flee from a geographic area or to conceal oneself without authorization, usually for the purpose of avoiding legal proceedings

acquit (uh KWIT) *v.* to relieve an accused from criminal charges

alibi (AL uh by) *n.* an excuse intended to avert blame

arraign (uh RAYN) *v.* to bring before a court of law to hear and answer charges

citation (sy TAY shun) *n.* summons to appear in court; an official praise, as for bravery; reference to legal precedent or authority

collusion (kuh LOO zhun) *n.* an agreement between two or more parties to defraud another of their property or rights

complicity (kum PLIH sih tee) *n.* association with or participation in a crime

duress (dyoo RES) *n.* actual or threatened force, violence, or imprisonment, causing another to act contrary to his or her will

extort (eks TORT) *v.* to demand payment based on threats

extradite (EKS truh dyt) *v.* to deliver (give up) a criminal from one state or nation to another

flagitious (fluh GIH shus) *adj.* scandalous, villainous

forgery, *n.* The false making or material altering, with intent to defraud, of any writing that, if genuine, might be the foundation of a legal liability

graft (GRAFT) *n.* illegal use of position of power for gain

homicide (HAH muh syd) *n.* killing of one person by another

illicit (ih LIH sit) *adj.* illegal; not licensed

immurement (ih MYOOR munt) *n.* confinement within walls

incarcerate (in KAR ser ayt) *v.* to imprison

indict (in DYT) *v.* to accuse (of a crime) formally

incendiary (in SEN dee ayr ee) *n.* an agitator, especially one who stirs up discontent by starting fires

indict (in DYT) *v.* to charge with a crime or accuse of wrongdoing

kleptomaniac (klep toh MAY nee ak) *n.* a person who has a compulsive desire to steal

larceny (LAR suh nee) *n.* theft of personal property

misdemeanor (mis duh MEEN er) *n.* petty minor legal offense.

parole (puh ROHL) *n.* conditional release (from prison) before full sentence is served

peccadillo (pek uh DIL oh) *n.* a slight or minor offense; misdemeanor

peculation (pek yoo LAY shun) *n.* stealing or misuse of public money entrusted to one's care; misappropriation; embezzlement

penal (PEE nul) *adj.* concerning legal punishment.

perjure (PER jer) *v.* to lie under oath, especially to give false testimony in court

pilfer (PIL fer) *v.* to steal repeatedly (especially, from one's workplace)

poach (POHCH) *v.* to take fish or game unlawfully from private or protected property

recidivism (rih SIH dih vih zum) *n.* habitual repetition of or return to criminal activity

regicide (REJ uh syd) *n.* murder of a monarch (king or queen)

vandalize (VAN duh lyz) *v.* to deface, damage, or destroy property

vigilante (vih juh LAN tee) *n.* one who takes justice into one's own hands

Ecology (Meteorology, Soil Science and the Environment)

agrarian (uh GRAYR ee un) *adj.* pertaining to agricultural land and its cultivation

biome (BY ohm) *n.* a discrete region characterized by the same life forms and conditions

cataclysm (KAT uh klih zum) *n.* a violent or overwhelming subversion of ordinary phenomena of nature (e.g., a flood, earthquake, or volcanic eruption)

debacle (dih BAH kul) *n.* a violent rush or flood of debris-filled waters; an overwhelming defeat

diurnal (dy YER nul) *adj.* referring to or occurring during the daylight hours

ebb (EB) *v.* to recede or fall back (as the tide)

ecology (ee KAHL uh jee) *n.* science of the relation of life to its environment

effluent (EF loo unt) *n.* waste matter emitted by a sewage treatment or industrial plant

eolian (ee OHL ee un) *adj.* affected by wind

estival (ES tuh vul) *adj.* pertaining to summer

fallow (FAL oh) *adj.* left idle (uncultivated) to restore productivity, usually referring to land used for agriculture

fumerole (FYOO mer ohl) *n.* a hole or vent (of a geyser, volcano, or spring) from which fumes or vapor rises

hibernal (hy BER nul) *adj.* relating to winter

humic (HYOO mik) *adj.* derived from the soil

humus (HYOO mus) *n.* decayed or decaying organic material in the surface layers of soil

indigenous (in DIJ uh nus) *adj.* native to a given area

leach (LEECH) *v.* to separate a liquid from a solid (usually waste) by flowing or percolating water into surrounding soil

littoral (LIT er ul) *adj.* pertaining to a shore (coastline), particularly the area of the shore between the high and low tide marks

maelstrom (MAYL strum) *n.* a whirlpool

pedology (pih DAHL uh jee) *n.* the study of soils

pluvial (PLOO vee ul) *adj.* relating to rain; drizzly

quagmire (KWAG myr) *n.* soft ground where footing is insecure; swamp; bog

simoon (sih MOON) *n.* desert wind or duststorm
spate (SPAYT) *n.* a sudden flood
squall (SKWAWL) *n.* a strong, sudden wind
vernal (VER nul) *adj.* relating to the spring
virazon (VEER uh zahn) *n.* a sea breeze
zephyr (ZEF er) *n.* a gentle breeze; a west wind

Gastronomy (the Art and Science of Good Eating)

baste (BAYST) *v.* to moisten meat in its own juices during cooking
braise (BRAYZ) *v.* to cook first by searing, then simmering in a small amount of liquid
bran (BRAN) *n.* the coat of a grain seed, used for cereal
brazier (BRAY zhyer) *n.* a pan for holding burning coals, used for open-flame cooking
calorie (KAL er ee) *n.* a unit of heat (not of nutrition)
colander (KAHL in der) *n.* a perforated basket used to strain water-filled foods
comestible (kuh MES stuh bul) *adj.* fit for eating; edible
confectionery (kun FEK shun ayr ee) *n.* any sweet food comprised primarily of sugar
cuisine (kwih ZEEN) *n.* particular style of prepared food
culinary (KUL uh nayr ee) *adj.* pertaining to cooking
decanter (dih KAN ter) *n.* a narrow-necked glass container used to hold and serve wine
desiccate (DES ih kayt) *v.* to dry or dehydrate

elixir (eh LIK ser) *n.* a liquid essence said to contain healthful properties

gastronomy (gas TRAHN uh mee) *n.* the science of preparing and serving food

larder (LAR der) *n.* a pantry; place where food is kept

pasteurize (PAS chyoor yz) *v.* to sterilize by raising and lowering temperature to prevent fermentation and growth of bacteria

percolate (PER kuh layt) *v.* to filter liquid though a permeable substance in order to extract the substance's essence

serrated (ser AY tud) *adj.* saw-toothed (especially, a knife)

sieve (SIV) *v.* to strain

spit (SPIT) *n.* a pointed skewer to hold meat over coals or fire

tripe (TRYP) *n.* the stomach and intestinal lining of an animal

truss (TRUS) *v.* to secure (hold together) with skewers or twine before cooking

tureen (ter REEN) *n.* a large, deep pot used to serve soup and sauces

viand (VY und) *n.* a dish or article of food serve at a fine meal; course

vintner (VINT ner) *n.* a dealer in or producer of wines

zest (ZEST) *n.* the outside rind of any citrus fruit which contains the essential oils used for flavoring

Geography

acclivity (uh KLIV ih tee) *n.* an ascending slope

accretion (uh KREE shun) *n.* gradual addition of new land to old by deposit of sediment carried by the water of a stream

aggrade (uh GRAYD) *v.* to build up a grade or slope by the deposit of sediment

alluvial (uh LOO vee ul) *adj.* pertaining to sediment deposited by flowing water, usually at the bottom of a body of water

alpine (AL pyn) *adj.* pertaining to great mountain heights

apex (AY peks) *n.* tip, point, or angular summit (of a mountain)

atoll (AT ahl) *n.* a coral island

avulsion (uh VUL shun) *n.* rapid erosion of a shoreline during a storm

benthal (BEN thul) *adj.* pertaining to the deepest zone or region of the ocean

berm (BERM) *n.* a narrow shelf or ridge

caldera (KAWL dayr uh) *n.* a crater formed at the top of a volcanic mountain

cataract (CAT uh rakt) *n.* a waterfall of great volume in which the vertical flow is concentrated in one sheer drop

confluence (KAHN floo ins) *n.* the point of convergence and uniting of two streams

cordillera (kor dil YAR uh) *n.* a system of mountain ranges

debouchure (dih BOO shyoor) *n.* mouth of a river or point at which tributaries connect with larger passages

eddy (ED ee) *n.* circular movement of water produced by counter currents

estuary (ES choo ayr ee) *n.* river basin affected by ocean tides, having a mixture of fresh and salt water

fell (FELL) *n.* a bare, uncultivated rocky hill or mountain

kame (KAYM) *n.* a short, conical, steep hill

longitudinal (lawn juh TOOD uh nul) *adj.* pertaining to geographic length, especially along the circumference from one of Earth's poles to the other

lotic (LOH tic) *adj.* pertaining to a flowing stream, river, or spring

meridian (muh RIH dee un) *n.* a line of longitude, passing over both north and south poles

occidental (ahk suh DEN tul) *adj.* pertaining to the earth's western hemisphere

piedmont (PEED mahnt) *adj.* lying or formed at the base of a mountain

riparian (ry PAYR ee un) *adj.* pertaining to a riverbank

scarp (SKARP) *n.* a steep slope or inland cliff

sedimentary (sed uh MEN tuh ree) *adj.* describing accumulation of material deposited by water, wind, or glaciers

spit (SPIT) *n.* a narrow strip of alluvial deposit projecting into the sea

tundra (TUN druh) *n.* a vast, cold, treeless region

Geology (Rock Formations, Minerals, and Metals)

anodize (AN oh dyz) *v.* to treat a metal in an electrolytic process so that it forms a protective coating of oxide

aven (AY vin) *n.* a vertical shaft leading upward from a cave passage

beneficiate (ben uh FISH ee ayt) *v.* to improve the grade of ore by milling, sintering, etc

chatoyant (shuh TOY unt) *adj.* having the luster or glow of certain gems, particularly cat's-eye

denude (dih NOOD) *v.* to wear away or remove overlying matter from underlying rocks, exposing them to view

facet (FAS it) *n.* the polished surface of a gemstone; a flat surface of a rock fragment

fault (FAWLT) *n.* a fracture in the earth's crust

fissure (FIH zher) *n.* crack.

hyaline (HY uh leen) *adj.* glassy; crystalline; transparent

igneous (IG nee us) *adj.* produced by volcanic eruption or fire

karat (KAYR ut) *n.* a unit for measuring the fineness of gold

lodestone (LOHD stohn) *n.* a natural mineral containing iron that acts as a magnet

magma (MAG muh) *n.* molten rock within the earth

monolith (MAH nuh lith) *n.* large piece of stone

nacreous (NAY kree us) *adj.* pearly; having the luster of mother-of-pearl

obsidian (ub SID ee un) *n.* black volcanic rock

quarry (KWOR ee) *v.* to extract stone from the surface

sectile (SEK til) *adj.* capable of being cut with a knife without breaking off in pieces

seismic (SYZ mik) *adj.* caused by or concerning earth-quakes

shard (SHARD) *n.* a spikelike fragment of glass

tufa (TOO fuh) *n.* a soft porous rock formed from lime deposits in springs

ventifact (VEN tuh fakt) *n.* a stone that has been shaped to some extent by the abrasion of wind-driven sand

vitreous (VIT ree us) *adj.* having the luster of broken glass

Government

amnesty (AM nis tee) *n.* a general pardon by a govern-ment for past offenses

apparat (uh PAYR it) *n.* the existing power structure or political organization

despot (DES put) *n.* a ruler having absolute ruler; tyrant; dictator

edict (EE dikt) *n.* an official order or proclamation having the force of law

hegemony (heh JEM uh nee) *n.* domination by one state over others

insurgency (in SER jin see) *n.* a minor revolt against a local government; uprising

junta (HOON tuh) *n.* a small group, usually composed of military officers, ruling a country in the absence of a civilian government

legislature (LEJ uh slay cher) *n.* lawmaking body

mandate (MAN dayt) *n.* authority conferred on an elected official by the electorate

moratorium (mor uh TOR ee um) *n.* an officially declared stoppage or delay

ordinance (OR duh nuns) *n.* statute (law) of a municipal (city) government

ombudsman (AHM boods mun) *n.* an intermediary between a citizen and the government who investigates complaints by citizens about government agencies or officials

polity (PAHL ih tee) *n.* a system or form of government

potentate (POH tun tayt) *n.* a monarch, dictator, or similar person possessing great political power

ratify (RAT ih fy) *v.* to approve officially; sanction

referendum (ref uh REN dum) *n.* popular vote on either proposed legislation or a popular initiative

regalia (rih GAYL yuh) *n.* emblems and trappings of a political or military office

regime (reh ZHEEM) *n.* the government of a specific leader; administration

secede (suh SEED) *v.* to separate from an organized body of government

sedition (sih DISH un) *n.* incitement to rebel against the government

subjugate (SUB joo gayt) *v.* to conquer or dominate a people or territory

subvert (sub VERT) *v.* to overthrow, ruin, corrupt, or otherwise undermine the stability or order of a government

suffrage (SUF rij) *n.* the right to vote

thralldom (THRAWL dum) *n.* slavery; serfdom

titular (TICH uh ler) *adj.* in title only (e.g., a monarch or president); nominal, and without actual power or authority

tribunal (try BYOO nul) *n.* court of justice

tyranny (TEER uh nee) *n.* absolute authority, usually exercised oppressively

usurp (yoo SERP) *v.* to assume political power or office by force or without right

Linguistics

alliteration (uh lih ter AY shun) *n.* repeating the same sound at the beginning of words

anachronism (uh NAK ruh nih zum) *n.* a word or expression not corresponding to the language of a given period of history; anything seemingly from another time

anagram (AN uh gram) *n.* a word (or group of words) made up of the same letters as those of another word or group of words

aphasia (uh FAY zhyuh) *n.* loss of the ability to speak

assonance (AS uh nuns) *n.* repetition of sounds, especially vowel sounds, in a word or phrase

cadence (KAY dins) *n.* the rise and fall in pitch, volume, or stress in speech

colloquial (kuh LOH kwee ul) *adj.* informal spoken or written expression

connote (kuh NOHT) *v.* to suggest or convey feelings or ideas in addition to the express meaning (denotation) of a word

dialect (DY uh lekt) *n.* a distinctive regional variety of a language

elocution (el uh KYOO shun) *n.* the study and practice of speaking properly and effectively in public oratory and in professional acting

etymology (et uh MAHL uh jee) *n.* origin and history of a word, study of the changes in words

euphonic (yoo FAHN ik) *adj.* having an agreeable or pleasing sound

evocative (ih VAHK uh tiv) *adj.* causing an emotional reaction in the listener (or reader)

expletive (EKS pluh tiv) *n.* any word used as a filler

idiom (ID ee um) *n.* a phrase which has a special meaning apart from the individual words used in the phrase

intonation (in toh NAY shun) *n.* the melodic pattern produced by the variation in pitch of the voice during speech

lexicon (LEK sih kahn) *n.* collection of vocabulary; dictionary

locution (loh KYOO shun) *n.* any utterance, expression, or phrase

mnemonic (nee MAH nik) *adj.* symbolic substitution or abbreviation, used for memorization (and in computer programming)

parlance (PAR luns) *n.* any particular manner of expressing oneself, using vernacular and idioms

pejorative (puh JOR uh tiv) *adj.* negative in connotation

peroration (per uh RAY shun) *n.* the concluding part of a public address or speech (especially, summing up and recapitulating key points and/or exhorting and uplifting the audience)

phonetic (fuh NET ik) *adj.* based on sounds (e.g., the phonetic spelling of a word)

pidgin (PIH jun) *n.* a mixture of different languages

polyglot (PAH lee glaht) *n.* a person who speaks or writes in several languages

proem (PROH um) *n.* an introduction, preface, or preamble (in speech or writing)

prosody (PRAH suh dee) *n.* the distinctive rhythm, stress, and intonation in a language (or of poetic verse)

rebus (REE bus) *n.* the representation of a word by pictures or symbols

rhetoric (RET uh rik) *n.* persuasion through argument

rostrum (RAHS trum) *n.* a platform for public speaking; dais

semantic (suh MAN tik) *adj.* involving signs (especially, words) and the things (ideas) they are intended to signify

syntax (SIN taks) *n.* construction of a sentence; arrangement of words in a sentence

vernacular (ver NAK yuh ler) *n.* distinct language or spoken and written expression of a particular region

Literature

allegory (AL uh gor ee) *n.* a collection of extended metaphors in narrative form used as a device for teaching a lesson

allusion (uh LOO zhun) *n.* a reference in a literary work to an identifiable person, event, place, or literary passage

analect (AN uh lekt) *n.* a literary fragment or passage

anthology (an THAH luh jee) *n.* a collection of selections from the writings of one or more authors

apocryphal (uh PAHK rih ful) *adj.* of unknown authorship or doubtful integrity

ballad (BAL id) *n.* a narrative poem meant for recitation or singing

bard (BARD) *n.* a prominent poet or other writer (of the Renaissance period)

bibliography (bib lee AHG ruh fee) *n.* list of sources of information on a particular subject

colophon (KAH luh fahn) *n.* a publisher's and/or printer's distinctive emblem, monogram, or cipher

denouement (day noo MAHN) *n.* the final unfolding of a plot; the final resolution or outcome following the climax

doggerel (DAW guh rul) *n.* poetic verse of generally poor quality; verse characterized by a crude, rough, irregular, or burlesque style

elegy (EL uh jee) *n.* a poem (or song) of mourning; a lament

epic (EP ik) *n.* a literary work recounting the travels and deeds of a legendary (heroic) figure

epitaph (EP ih taf) *n.* an inscription on a monument in memory of a deceased person

euphemism (YOO fuh mih zum) *n.* a pleasant or complimentary word or phrase used instead of one that is harsh or derogatory to prevent the conveyance of a bluntly honest opinion

figurative (FIG yoor uh tiv) *adj.* metaphoric; not to be interpreted literally

fustian (FUS chun) *n.* describing pretentious, pompous, or bombastic writing

imprimatur (im pruh MAH ter) *n.* license to publish

lampoon (lam POON) *n.* harsh satire, usually directed against a particular person

litotes (LY toh teez) *n.* an understatement made for rhetorical emphasis

masthead (MAST hed) *n.* a statement of the name, ownership, etc. of a publication

missive (MIS iv) *n.* a letter, usually formal or official

motif (moh TEEF) *n.* a literary, artistic, or musical device that serves as the basis for suggestive expansion; the basic element repeated throughout the work

ode (OHD) *n.* a lyric poem marked by exalted feeling

opus (OH pus) *n.* a literary or musical work

parody (PAYR uh dee) *n.* a distorted and usually humorous imitation of a particular style of writing

pastiche (pas TEESH) *n.* a composition made up of bits from various sources; an imitation of another writer's style or technique, usually done for satirical or humorous purposes

pathos (PAY thohs) *n.* the quality of evoking a feeling of pity or compassion (in literature, art, or music)

plagiarism (PLAY jer iz um) *n.* The act of taking an idea, plot, or actual written work from another and passing it off as one's own.

protagonist (proh TAG uh nist) *n.* the leading character in a story

pseudonym (SOO duh nim) *n.* a fictitious name used by an author

satire (SAT yr) *n.* a literary form employing irony, ridicule, and sarcasm

scholiast (SKOH lee ast) *n.* an ancient commentator or annotator of classic texts

thesaurus (thih SOR us) *n.* dictionary of synonyms

tome (TOHM) *n.* a very large or scholarly work

treatise (TREE tis) *n.* a comprehensive and systematic literary examination of a particular subject

vignette (vin YET) *n.* a short, sketchy story

vita (VEE tuh) *n.* a brief, autobiographical sketch

Mathematics

conflate (kun FLAYT) *v.* to integrate two separate sets to produce a single set

congruent (kun GROO unt) *adj.* equivalent; having exactly the same size and shape

conjugate (KAHN joo git) *adj.* having the same or similar properties

corollary (KOR uh layr ee) *n.* a theorem proved by a previously proved theorem

innumerate (ih NOO mer it) *adj.* mathematically illiterate

interpolate (in TER pul ayt) *v.* to estimate a value of a function between two known values (by a method other than that defined by the equation or law that represents the function)

involution (in vuh LOO shun) *n.* the process of multiplying a quantity by itself a given number of times (i.e., taking a number to a "power")

iteration (ih ter AY shun) *n.* one step in a sequence of repeated steps in the solution of a problem (iterative: *adj.* repeating)

matrix (MAY triks) *n.* an array of terms (numbers) arranged in columns and rows

median (MEE dee un) *adj.* middle; *(n)* middle item in a series

ordinal (OR duh nul) *adj.* indicating the order, position, or rank of an item among others in a group or set

permutation (per myoo TAY shun) *n.* an operation on a set of elements (numbers) in which each element is replaced by itself or by some other element of the set

quotient (KWOH shunt) *n.* in arithmetic, the number resulting from the division of one number by another

ratio (RAY shee oh) *n.* proportion, fixed relation of number or amount between two things

ratiocination (rash ee ah suh NAY shun) *n.* the act of drawing conclusions from premises; reasoning

scalar (SKAY ler) *n.* an element of a set or field (e.g., of numbers)

stochastic (stuh KAS tik) *adj.* referring to a sequence of uncertain outcomes over time (usually used in statistics and linear programming)

tertiary (TER shee ayr ee) *adj.* third

Medicine and the Health Professions

asphyxiation (as fik see AY shun) *n.* death or loss of consciousness caused by lack of oxygen

astringent (uh STRIN junt) *n.* a substance that causes binding by contraction; a harsh, biting substance

autopsy (AW tahp see) *n.* examination and partial dissection of a body to determine the cause of death

chronic (KRAH nik) *adj.* continuous; constant; prolonged; recurring periodically

coma (KOH muh) *n.* a state of deep unconsciousness caused by injury or disease

congenital (kun JEN ih tul) *adj.* existing or dating from birth; inbred; inborn; innate

cranium (KRAY nee um) *n.* skull of a human or other vertebrate animal

endocrine (EN duh krin) *adj.* of a system of glands and their secretions that regulate body functions

emetic (uh MET ik) *n.* any substance used to induce vomiting

febrile (FEE bryl) *adj.* feverish

geriatric (jayr ee AT rik) *adj.* relating to medical care and treatment of the elderly

hallucination (huh loo suh NAY shun) *n.* apparent perceiving of things not present

hospice (HAH spis) *n.* a shelter for the sick, dying, or underprivileged (or for travelers)

hypertension (hy per TEN shun) *n.* high blood pressure

intravenous (in truh VEE nus) *adj.* through a vein

longevity (lawng JEV uh tee) *n.* life span, long life

morbidity (mor BID ih tee) *n.* the incidence or prevalence of disease (or death)

natal (NAY tul) *adj.* pertaining to birth

neuralgia (nyoo RAL juh) *n.* pain along the course of a nerve

pathology (path AHL uh jee) *n.* the study of the processes and causes of disease

prognosis (prahg NOH sis) *n.* a medical prediction or forecast of the course of an illness and chances of recovery

prosthesis (prah STHEE sis) *n.* an addition to the end of (esp., an artificial limb)

quarantine (KWOR un teen) *n.* sequestration (isolation) of a person to prevent spread of disease (also used as a verb)

remission (ree MIH shun) *n.* abatement or lessening (of the symptoms of a disease)

senescent (suh NES unt) *adj.* growing old; aging

suture *n.* stitch on a wound

syncope (SING kuh pee) *n.* a brief loss of consciousness; fainting or swooning

syndrome (SIN drohm) *n.* a cluster of symptoms, all thought to be caused by the same disease or illness

varicose (VAYR uh kohs) *adj.* swollen, said of veins

vellicate (VEL uh kayt) *v.* to cause convulsive twitching

venous (VEE nus) *adj.* pertaining to a vein or veins

vertigo (VER tih goh) *n.* dizziness and the sensation of head-spinning

veterinary *adj.* concerning the medical treatment of animals

Metaphysics and the Afterlife

anagogic (an uh GAHG ik) *adj.* relating to spiritual or lofty ideals

animism (AN ih mih zum) *n.* the belief that natural objects and phenomena possess souls or spirits

apocalypse (uh PAH kuh lips) *n.* a cataclysmic, violent event in which forces of good destroy those of evil

apostate (uh PAH stayt) *n.* one who defects from or abandons one's faith, church, or principles

apotheosis (uh pah thee OH sis) *n.* the elevation of a mortal to the rank of deity (god); deification; glorification

deity (DEE uh tee) *n.* a divine or supreme being

ethereal (ee THEER ee ul) *adj.* nonmaterial; heavenly

expiate (EKS pee ayt) *v.* to atone for one's wrongful acts (sins)

hallow (HAL oh) *v.* to make holy; consecrate

heathen (HEE thin) *n.* a nonbeliever; pagan; infidel; kafir

heresy (HAYR uh see) *n.* a dissenting or unorthodox religious belief; sacrilege

kismet (KIZ mut) *n.* fate; destiny; fortune

mammonism (MAM un ih zum) *n.* the personification of material wealth as evil

manitou (MAN ih too) *n.* a supernatural being that controls nature

oracular (or AK yoo ler) *adj.* prophetic; foretelling; portentous (oracle: *n.* a divinely inspired utterance)

perdition (per DIH shun) *n.* a place of damnation; hell

pious (PY us) *adj.* acting dutifully in reverence (whether or not genuine) to God

prescience (PRESH uns) *n.* direct acquaintance with the future, as opposed to foreknowledge based on inference

recreant (REK ree unt) *adj.* failing to maintain faith

sacrilege (SAK rih lij) *n.* a statement or act that degrades that which is sacred; heresy

sacrosanct (SAK roh sankt) *adj.* sacred; holy inviolable; hallowed

secular (SEK yoo ler) *adj.* rejecting religion as necessary in understanding or interpreting the world

veneration (ven er AY shun) *n.* reverence; devotion

Military Science

armistice (AR muh stis) *n.* a general truce; cessation of war

belay (buh LAY) *v.* to cancel a command (also, to make secure or fast)

bivouac (BIV wak) *n.* a temporary encampment, usually with little or no shelter

brassard (BRAS erd) *n.* a distinctive insignia worn on the shoulder of a uniform to indicate task or rank

breach (BREECH) *n.* an expedient passage through an obstacle

brigade (brih GAYD) *n.* a type of military unit; sub-unit of a battalion

citadel (SIT uh dul) *n.* a fortress or stronghold, especially for defending a city

clandestine (KLAN DES tin) *adj.* secret; concealed

coup (KOO) *n.* a highly successful maneuver; a surprise attack

covert (KOH vert) *adj.* secret; hidden

debark (dee BARK) *v.* to unload or leave a ship or aircraft

decrypt (de KRIPT) *v.* to convert encrypted (coded) text to plain text through the use of a decoding system

defect (duh FEKT) *v.* to repudiate one's native country in favor of an opposing nation

deploy (dih PLOY) *v.* to send troops or equipment to a foreign area for duty

foray (FOR ay) *n.* an incursion or raid

garrison (GAYR uh sun) *n.* a fortified, secured area or building for stationing troops

interdiction (in ter DIK shun) *n.* disruptive action designed to prevent an enemy from gaining access to routes, areas, or supplies

mercenary (MER suh nayr ee) *adj.* for hire; not motivated by political loyalty or allegiance

perfidy (PER fuh dee) *n.* deceptive tactics that tend to destroy the basis for restoring peace

preemptive (pree EM tiv) *adj.* launched or initiated because of evidence that the enemy is about to move or attack

reconnaissance (rih KAH nuh suns) *n.* observation of an area of military significance

sabotage (SAB uh tahzh) *n.* intentional destruction or obstruction aimed at disrupting military or government activities

sentry (SEN tree) *n.* a soldier whose job is to maintain a watch against threats from the enemy

shrapnel (SHRAP nul) *n.* destructive fragments resulting from the explosion of a bomb or projectile

sortie (SOR tee) *n.* an air mission

triage (TREE ahzh) *n.* a method of ranking sick or injured people according to severity of sickness or injury for the purpose of determining priority of treatment

vanguard (VAN gard) *n.* troops (forces) sent in advance; the forefront of an army

waylay (WAY lay) *v.* to lie in wait for the purpose of ambushing or intercepting

Music and Musicology

anthem (AN thum) *n.* a short choral song of a serious (e.g., religious or patriotic) nature

aria (AR ee uh) *n.* part of an opera, oratorio, etc., where the action is stopped and characters sing their reaction to the dramatic situation

ballad (BAL ud) *n.* a (vocal) song whose words tell a story

ballade (buh LAHD) *n.* an instrumental piece, usually long, that is lyrical and romantic in style

baroque (buh ROHK) *adj.* attempting to achieve artistic effect (in music, literature, or art) by startling and irregular movement in style and form

cadence (KAY duns) *n.* a point of rest or conclusion; modulation in tone; measured movement

cadenza (kuh DEN zuh) *n.* an extended cadence just before a point of rest, allowing for a soloist to improvise or play a composed passage to display his or her technical ability

canon (KAN un) *n.* a musical form in which the voices enter successively with the same material; a round

chorale (kuh RAL) *n.* a hymn or psalm sung to a melody

clarion (KLAYR ee un) *n.* a shrill-toned trumpet

coda (KOH duh) *n.* passage added to the final section of a musical piece

concerto (kun CHAYR toh) *n.* a composition for a solo instrument (or group of instruments) and orchestra

conservatory (kun SER vuh tor ee) *n.* a special school which offers instruction in all aspects of music

forte (FOR tay) *adj.* strong; loud

fugue (FYOOG) *n.* a musical form consisting of a number of imitative explorations of a theme

glissando (glih SAHN doh) *n.* a series of ascending or descending notes played quickly so as to give the impression of sliding from the first to the last note

libretto (lih BRET oh) *n.* the words or text for an opera, oratorio, etc

madrigal (MAD ruh gul) *n.* a Renaissance form of unaccompanied choral music based on a non-sacred text

melisma (muh LIZ muh) *n.* a florid melody with a free rhythm structure

nocturne (NAHK tern) *n.* a slow, quiet, lyrical piece

oratorio (or uh TOR ee oh) *n.* a large multisectional musical form which is really an unstaged sacred opera

ostinato (ah stih NAH toh) *n.* a repeated melodic pattern whose insistence becomes a characteristic of the piece

overture (OH ver cher) *n.* an instrumental introduction to a musical play or opera

polyphony (puh LIF uh nee) *n.* the simultaneous combination of two or more melodies

prosody (PRAH zuh dee) *n.* the art of setting text to music

reprise (rih PRYZ) *n.* repetition of a musical phrase

requiem (REK wee um) *n.* a composition written for a funeral Mass

sonata (suh NAH tuh) *n.* a musical piece composed for solo instrument, sometimes with piano accompaniment

syncopation (sing kuh PAY shun) *n.* a shifting of the normal accent (stress) in music, so that "offbeats" are stressed

timbre (TIM ber) *n.* the unique quality of a sound produced by a particular instrument or voice

troubadour (TROO buh dor) *n.* a poet-musician of the Medieval period

Philosophy, Critical Thinking and Logic

autonomy (aw TAH nuh mee) *n.* independence from external constraints; self-determination

canon (CAN un) *n.* a rule, norm, tenet, or principle that is logically consistent

corporeal (kor POR ee ul) *adj.* relating to the body or to physical matter

dialectic (dy uh LEK tik) *n.* a question-and-answer method of investigation

discursive (dis KER siv) *adj.* characterized by analysis

empirical (em PEER ih kul) *n.* based on direct or practical observation and experience

epicurean (ep ih KYOOR ee un) *adj.* pertaining to the pursuit of pleasure

fallacious (fuh LAY shus) *adj.* logically unsound; misleading or deceptive

heuristic (hyoo RIS tik) *adj.* serving to persuade through discovery and revelation rather than through logic or rhetoric

hypothesis (hy PAH thuh sis) *n.* theory, tentative explanation yet to be proven

immanent (IM uh nunt) *adj.* existing within the mind; indwelling or inherent

infer (in FER) *v.* to conclude from reasoning or implication

irrefragable (ih REF ruh guh bul) *adj.* irrefutable; undeniable

metaphysics (met uh FIZ iks) *n.* the philosophy of being; the study of being in its universal aspects

nihilism (NY uh liz um) *n.* the belief that that there is no purpose to existence; rejection of established laws and institutions

nonsequitur (nahn SEK wih ter) *n.* that which does not follow logically

ontology (ahn TAHL uh jee) *n.* the branch of metaphysics dealing with the nature of existence (being)

paradox (PAYR uh dahks) *n.* a seemingly contradictory assertion that may nevertheless be true or valid

polemics (puh LEM iks) *n.* the art of disputing (debate)

postulate (PAHS choo lut) *n.* a hypothesis that cannot be demonstrated

premise, (PREM us) *n.* A previous statement or assertion that serves as the basis for reaching a conclusion of an argument.

presumption, (prih ZUM chun) *n.* The act of accepting as true, lacking proof to the contrary.

prolepsis (proh LEP sis) *n.* a preconception or necessary assumption or principle; anticipation of possible objections in order to answer them; an error in chronology in which an event is dated before the actual time of occurrence

Physics

amplitude (AMP lih tood) *n.* height or depth (range) of the crest (or trough) of a wave

attenuate (uh TEN yoo ayt) *v.* to reduce in size or amount

buffer (BUF er) *n.* a temporary storage area for data or signals as they pass from one system to another

centrifugal (sen TRIF uh gul) *adj.* conveyance outward by force from a rotating center

cryogenics (kry oh JEN iks) *n.* production and effects of extremely low temperatures

damp (DAMP) *v.* to lessen a vibration

decibel (DES uh bul) *n.* a unit of measurement of the intensity (loudness) of sound

entropy (EN truh pee) *n.* the degree of disorder or tendency toward the breakdown of a system

fission (FIH zhun) *n.* the process of splitting apart or disjoining

fulcrum (FUL krum) *n.* the point of pivot of a lever

galvanize (GAL vuh nyz) *v.* to excite (stimulate) by electrical current; to coat iron with zinc in order to prevent rust

incandescent (in kun DES unt) *adj.* emitting light due to production of heat

inertia, (in ER shuh) *n.* the tendency of matter to remain at rest if at rest, or, if moving, to keep moving in the same direction, unless affected by some outside force.

irradiate *v.* to spread out, expose to radiant energy, heat by radiant energy

joule (JOOL) *n.* a unit of energy or work used in scientific measurement

kinetic (kih NET ik) *adj.* produced, creating, or characterized by motion

luminous (LOO min us) *adj.* giving off light

modulate (MAHJ yoo layt) *v.* to vary

opaque (oh PAYK) *adj.* describing a material that is unable to transmit light

parallax (PAYR uh laks) *n.* a shift in the relative position of objects due to a change in perspective

photic (FOH tik) *adj.* pertaining to light

quantum (KWAHN tum) *n.* a discrete and indivisible unit of energy

radiation (ray dee AY shun) *n.* divergence in all directions from a point, especially of energy

refraction (ree FRAK shun) *n.* the bending of a wave as it passes obliquely from one medium to another

resonate (REZ uh nayt) *v.* to vibrate greatly as a response to an external stimulus

sonic (SAH nik) *adj.* pertaining to sound waves

spectrum (SPEK trum) *n.* the entire range of wavelengths produced when a beam of electromagnetic radiation is broken up into its array of entities

thermal (THER mul) *adj.* pertaining to heat

torque (TORK) *n.* a force that produces a twisting or rotating motion

viscosity (vis KAHS ih tee) *n.* internal friction of a fluid; resistance to flow

Political Science

cabal (kuh BAL) *n.* a secret group of political conspirators

cadre (KAH dray) *n.* close-knit group of leaders who advocate particular views

caucus (KAW kus) *n.* a closed meeting, usually by a political party to plan a strategy

clout (KLOWT) *n.* political power or influence

coalition (koh uh LIH shun) *n.* an alliance of political parties or states based on a common purpose

constituency *n.* body of voters

electorate (il EK ter it) *n.* body of persons entitled to vote in an election

emissary (EM uh sayr ee) *n.* one sent to influence opponents politically

gerrymander (JAYR ee man der) *v.* to alter voting district lines so as to further one's own interests in obtaining votes

graft (GRAFT) *n.* money or property gained through political corruption

ideologue (Y dee uh lawg) *n.* one who believes in and propagates a political or social doctrine

incumbent (in KUM bunt) *adj.* currently in office; running against a challenger

jingoism (JING goh ih zum) *n.* belligerent or excessive patriotism

junket (JUNG kit) *n.* a personal trip of a public official financed by public funds

nepotism (NEP uh tih zum) *n.* political favoritism toward friends and relatives, especially in granting favors

partisan (PAR tih zun) *adj.* advocating or favoring the views of one party

ploy (PLOY) *n.* a clever and deceptive maneuver designed to achieve an objective without revealing one's intent or goal

quisling (KWIZ ling) *n.* a traitor who collaborates with an enemy occupying his country

stalwart (STAWL wert) *n.* an unwavering, staunch supporter

Psychology

agoraphobia (uh gor uh FOH bee uh) *n.* unreasonable fear of open (public) places

anaclitic (an uh KLIH tic) *adj.* dependent on another person

anemia (uh NEE mee uh) *n.* deficiency of red blood corpuscles or hemoglobin in the blood

angst (ANGST) *n.* anxiety

cataplexy (KAT uh plek see) *n.* a sudden paralysis of all voluntary movement, resulting in a collapse of the entire body

catharsis (kuh THAR sis) *n.* a discharge of strong emotions

cathexis (kuh THEK sis) *n.* placing special emotional significance on an object or idea

dereistic (der ee IS tik) *adj.* not in accord with reality, experience, and logic

empathy (EM puh thee) *n.* the ability to participate in another person's feelings and experiences and to understand them

gestalt (guh SHTAWLT) *n.* a unified whole, especially the human psyche, having properties distinct from the sum of its parts

hypochondria (hy poh KAHN dree uh) *n.* abnormal anxiety about health

idiotropic (id ee oh TROH pik) *adj.* introspective

libido (lih BEE doh) *n.* sexual or psychic energy

ludic (LOO dik) *adj.* pertaining to play and playful curiosity

misogynist (mih SAH juh nist) *n.* a person who hates women

narcissism (NAR sih sih zum) *n.* excessive love of oneself

neurosis (nyer OH sis) *n.* any mild emotional disorder

placebo (pluh SEE boh) *n.* a treatment that has no effect except in the patient's own mind

sublimate (SUB luh mayt) *v.* to express repressed desires or wishes in acceptable forms

subliminal (suh BLIM uh nul) *adj.* beneath the threshold of consciousness

surgent (SER junt) *adj.* extroverted

vicarious (vy KAYR ee us) *adj.* experienced indirectly through observation

xenophobia (zee nuh FOH bee uh) *n.* an unreasonable fear of strangers, foreigners, or anything foreign, strange, or different

---

Religion (Institutions and Customs)

---

advent (AD vent) *n.* signifying arrival

apostle (uh PAH sul) *n.* an agent or deliverer through which the will of the sender of a message is expressed

atone, *v.* To make amends or reparation for one's wrong-doing or sins

benediction (ben uh DIK shun) *n.* a recitation of praise (to God)

canon (KAN un) *n.* a religious doctrine, code, or law, usually written

cherub (CHAYR ub) *n.* a type of angel, represented as a child

cleric (KLAYR ik) *n.* a member of the clergy; an ordained priest, minister or rabbi

creed (KREED) *n.* a system or formal statement of religious beliefs

doxology (dahk SAH luh jee) *n.* a hymn of praise (to God)

ecclesiastical (eh klee zee AS tih kul) *adj.* pertaining to the church as an institution

ecumenical (ek yoo MEN ih kul) *adj.* universal; world-wide; pertaining to a unified whole

exegesis (ek sih JEE sis) *n.* analysis, interpretation, and criticism of a literary work (usually a sacred text), especially its metaphoric and symbolic patterns

heterodox not conforming or conventional (orthodox), especially in religious belief

idolatry (y DAHL uh tree) *n.* worship of idols or false gods

impetration (im puh TRAY shun) *n.* a petition; request; prayer

laity (LAY uh tee) *n.* any persons other than clergy; lay-persons

liturgy (LIH ter jee) *n.* the rites, practices, and ceremonies of religious worship

martyr (MAR ter) *n.* a person who is persecuted—usually put to death—for defending his or her religious principles

orthodox (OR thuh dahks) *adj.* conventional; traditional

penance (PEN uns) *n.* a specific act of repentance for wrongful acts (sins)

predicant (PRED uh kunt) *n.* a preacher (curate, vicar, parson, minister, etc.)

sacrament (SAK ruh munt) *n.* sacred rite (ritual)

schism (SKIH zum) *n.* a separation or division into groups or sects due to differing beliefs

sect (SEKT) *n.* a religious group deviating from orthodox faith

Sociology

ableism (AY bul ih zum) *n.* discrimination against mentally or physically disabled people

acculturate (uh KUL cher ayt) *v.* to adopt the cultural traits and patterns of another group through continual firsthand exposure

anomie (AN uh mee) *n.* a societal condition in which the social norms have weakened or disappeared

atomism (AT uh mih zum) *n.* a society composed of clearly distinct elements and factions

bourgeois (boor ZHWAH) *adj.* middle-class

caste (KAST) *n.* a hierarchical social system, characterized by minimal social mobility

deracination (dih ras ih NAY shun) *n.* uprooting from one's cultural or social environment

enculteration (en kuhl cher AY shun) *n.* the process of learning the culture of one's own group or society by observation, experience, and instruction

ethnocentric (eth noh SEN trik) *adj.* evaluating the behavior and values of others only according to the criteria of one's one ethnic group

guild (GILD) *n.* an association for the promotion of common goals

insular (IN suh ler) *adj.* pertaining only to an isolated region or group of people; parochial; provincial; local

labefaction (LAB uh fak shun) *n.* a decline in or weakening of public morality and social order

more (MOR ay) *n.* a custom or folkway considered essential to the welfare of a society

solecism (SAH lih sih zum) *n.* a violation of accepted conventions or customs (especially in language or etiquette)

taboo (tab OO) *adj.* prohibited behavior, where the prohibition is established through social custom

telesis (TEL uh sis) *n.* planned progress through the use of both social and natural forces

yeoman (YOH man) *n.* the owner of a small estate; a middle-class farmer

Theater Arts and Public Speaking

debut (day BYOO) *n.* an actor's first performance
hamartia (hah mar TEE uh) *n.* a flaw in a tragic character

harlequin (HAR lih kwin) *n.* masked, comic character

histrionics (his tree AH niks) *n.* acting in highly theatrical or overly dramatic, exaggerated style

impresario (im preh SAR ee oh) *n.* a manager, promoter, or sponsor for performing artists

librettist (lih BRET ist) *n.* writer of song lyrics for a musical

loge (LOHZH) *n.* balcony seating area of a theater

marquee (mar KEE) *n.* sign on the front of a theater advertising a play

minstrel (MIN strul) *n.* traveling entertainer of the medieval period

odeum (OH dee um) *n.* a small theater or concert hall

pantomime (PAN tuh mym) *n.* acting without dialogue

peripeteia (per uh pih TY uh) *n.* a striking reversal in the action of a play

podium (POH de um) *n.* raised platform, as for use by speakers or musical conductors

proscenium (proh SEE nee um) *n.* the front of a stage, marked off at the top by an arch

repertory (REP er tor ee) *n.* a theatrical company

scrim (SKRIM) *n.* a curtain that may be transparent or opaque, depending on how it is lit

soubrette (soo BRET) *n.* a frivolous girl character, often a lady's maid

tableau (tab LOH) *n.* a stage picture created by actors posing motionless

Visual Arts—General/Sculpture

armature (AR muh cher) *n.* a skeleton construction upon which a sculptor builds up a sculpture

burnish (BER nish) *v.* to rub or polish to a high gloss

collage (kuh LAHZH) *n.* artwork resulting from the piecing together of different, often unrelated, pieces of material

contrapposto (kahn truh PAH stoh) *n.* a pose in which the parts of the body are twisted or distorted into opposite directions

crop (KRAHP) *v.* to trim off

curator (KYER ay ter) *n.* person in charge of the artwork in a museum

docent (DOH sint) *n.* a tour guide at a museum

ectype (EK typ) *n.* a replica of an original artwork

emboss (em BAWS) *v.* to create raised figures or designs on a surface

etch (ECH) *v.* to partially eat away a glass or metal surface by using a chemical in order to create a design

festoon (fes TOON) *n.* a decorative design of looped, curved lines

gilded (GIL did) *adj.* covered with a gold finish

gisant (gee ZAHNT) *n.* the sculptured representation of a deceased person, usually part of a monumental tomb

medium (MEE dee um) *n.* the particular material used to create a picture or sculpture

montage (mahn TAHZH) *n.* a combination of several pictures or parts of pictures blended into a single unit

mosaic (moh ZAY ik) *n.* an illustration formed by a matrix of tiles or stones set in cement

patina (puh TEE nuh) *n.* green film on the surface of bronze, resulting from exposure to atmosphere or chemicals

relief (rih LEEF) *n.* raised; projecting from a background surface

slip (SLIP) *n.* a fluid mixture of clay and water used for pottery

tessellated (TES uh lay tid) *adj.* inlaid; mosaic

Visual Arts—Painting

abozzo (uh BOHT soh) *n.* a sketch; in painting, the first outline or drawing on a canvas

calligraphic (kal uh GRAF ik) *adj.* the free and rhythmic use of pen markings to approximate handwriting

caricature (KAYR ih kuh choor) *n.* a pictorial ridicule or satire in which the subject's physical characteristics are distorted

cartoon (kar TOON) *n.* a preliminary drawing or sketch

chiaroscuro (kee ar uh SKYOOR oh) *n.* the use of light and shade to give forms a three-dimensional appearance

chroma (KROH muh) *n.* the distinctive quality, excluding color, that identifies a particular color

cursive (KUR siv) *adj.* free-flowing, in the manner of running handwriting

fictile (FIK tul) *adj.* molded or capable of being molded into form by sculpture

fresco (FRES koh) *n.* a mural painting on freshly laid plaster

impasto (im PAHS toh) *n.* heavy layers or strokes of paint, creating a rough surface with deep brush marks

palette (PAL ut) *n.* the range of colors or pigments available to an artist; a wooden board used by a painter to hold paint while painting

siccative (SIK uh tiv) *n.* a substance added to oil paint to make it dry more quickly

tempera (TEM per uh) *n.* pigment mixed with water and egg yolk or similar material

tondo (TAHN doh) *n.* a picture in the round

varnish (VAR nish) *n.* a solution used as a protective coating over paint

vignette (vin YET) *n.* an illustration that fades into the space around it without a definite border; also, a small illustration at the beginning or end of a chapter or book to fill up space

Zoology

agonistic (ag uh NIS tik) *adj.* displaying fighting behavior

aliped (AL uh ped) *n.* an animal whose toes are connected by a membrane, serving as a wing (e.g., a bat)

apiary (AY pee ayr ee) *n.* a place where bees are kept

aviary (AY vee ayr ee) *n.* an enclosure for birds

carapace (KAR uh pays) *n.* a shell or protective covering over all or part of the back of certain animals (e.g., turtles and crabs)

diurnal (dy YER nul) *adj.* referring to or occurring during the daylight hours

equine (EK wyn) *adj.* pertaining to horses; horselike

ewe (YOO) *n.* a female sheep

fauna (FAW nuh) *n.* the animal species of a given region or period

forage (FOR ij) *v.* to wander or rove in search of food; to collect food; *n.* food of any kind for animals, especially for horses and cattle

genus (JEE num) *n.* kind or class; biologists classify similar species as members of the same *genus*

herpetologist (her pih TAHL uh jist) *n.* a person who studies reptiles

ichthyology (ik thee AHL uh jee) *n.* the study of fish

leonine (LEE uh nyn) *adj.* pertaining to lions; suggestive of a lion

matutinal (muh TOO duh nul) *adj.* pertaining to or functioning in the morning

nidus (NY dus) *n.* a nest in which insects deposit eggs

nocturnal (nahk TER nul) *adj.* pertaining to the darkness or to organisms active or functional at night

omnivorous (ahm NIV er us) *adj.* eating both plants and animals

ornithology (or nih THAHL uh jee) *n.* the study of birds

pabulum (PAB yuh luhm) *n.* any nourishment for an animal (or plant)

prehensile (pre HEN sul) *adj.* capable of grasping and holding

rookery (RUH ker ee) *n.* a breeding or resting place, especially for birds

sedentary (SED in tayr ee) *adj.* living in one place; not
   migratory
taxidermy (TAK sih der mee) *n.* preparing, stuffing, and
   displaying animal skins
taxonomy (tak SAH nuh mee) *n.* the science or technique
   of classification (of animals, plants, etc.)
ursine (ER syn) *adj.* pertaining to bears; bearlike
vagility (vuh JIL ih tee) *n.* the innate ability to disperse
vespiary (VES pee ayr ee) *n.* a nest of wasps
vestigial (ves TIJ yul) *adj.* describing a body part that no
   longer functions usefully (*n* vestige)
vulpine (VUHL pyn) *adj.* pertaining to foxes; like a fox

Level 7

Confusing Word Groups

Level 7 features the most advanced vocabulary study. Each word group in this level contains words often confused with one another. By studying words in these groups you can clearly see their difference in meaning, spelling, and usage, thereby sharpening your vocabulary.

abatement *adj.* alleviation; lessening; mitigation
abeyance *n.* cessation; discontinuation

aberration *n.* a deviation from what is normal, common, or morally right
abhorrence *n.* detesting; despising; loathing
apparition *n.* a ghost, phantom, or other such appearance

abet *v.* to assist
abut *v.* to border upon; adjoin

abdicate *v.* to give up; relinquish

abnegate *v.* to deny oneself (e.g., a pleasure or right); to relinquish or give up

abrogate *v.* to repeal; abolish

abjection *n.* utter hopelessness; despicableness (*adj.* abject)

abjuration *n.* renunciation; giving up (*v* abjure)

adjuration *n.* an earnest appeal; solemn urging (*v* adjure)

adulation *n.* flattery; admiration

abrade *v.* to irritate; chafe

upbraid *v.* to scold; reproach; censure; reprove; reprimand

absolve *v.* to release from an obligation; to free from blame

resolve *n.* determination made, especially to solve a problem; *v.* to determine to do something by will

accede *v.* to adhere to an agreement

cede *v.* to relinquish or give up something—especially, territory

exceed *v.* to surpass

secede *v.* to withdraw and split off from a group

adapt *v.* to adjust

adept *adj.* proficient

affable *adj.* agreeable; friendly

effable *adj.* expressible; utterable

alleviate *v.* to provide relief; lessen
ameliorate *v.* to improve

allude *v.* to refer to indirectly
elude *v.* to avoid; escape detection

allusion *n.* indirect reference
delusion *n.* error in judgment
illusion *n.* error in vision

amend *v.* to alter; change
emend *v.* to correct or improve

amerce *v.* to punish by inflicting an arbitrary penalty
immerse *v.* to plunge completely into a liquid; dunk

amity *n.* friendship
amnesty *n.* a general pardon by a government for past offenses
amorous *adj.* moved by sexual or romantic love
amorphous *adj.* vague; shapeless

amulet *n.* a good-luck charm (a safeguard against misfortune)
annulet *n.* a ring-shaped molding or ridge

anaphora *n.* in speech, repeating the first words of sentences

anathema *n.* a thing cursed or condemned

anecdote *n.* narrative of a particular incident; brief personal story

antidote *n.* remedy to counteract a harmful substance (poison)

annunciate *v.* to proclaim or promulgate

enunciate *v.* to pronounce clearly

averse *adj.* disinclined; unwilling

adverse *adj.* opposing

apiary *n.* a place where bees are kept

aviary *n.* an enclosure for birds

apostate *n.* one who defects from or abandons one's faith, church or principles.

prostate *n.* male glandular organ

prostrate *adj.* lying down; prone

apocalyptic *adj.* describing a cataclysmic and violent event in which forces of good destroy those of evil

apocryphal *adj.* describing a literary work of unknown authorship or doubtful integrity

apothecary *n.* druggist; pharmacist

apotheosis *n.* elevation of a mortal to the rank of god; deification; glorification

appraise *v.* to determine a monetary value
apprise *v.* to inform; notify

archetype *n.* anything that serves as a model for (example of) all other similar things
prototype *n.* the first of a type

ardent *adj.* eager, zealous, fervent
arduous *adj.* requiring great exertion; laborious; difficult

arrant *adj.* downright; complete or total; unmitigated
errant *adj.* wandering; deviating from the regular course

articulate *adj.* clear and precise in expression
reticulate *adj.* having a veined, fibrous, or netlike quality

ascend *v.* to rise or climb
assent *v.* to agree to

asperse *v.* to slander, defame, or insult
disperse *v.* to separate or scatter

auger *n.* a tool for boring holes in wood
augur *v.* to predict, presage; forebode; portend (*n* a sooth-sayer or prophet)

autonomic *adj.* referring to movements produced by some internal stimulus
autonomous *adj.* independent from external constraints; self-governing

avocation *n.* minor occupation
invocation *n.* a call for assistance to a spiritual power

banal *adj.* commonplace; trite; hackneyed; unoriginal
bane *n.* any cause of ruin or destruction, lasting harm or injury, or woe

baneful *adj.* destructive or poisonous
baleful *adj.* evil or destructive; sorrowful

biannual *adj.* twice a year; semiannual
biennial *adj.* every two years

broach *v.* to open up; to mention a subject; propose; introduce
brooch *n.* a decorative pin (jewelry item)

canvas *n.* strong cloth for making tents
canvass *v.* to solicit for orders, votes

capacious *adj.* spacious; roomy
capricious *adj.* impulsive; arbitrary
captious *adj.* fault-finding; carping

censor *v.* to criticize, object to, and possibly delete (from a broadcast or publication), especially on moral grounds

censure *v.* to severely criticize or find fault with; reproach; reprove; rebuke; reprimand; scold

cite *v.* to quote or refer to as authority; also, to summons for a court appearance

site *n.* a place; location

climactic *adj.* relating to climax

climatic *adj.* relating to climate

collegial *adj.* easy to work with; amiable

collegiate *adj.* pertaining to college

commensurate *adj.* proportionate; equivalent

commiserate *v.* to empathize; sympathy; share sorrow

complacent *adj.* self-satisfied; smug; content

complaisant *adj.* willing to please (comply with)

condole *v.* to express sympathetic sorrow

condone *v.* to approve tacitly; overlook; forgive

congeal *v.* freeze; coagulate

congenial *adj.* gracious; warm-hearted; friendly

congenital *adj.* from or existing at birth; inborn; innate

council *n.* an assemblage or group gathered to confer
counsel *v.* to advise

credible *adj.* worthy of acceptance; having integrity; believable
credulous *adj.* believing easily; gullible

deceased *adj.* dead
diseased *adj.* characterized by illness

delegate *v.* to appoint; authorize; deputize
relegate *v.* to transfer or consign to an inferior position

demagogue *n.* a false leader
pedagogue *n.* a teacher

demur *v.* to object
demure *adj.* serious; grave; coy (feigning shyness)

denigrate *v.* to smear or blacken, especially the reputation of another
deprecate *v.* to express strong disapproval
depredate *v.* to plunder; to rampantly destroy and vandalize

denounce *v.* to accuse or inform against
renounce *v.* to give up a right or opinion; retract; abdicate; repudiate

desecrate *v.* to violate the sanctity of
desiccate *v.* to dry up

device *n.* tool; implement
devise *v.* to give (a gift) of property

discreet *adj.* tactful; prudent
discrete *adj.* distinct; distinguishable; separate

disillusioned *adj.* free from illusion; disenchanted
dissolution *n.* a dissolving or breaking up

disparage *v.* to speak ill of; belittle
disparate *adj.* scattered; unrelated

dissident *adj.* rebellious; dissenting
dissonant *adj.* unpleasant or disagreeable; discordant;
  clashing (especially sound)

dissolute *adj.* lewd; licentious; morally lax
resolute *adj.* determined; full of resolve

distrait *adj.* absent-minded
distraught *adj.* worried; anxious; upset

effervescent *adj.* bubbling
efflorescent *adj.* busting into bloom; blossoming
evanescent *adj.* fleeting; fading quickly; passing away;
  vanishing

eminent *adj.* distinguished; lofty
immanent *adj.* inherent; indwelling; invading all creation
imminent *adj.* impending; about to happen; threatening

empirical *adj.* based upon experience or observation
imperial *adj.* pertaining to a state's sovereign rule over
persons or other states
imperious *adj.* dictatorial; domineering

epic *n.* great in size or extent; a type of poem about a heroic adventure
epoch *n.* a specific time period marked by distinctive
events or features

epigram *n.* a clever, pithy saying; aphorism
epitaph *n.* an inscription on a monument in memory of a
deceased person
epithet *n.* a word or phrase describing a person used instead of or added to the person's name

escheat *v.* to transfer title by default to the state (government)
eschew *v.* to avoid

evoke *v.* to call up past emotions
inveigh *v.* to denounce; censure
invoke *v.* to call up a spirit or emotion for assistance or
inspiration
revoke *v.* to take back; rescind; cancel; annul

exacerbate *v.* to increase the harshness or severity of; aggravate; worsen

exaggerate *v.* to distort by overstatement

exasperate *v.* to annoy, irritate, or infuriate

exigent *adj.* urgent

exiguous *adj.* meager; trifling; scanty

expatiate *v.* talk at length

expatriate *v.* to banish or exile

expiate *v.* make amends for an offense or sin

expedient *adj.* suitable for a particular purpose; practicable; fitting for one's advantage or interest

expeditious *adj.* speedy; quick

explicate *v.* to explain, interpret, or clarify

expurgate *v.* to clean; remove offensive parts (of a book)

extirpate *v.* to root up

extricate *v.* to free; disentangle

factious *adj.* given to dissent; hostile; seditious; insurgent

factitious contrived; not genuine; artificial; counterfeit; sham

fractious *adj.* unruly; given to breaking rules

feculent *adj.* relating to feces (excrement)

fecund *adj.* fertile; productive; fruitful

felicitous apt; suitable; appropriate
filaceous *adj.* composed of threads
fallacious misleading; deceptive; logically unsound

fervent *adj.* adamant; feverish; impassioned
furtive *adj.* sneaky; surreptitious

germane *adj.* pertinent; relevant
germinal *adj.* creative; pertaining to a germ; seminal

glutinous *adj.* gluey; sticky; adhesive
gluttonous *adj.* ravenous; indulgent

hapless *adj.* unlucky; unfortunate
helpless *adj.* unable to help oneself

hoard *v.* to stockpile, collect, or accumulate for future use
horde *n.* a crowd

hypercritical *adj.* overly critical
hypocritical *adj.* insincere

igneous *adj.* caused or created by volcanic eruption or by fire
ligneous *adj.* like wood; having the quality of wood

imprudent *adj.* careless; reckless; indiscreet
impudent *adj.* rude; insolent; audacious; brazen; impertinent

impugn *v.* to challenge; call into question; contradict
impunity *n.* privilege; license; exemption

incipient *adj.* coming into being; nascent; inchoate
insipid *adj.* tasteless; uninteresting; banal

incubate *v.* to hatch; scheme
incubus *n.* burden; nightmare
inculcate *v.* to teach; indoctrinate

indict *v.* to charge with an offense
indite *v.* to compose or express in words

indigenous *adj.* native to or characterizing a particular
region
indigent *adj.* poor; destitute
indulgent *adj.* permissive; tolerating

indurate *adj.* hardened; unyielding; obstinate
inundated *adj.* flooded; overflowed

inevitable *adj.* unavoidable
inexorable *adj.* relentless; unyielding; implacable

ingenious *adj.* inventive; clever (*n* ingenuity)
ingenue *n.* a naive and unsophisticated young woman
ingenuous *adj.* naive; unsophisticated (*n* ingenuousness)

insidious *adj.* wily; crafty; sly; treacherous

invidious *adj.* likely to cause ill will, resentment, or discontent

insolent *adj.* rude; insulting; brazen; audacious
insular *adj.* isolated; narrowly exclusive

inveigh *v.* to criticize vehemently with words
inveigle *v.* to lure or entice by inducements

jocose *adj.* playful; jesting; humorous
jocular *adj.* joking; not serious; jesting; facetious
jocund *adj.* cheerful; merry

labile *adj.* unstable; likely to change
liable *adj.* responsible for a debt; owing

lassitude *n.* weariness; depression; languor
latitude *n.* leeway; freedom from limitation
platitude *n.* commonplace or trite expression

lathe *n.* a rotating tool for rounding wood objects
lithe *adj.* flexible; supple; labile

loath *adj.* averse; reluctant
loathe *v.* to detest; hate

literal *adj.* word for word; express
literate *adj.* able to read
littoral *adj.* pertaining to a coastal region (shoreline)

livid *adj.* enraged; extremely angry

lurid *adj.* sensational or shocking; shining with an unnatural glow; gruesome or revolting

macerate *v.* waste away or fall apart; to soften by soaking in liquid

maculated *adj.* spotted or stained

masticate *v.* chew

meddlesome *adj.* interfering; intrusive

mettlesome *adj.* courageous; ardent

nettlesome *adj.* prickly or barbed; annoying or vexing

mendacity *n.* deceit or fraud (*adj.* mendacious)

mendicancy *n.* the practice of begging or living off alms (charity) of others

meritorious *adj.* worthy of merit; of value

meretricious *adj.* gaudy; tawdry; flashy

miscreant *n.* an evil person

recreant *n.* one who yields in combat and begs for mercy

multifarious *adj.* greatly diversified; of various kinds

multiparous *adj.* producing more than one offspring at a birth

obfuscate *v.* confuse; muddle

obdurate *adj.* stubborn; persistent

obloquy *n.* condemnation or verbal abuse, or the disgrace resulting therefrom

obsequious *adj.* overly servile or obedient

obsequies *n.* funeral rites or ceremonies

odious: *adj.* deserving or causing hatred or scorn; detestable; despicable; offensive

odorous: having a distinct or strong smell

onerous *adj.* burdensome; difficult

ominous *adj.* looming; threatening; foreboding; impending

opalescent *adj.* iridescent; shining

opulence *n.* luxury; extreme wealth

oratorio *n.* a large multisectional musical form which is really an unstaged sacred opera

oratory *n.* discourse or speech

pablum *n.* banal (trite or hackneyed) intellectual ideas or writings

pabulum *n.* any nourishment for an animal (or plant)

palatable *adj.* agreeable; tasty

palpable *adj.* obvious; evident; unmistakable

palette *n.* a board on which a painter mixes pigments

palliate *v.* gloss; veil; varnish

pallet *n.* cot (small bed)
pallid *adj.* pale; wan

paradigm *n.* a model, example, or pattern
paragon *n.* a model of perfection; an ideal

paramount *adj.* highest in rank or value
tantamount *adj.* equivalent in meaning, value, or effect

parity *n.* equivalence; resemblance
parody *n.* humorous imitation

parley *n.* a conference or discussion
parlance *n.* a way or manner of speaking
parlay *v.* to bet one's winnings on a subsequent bet

patriarch *n.* father and ruler of a family or tribe
patrician *adj.* aristocratic; having the elegance of nobility

pedagogy *n.* the science of teaching methods
pedology *n.* the study of children

peremptory *adj.* final; with authority; absolutely
preemptive *adj.* claimed or initiated before or in preference to others

perquisite *n.* fringe benefit, privilege, or bonus
prerequisite *n.* necessary beforehand

perspicacious *adj.* insightful; penetrating; astute
perspicuous *adj.* clearly or plainly expressed
pertinacious *adj.* stubborn; persistent
pertinent *adj.* appropriate; relevant

plaintiff *n.* party initiating a law suit
plaintive *adj.* mournful; baleful

practicable *adj.* feasible; capable of being put into practice
practical *adj.* useful; sensible

preciosity *n.* fastidiousness or over-refinement
precocity *n.* maturity beyond one's years
prescience *n.* foreknowledge (of future events)

prescribe *v.* to set forth a rule, policy, or course of action
proscribe *v.* to prohibit; forbid

principal *n.* chief; primary
principle *n.* fundamental truth, axiom, or presupposition

prodigal *adj.* wasteful; reckless with money
prodigious *adj.* immense or enormous; extraordinary or marvelous (*n* prodigy)

profligate *adj.* degenerate; depraved; lascivious
proliferate *v.* to multiply; spread; breed

promulgate *v.* to make known by announcement; proclaim; disseminate

propagate *v.* to breed; reproduce; generate

propitiate *v.* to appease

propiteous *adj.* pitiful

propitious *adj.* favorable to; auspicious; advantageous

provenance *n.* origin or source

providence *n.* destiny; fate; divine guidance

provident *adj.* prepared; ready; thoughtful

provisional *adj.* temporary; interim; tentative

pugnacious *adj.* defiant; rebellious; belligerent

pungent *adj.* sharp or acidic in taste or smell

repugnant *adj.* repulsive; offensive; revolting

querulous *adj.* full of complaints; whining; peevish

query *v.* to inquire or question

rake *n.* a wasteful or morally lax person

rakish *adj.* stylish; sportive

refectory *n.* a large dining hall (at a church, college, etc.)

refractive *adj.* changing direction obliquely (as light when moving from one medium to another)

refractory *adj.* stubborn; unmanageable

regime *n.* a system of government (especially, the administration of a specific leader)

regimen *n.* a prescribed routine or habit

requisite *adj.* necessary; required; mandatory; indispensable

requite *v.* to repay; compensate; recompense; remunerate

respectful *adj.* showing respect; courteous

respective *adj.* in the order (sequence) given

salient *adj.* prominent or conspicuous; notable, significant, or important

saline *adj.* pertaining to salt

satire *n.* a literary form employing irony, ridicule, and sarcasm

satyr *n.* a mythological deity, appearing as half-man, half-goat, and known for its riotous and lascivious behavior

sedentary *adj.* staying in one place; inactive

sedimentary *adj.* describing accumulation of material deposited by water, wind, or glaciers

seditious *adj.* resistant to authority; unruly; defiant; insubordinate; factious

sedulous *adj.* diligent; persistent; assiduous; industrious

sinewy *adj.* strong; sturdy; tough

sinuous *adj.* winding; twisted; serpentine

specie *n.* a coin or coined money
species *n.* type; sort; variety; kind

succor *n.* aid; relief; assistance
succumb *v.* to yield; give in

superfluent *adj.* frictionless; easily flowing
superfluous *adj.* adding nothing necessary or important;
    excess; unnecessary; surplus

supine *adj.* lying on one's back
supple *adj.* soft; pliable

synergy *n.* teamwork; cooperation
syzygy *n.* alignment of three celestial bodies

temerarious *adj.* foolhardy; rash; audacious (*n* temerity)
timorous *adj.* fearful; timid

temporal *adj.* pertaining to time
temporary *adj.* lasting for a time only
temporize *v.* to avoid committing oneself in order to de-
    lay or gain time

tenacious *adj.* holding firm and fast, as with a strong grip
    (*n* tenacity)

tendentious *adj.* tending to; having a propensity to; leaning toward a direction
tentative *adj.* temporary; uncertain

torpid *adj.* inactive; sluggish; lethargic; phlegmatic
turbid *adj.* clouded; muddy
turgid *adj.* swollen; inflated

tortuous *adj.* twisting
torturous *adj.* cruelly painful

ululate *v.* to wail; howl; lament loudly
undulate *v.* to move in a wavelike motion

vagary *n.* an impulse; whim; caprice
vagrancy *n.* the condition of having no home; vagabondage
vague *adj.* imprecise; obscure; nebulous

venal *adj.* corrupt; capable of being bribed; mercenary
venial *adj.* excusable; forgivable; trivial

venerable *adj.* worthy of respect, praise, or honor
veritable *adj.* truly; very much so; genuine

veracious *adj.* truthful; honest; credible
voracious *adj.* ravenous; gluttonous; rapacious

virile *adj.* possessing masculine strength

virulent *adj.* poisonous; extremely injurious; deadly

visceral *adj.* physiological; felt in one's inner organs
viscous *adj.* sticky; gluey

waiver *n.* giving up of a claim or right
waver *v.* to hesitate

Index